SHOW ME

THE

FUNNY!

SHOW ME

FUNNY!

AT THE WRITERS' TABLE WITH

HOLLYWOOD'S
TOP COMEDY
WRITERS

PETER DESBERG & **JEFFREY DAVIS**

STERLING

New York / London
www.sterlingpublishing.com

STERLING and the distinctive Sterling logo are registered trademarks of
Sterling Publishing Co., Inc.

Library of Congress Cataloging-in-Publication Data
Desberg, Peter.
  Show me the funny! : at the writers' table with Hollywood's Top Comedy
Writers / Peter Desberg and Jeffrey Davis.
    p. cm.
  Includes index.
  ISBN 978-1-4027-6841-5
  1. Television comedies--Authorship. 2. Comedy films--Authorship.
  3. Television comedy writers--United States--Interviews. 4. Screenwriters--
United States--Interviews. I. Davis, Jeffrey.
  PN1992.8.C66D37 2010
  808.2'25--dc22
                    2010007181

10 9 8 7 6 5 4 3 2 1

Published by Sterling Publishing Co., Inc.
387 Park Avenue South, New York, NY 10016
© 2010 by Peter Desberg and Jeffrey Davis
Distributed in Canada by Sterling Publishing
ᶜ/o Canadian Manda Group, 165 Dufferin Street
Toronto, Ontario, Canada M6K 3H6
Distributed in the United Kingdom by GMC Distribution Services
Castle Place, 166 High Street, Lewes, East Sussex, England BN7 1XU
Distributed in Australia by Capricorn Link (Australia) Pty. Ltd.
P.O. Box 704, Windsor, NSW 2756, Australia

Sterling ISBN 978-1-4027-6841-5

For information about custom editions, special sales, premium and
corporate purchases, please contact Sterling Special Sales
Department at 800-805-5489 or specialsales@sterlingpublishing.com.

Dedication

This book is dedicated to the memory of Jerry Davis, who inspired almost every aspect of it. His warm relationships with more than a few of the writers interviewed didn't hurt, either.

In addition, we'd like to extend the dedication to include our loving and patient families for putting up with us as we worked, complained about, and were consumed by this book:

Cheryll and Lauren Desberg

Louise, Nora, and Michael Davis

Contents

Preface

Years ago, I got a phone call from a woman named Susie who said she was getting her master's degree in psychology from Antioch West University. She said she was interested in the psychology of humor and had gotten my name from one of her professors. She asked if I would be willing to help with her thesis and serve on her thesis committee.

It was the tail end of a grueling day and the thought of working for no compensation was doing nothing for my mood. But being polite to a fault, I asked her to describe her thesis. In a droning voice she outlined a plan to write a chapter on the psychology of humor, a chapter on the sociology of humor, and a chapter on the anthropology of humor. I was about to cut her off, politely, of course, when she said she was going to interview a famous Hollywood comedy writer. I asked who the writer was. "Edmund Hartmann," she said. He was the first president of the Writers Guild of America. He'd written several classic Bob Hope movies, including *The Lemon Drop Kid*, *Sorrowful Jones*, *Paleface*, and *Fancy Pants*. He also wrote several movies for Abbott and Costello and much, much more. I asked how she knew him and she said offhandedly, "Oh, he's my dad."

I suggested that we drop the first three chapters and asked if her father would ask some of his comedy writer friends to be interviewed. This seemed like a once-in-a-lifetime opportunity. I had an idea that was different from books on the subject in which writers were asked, "How did you get into comedy writing?" Instead, we would give the comedy writers a task that they performed as part of their work. They would tell us how they solved comedy writing problems while our tape recorder was rolling.

We were lucky enough to get some of the top writers in Hollywood at that time, including people like Hal Kantor and Herbie Baker. We completed eight interviews and then I got a disasterous call from Susie announcing that she was moving to Illinois. The project, which, by this time, had worked its way into my heart, was dead.

Fast-forward twenty years. Jeffrey was sitting in his car in front of my house. He had come to pick up his son, who had a playdate with my daughter. He was sulking in the front seat, waiting for his son to come out, knowing that if the kid didn't come out soon, he would have to make small talk with yet another set of parents. His luck ran out, as often happens when you are waiting on fifteen-year-olds. He came in and we introduced ourselves.

Within a minute or two, we found out that we were both college professors and wallowed in a few minutes of commiseration. Jeffrey said he taught screenwriting, mostly comedy, at Loyola Marymount University. He had written many plays and sitcoms, but had never done any academic-type writing or research, which was now something that was expected of him if he wanted to continue down an academic path. He asked me if I had done much of it. I reluctantly admitted that I had. On a hunch, I told him about the comedy writer project I had begun so many years before. He asked me who some of the writers were. As I reeled off the names, his eyes began to open wider and he began to smile. "All those guys were around my crib . . . probably playing poker." Jeffrey's father was a well-known comedy writer from that era. "He was a show runner for *Bewitched*, *That Girl*, and *The Odd Couple* and had credits a mile long." Jeffrey said, "Let's do it!"

We decided to start from scratch, and on Jeffrey's suggestion, we changed the task. We wrote a generic comedy premise—reprinted in its entirety in the Introduction—which we gave each of our twenty-seven writers. Then we asked each writer to develop it while we watched. Not only is the rest history, but you'll be reading this history very soon because it's the rest of this book.

We have been fortunate to work with some of the most talented and generous comedy writers in Hollywood. We want to thank them for opening up and sharing their artistic processes with us.

Peter Desberg and Jeffrey Davis

Introduction

BEING THERE AS TOP COMEDY PROFESSIONALS CREATE

As veteran comedy writer Elliot Schoenman (Maude, Home Improvement) *is retracing the cab ride his father took on the way to his suicide, he wonders how much his famously cheap father tipped the cabbie.*

Ken Daurio is listening to notes on his film project, Bubble Boy, *when the producer suggests that they lose the bubble after the first act. Ken turns to his writing partner, Cinco Paul, and whispers, "We can just call it Boy."*

Why start with these stories? Because they illustrate just how different comedy writers are from the rest of us. They notice character quirks and conflicts they can turn into interesting and off-kilter situations. If there's no quirk or conflict, they think, "Yeah, but what if . . .?" Then they create one. How do they do it? That's the question *Show Me the Funny!* sets out to answer in twenty-two unconventional interviews.

We're in Hollywood, Not France

In Paris, people line up and pay to see the paintings at the Picasso Museum. What would you pay to have been in Picasso's studio at Montmartre, watching him as he created his paintings? Now, imagine if you could also have been in the studios of Monet, Renoir, Degas, Chagall, Manet, and Matisse and you could have watched each of them as they painted. Each had a unique style and a unique approach to painting. Now imagine if each of them began by painting the same model. Well, we're not in France, but we are in Hollywood (those painters are all dead anyway) and this book puts you in a seat at the table in the writers' room to see how some of the best comedy writers apply their brushstrokes to the word processor.

When Hollywood luminaries are interviewed, they're typically asked, "How do you create comedy?" They're really being asked, "How *did* you do it?" *We* wanted to know what their writing process actually looks like. We wanted to see them at work, so we asked them to *show* us.

What you're about to dive into is a different approach to the interview book. We gave all twenty-five writers the same loosely structured comedy premise and asked them to develop it any way they wanted. We told them there were no rules, no boundaries, and no limits. That was just as well because they wouldn't have followed them anyway. That's why they're comedy writers, not accountants.

Encouraging them to play with the premise results in lots of memorable new stories, as unique as each of the writers in this book, proving that there is no "one size fits all" way to create comedy. While you're sitting next to them, the writers jump in, ask questions, develop characters, create conflicts, pitch jokes, and make casting decisions. Some stay within the original premise, while others turn it on its head. However it goes, the process is always absorbing. Many of the writers who gave their time and passion to this project told us how much more stimulating this process was compared to other interviews they've done. They suggested that it may prove the old saying, "Autobiography is the highest form of fiction." Along the way you'll also be treated to inside Hollywood anecdotes that flow naturally from each of the interviews. And it all happens in real time.

The writers in this book span the history of show business comedy from the Golden Age of television to some of today's hottest young movie and television writers. In addition to being writers, many are also show creators, show runners, producers, and directors.

And a Little Something Extra

When we read interview books, we always hope that a photo of the person interviewed is included. We have gone a step further. Go to the website http://www.showmethefunnyonline.com and you can view short video excerpts of each interview to see the writers in action and get a feel for who they are. We were pleased that many of the writers told us they usually repeat the same rehearsed answers in every interview they do, but revealed themselves here in a way they have never done before. A few told us that they actually used material that came out of the interviews in their own work.

How to Approach This Book

Any way you want. Many readers will read this book from beginning to end and then rush out and purchase multiple copies to give as gifts to people they want to impress. However, you don't have to read this book in order. If you're a daring type, here are a few additional suggestions. Whether you're an aspiring writer, a seasoned professional, or anthropologically inclined (a student of the history and culture of the entertainment industry), you can try to identify similarities and differences in these writers' approaches. If you are really adventurous, you can read the premise first, try your hand at developing it, and then compare your efforts with those of the pros. Then you can send your efforts to us and have them displayed on the website.

Have a look at the premise we gave the pros.

The Premise

If you want something done . . . give it to Sarah. She will do it creatively, thoroughly, and have it done a week early. Her problem is that her boss is afraid there's only room for one woman vice president—her. Sarah is so focused on her work that she is unaware that she is relationship-challenged as far as men are concerned.

In a generation where it isn't fashionable, Sarah has a great relationship with her parents. Of course, it helps that they live two thousand miles away. At their end of the country, her parents had a great life. Stylish apartment, expensive car, beautiful clothes and jewelry. Her father made sure of all that. When he suddenly dies, Sarah's mother, Molly, is stunned to find that their financial situation is not an iceberg with a firm 80 percent below the water level. He was obsessed with appearances. He made it, they spent it. What she sees is all she has.

Molly is fiftyish, broke, unprepared for even the most unskilled job. Sarah invites her mother to move in with her. Molly reluctantly agrees, if it's just for a few weeks. A few weeks turns into a permanent arrangement as Molly decides that Sarah's apartment, friends, and lifestyle are the perfect launching pad for her new life. To complicate things even further, Molly's mother and father both have a strong work ethic and find their free-spirited daughter baffling. Sarah is actually the daughter they never had and always wanted.

Molly may not have any work skills, but she has a gift when it comes to people, especially men. She wants to boost her daughter's social life, but somehow she always ends up stealing the show.

Sarah wants Molly to get a job or go back to school. Molly wants to "examine all her options," which she now has for the first time in her life. Sarah wants the mother-daughter relationship she never had. Molly wants to be best friends.

LAUGHTER OFF THE TWUCK

 An Interview with Walter Bennett

A partial list of Walter Bennett's credits as a writer include *The Bill Cosby Show*, *The Steve Harvey Show*, *In the House*, *Here and Now*, *Buddies*, and *Contradictions of the Heart*.

Walter Bennett has an infectious kettle-drum laugh that comes from somewhere deep inside and serves as his comedic barometer. As you read the interview, notice how he uses it to test out material, breaking himself up when he hits a line or a character bit that pleases him. His laugh is his personal transition from writer to audience.

In the way Walter approaches process, he reminds us of great jazz improvisers like Miles Davis who said, "There are no mistakes." As he moves from idea to idea, his "playing" is so effortless that you can easily miss his flawless technique and all you hear is the music accompanied by his laughter.

�֎ �֎ ✖

WB (WALTER BENNETT): The first thing I usually do is try to put myself in the place of Sarah. I try to figure out, Whose story is this? What's this really about? You've got your mom—she's got to be "out there." I feel kind of bad for her, but the crazy thing is you think you have a great relationship, until she's a block away. And then, when she's in the house with you, I want to make it as bad as I can for Sarah. I think she's doing okay. I guess I'm trying to figure out what her job is. It's not good enough that she has a room. Sarah is saving money so that they're in an apartment, but, where they're right on top of each other. I see a moving van pulling up to this single, efficiency, one-bedroom apartment. The story's about their proximity. So that's where I start. And then you can't go any further without really knowing who these people are.

I'm thinking Sarah takes on a few of the traits of her father, meaning that her life is 80 percent underwater, and only 20 percent is above, and Molly only really knows the 20 percent. Maybe some discovery on the daughter's part because she's not really aware of guys. I would say that she's finally taken notice of somebody, and in a perfect world, while she starts to figure this out, she doesn't need her mom around. This has got to be the worst time that her mom could show up, so I'm trying to figure out what would be the absolute worst time.

PD (PETER DESBERG): Well, in your own life what would be the worst time for a parent to show up?

WB: Unannounced. Maybe she didn't call and say, "I'm shutting down the house." Maybe the phone call was on a message machine, like, "One of these days maybe I should get out there." That was the whole message. "Call me, we'll talk about it" or something like that. So Sarah finally meets this guy. I just see her coming to the door in a towel, you know, and there's a van outside. And Mom's had Cousin Derrick drive it, Derrick with a lisp. But, you've got to be able to understand him. Meanwhile, the guy she's just started going out with is in the other room. They've just . . . you know . . .

The worst time. And so Mom's here, and she's looking at the 20 percent. But, the 80 percent is represented by what just went on in the room there. And you've got this guy with the lisp . . . "What you want off the twuck?" Sarah says, "That's not going to fit." And Derrick keeps moving things in. So Sarah's going back and forth. She whispers into the bedroom, "You've got to get out of here." He whispers back, "I thought you said your mom was cool."

So Mom is actually leaving a situation where, financially, things were not what they appeared to be and now she's coming into a relationship with her daughter that's not what it seems. So now we need to know, how often did they visit each other? Did Sarah want to move out because Molly was a little bit overbearing? And, the new guy's got to be in the bathroom, trying to make it a one-room kind of situation. Maybe Sarah shoved him into the bathroom, and her mom says, "You just got up? Whose shoes are these?"

JD (JEFFREY DAVIS): So it's a way of using the confined space to make conflict?

WB: To make conflict. When I start to look at it, I say, "Okay, that's surface. That can only go for so long." Let's get some laughs, but now we've got to talk about their needs, which is not really funny sometimes. Comedy is drama, but the "worst moment" drama. And surprise. Our laughter gives us a chance to be one step removed from drama.

JD: Do you think comedy is harder to write?

WB: It's harder to write. I break it down as an actor, because I was an actor for ten years, off-Broadway. And so what I need to know as an actor is what happens just before the doorbell rings. And some of these are writing things, too: Who am I expecting? And then I take that back a little bit. What was I doing? What was going on? What was the last conversation, or relationship, I had with Mom? What was she trying to get me to do? Or, What did I promise her I was doing, and why?

So now, I've got to get into what does Sarah do for a living? Her job makes her a fish out of water. So whoever she is, she's in a situation where she's working around cool people, or, her work partner is Salma Hayek. Somebody who she thinks she could never be like. But when she looks into the mirror at home, she's saying, "*Me gusta que miro . . .*"

I'm going to put Sarah at Target . . . She's a manager at Target . . . No, no, she's a trainee at Target. And she told Molly she was a VP. And the boyfriend works in the popcorn thing . . . And the Salma Hayek woman is at Register 4. So Sarah came from this splendid background, and she was two thousand miles away. But this is the way she lives now. And her mom said, "Your dad passed away," whatever, ". . . and the money's tied up." I don't know if she can break it to her daughter.

PD: They're all living a 20 percent.

WB: Yeah, we start to find out who this family is. And so, there's constantly layers every time there's something new that comes out. And I think Sarah gets found out. I think her mother becomes a secret shopper. "I've got a job . . ." "What are you doing here?" But then, storywise, I've got to know my ending here. It's about closing a gap. The big thing is they're too far away—they're two thousand miles away. They come together, and what do they get out of that? What are they avoiding? What are they afraid of? And why are they afraid to close this gap?

PD: When you close the gap you go from 20 to 40 percent . . . or 20 to 90 percent?

WB: I think in the end Molly and Sarah may stay at 20 to 80, but they know they're at 20/80. They respect the gap, and that's where you get the juice from.

PD: You get stories there?

WB: You get stories about Sarah saying, "I've just been promoted." And Molly asking, "To what?" "And where?" Mom is like fifty to fifty-five.

JD: What would you have to do to sex Molly up and keep it commercial?

WB: You know what they did to Fran Drescher—they made her a young, hot mom—that's going too far. I think I would look at an actress we generally don't see as a mom, like Sharon Stone. The other question is, an overpowering mom?

PD: Does it help you to find a person to do it?

WB: Yeah, it helps me to start thinking of a person. "Oh, man, I remember . . ." Sometimes it's not even like a mom. It was a teacher or it was a cousin or a friend's mom, a friend's cousin. But nowadays, you really have to think, who do you know? Shirley MacLaine. Yeah, Shirley MacLaine might be good at something like this. In fact, she would be.

I think the mom has a daughter who's out there, almost like a guy who says, "I got a son who's out there. And, wow, my daughter lives two thousand miles away, and she is the vice president of such-and-such. And by golly, I may only have what I see here financially, and that 80 percent isn't there, but hey, you know who's out there, that's my 80 percent." And that's what she feels. It's like someone telling you, "You want to become a dealer in Vegas?" and someone saying, "Well, I'm a big guy at this big casino, and one day when you get here," thinking they'll never get here. "When you get here, I'll introduce you to Steve Wynn," and you show up and you find out he's at the end of the Strip doing a little lounge act. He also has to bus tables. And this is what the Debra Messing character is all about. I think her character has a personal flaw with regard to almost getting somewhere. And she's scared, and she's always had the potential, and Mom is living through the eyes of her potential, rather than reality.

PD: So Sarah was on the fast track a few times and got knocked off.

WB: Yeah, or knocked herself off. She's presented herself in one way, but she's really at Target! And that's a dead end unless you're in the executive-training program. Which she's constantly trying to get into. Again, at one point I go, "Where did Molly settle?" She met a man who provided a lavish lifestyle. Well, let's just say upper middle class, not exceedingly rich, or anything like that, but I think the downside of that is it can make a person lazy, it can make her complacent. "Do I have to do this anymore?" or "Why am I doing this? I'm just happy raising my daughter." And at a point, the dad starts to realize that this is what she expected, because I don't think it's all his fault that he didn't come to her and say, "I'm broke. We've got to downsize." I don't think he ever said that to her because this was her world—it would crumble around her. And since Sarah was now out of the house, why do that now?

But the question is how long had they been living like that? Did the dad leave every morning with a briefcase, change clothes to do whatever kind of work he really did, and then put his suit back on and come back home? I think the father's side of it was the true drama side of it.

PD: Would you actually bring him on in flashbacks or in her recollections?

WB: I've got another way. Molly says she sees him and the daughter's sitting there. "Mom, what's wrong?" I think the daughter's teaching her how to drive. She's never had to drive. And she says, "I just saw your father." "No, Mom, it was closed casket." "Well, it could have been your father."

PD: So is it a vision? Wish fulfillment? Or is it really him?

WB: It's left open. And I think throughout the piece, she keeps seeing her husband. And at some point, we've got to ask, "Does she see her husband?" And the hard thing is that if she did, then what really happened? But if she didn't, she meets this guy who just looks like him, and she brings him home, and Sarah is shocked. "It's crazy!" But maybe he is everything her father wasn't.

I think if we have this element, we have the family album. In comedy, there's that element of reliving a relationship, keeping the funny there. But, through that story line, we get a chance to find out what was she with Dad. I think there would then be a point where the guy who looks like her father stumbles across a picture. He hasn't seen a picture of all this and he stumbles across a picture, and he realizes what's going on here.

I would love to do a story where both Molly and Sarah pull jury duty. They each have different versions, so other people have to deal with these two. So we have times where they're far apart, but when they're in sync—"These guys are nuts. These two are just . . ." And then we see them move on different sides of the street in that kind of setting.

PD: When you're writing comedy, how do you know when something's funny?

WB: Usually the first thing that comes out is funny. Then you go, "Oh, I'll tweak it here, I'll tweak it there." Then there's a point where I go past that, and I go, "No." But first, it's got to make me laugh.

PD: You have this infectious laugh and you have a really nice meter inside that says, "That would be funny."

WB: I do it so fast now. It's like, "No, no, no, yeah." And sometimes I don't even know what the "no" was.

PD: How do you go about making stuff funnier when you get feedback that you need more laughs?

"If it's not funny, it's usually because it's not the worst thing that can happen."

WB: First I'd look at what the original joke is, and a lot of times when it doesn't work, it's because there's no surprise in the joke; it's expected. If it's not funny, it's usually because it's not the worst thing that can happen. There's something worse that could happen. And you can't get any worse than this. Let me give you an example: "Well, the camera fell over." And I go, "Wow, now that's bad," but where did it fall? But it's not specific enough. And a lot of times, it will be something specific that plays into the fear of your character that you've built up. You can get comedy out of that.

PD: How did you get schooled in comedy writing?

WB: My first school in comedy writing was television. Watching Norman Lear at the time *Good Times* was on, and *Maude*, it was the heyday of half-hour comedy. I used to think of half-hour sitcoms as a play. Whatever I thought was funny I would put down on paper. And going back to the "What if" idea, I would put down what happened. And a lot of it I learned along the way. It started to turn into a curiosity because I started to get my own books on comedy. In theater, for some reason, drama is king, and you're trying to be

Oscar Wilde. I was drama all the way to Yale. I was known for writing drama and social criticism. And then I wrote a piece in New York called *Snapshots: An American Slide Show*, and it was done as part of a performance at Lincoln Center and Alice Tully Hall. I had to direct this thing, and I just said it was social commentary. I thought it was kind of funny, but I think the worst thing for a writer to hear is laughter. Live laughter.

JD (JEFFREY DAVIS): Did Norman Lear mentor you?

WB: No, actually we worked together for a brief time on the show *704 Hauser.*

I've spent time with Bill Cosby. Cosby said, "Let me help you out here." And so he would talk about his take on comedy. I remember what he told me. He said, "Don't go for the joke"—that's what he kept saying. "Don't go for the joke. Go for what's real. If it's real, you can always build off something that's real. But it's more difficult to try to build off a joke, because that's not real. And everybody laughs because they relate to it—it's something real to them."

A problem I had in the beginning was trying to emulate the joke I'd seen on television, and it wasn't very good. But when I started to learn it's like Cosby was saying—it's real, it's real, keep these people real—you can keep coming back to the well.

JD: What are your feelings are about writers' rooms, and the politics of a room?

WB: I like the writers' room; I hate the politics. When I first went to *The Cosby Show*, I had never written for a sitcom—never. In fact, it was embarrassing. I didn't know how a sitcom script lined up on the page. I only knew plays and screenplays. When I got the job, I told one of the writers' assistants, "Can you get me a script? Between you and me, I don't know what one looks like." And they laughed. What they said to me was, "Do you know what it's like to be at a table?" And this is my interview, and I go, "Ah . . . yeah, yeah . . ." "No, no, no . . ." It's writers who sit around the table and they explained it to me. And I went, "You mean like improv, you mean working off somebody." And they went "Yeah." And they hired me. I really loved working off the other writers.

Another one: You make an incredible pitch, and everyone goes, "Oh, no, that's not it," and then someone else says the exact same thing that you said, and someone says, "That was brilliant," and then you say, "I just said that." "Oh come on now, let's not get that way."

KEEPING IT CLEAN

 An Interview with Yvette Bowser

A partial list of Yvette Bowser's credits as a creator,
show runner, and writer include *Living Single* (created),
A Different World, *Half and Half* (show runner),
and *Hanging with Mr. Cooper* (show runner).

Imagine graduating from college, calling Bill Cosby for a
writing job, and getting it. Yvette Bowser imagined it, did it,
and has moved forward to create her own shows. While many
comedy writers struggle with the constraints of writing for network
television, Yvette took on this challenge and won. She uses her
background in psychology and political science to tap into the ebb
and flow of everyday conflicts. They have a universal theme that
enables her to make a statement without having to ruffle feathers
and be edgy. She has made a career of tackling the situations that
meet her criteria of being important and entertaining and going
with the flow rather than fighting to swim upstream. The result has
been the creation of shows like *Living Single*.

✪ ✪ ✪

YB (YVETTE BOWSER): I would break down each of the characters and
give them different attributes. *You want me to do that!!!* Now you
want me to do what I do over the course of weeks . . .

PD (PETER DESBERG): Pick a character.

YB: I would start with Sarah. Obviously, she's the lead, she's the center. I'd make a little list: What's her take on relationships? What's her take on financial success?

PD: So give her some attributes.

YB: Well, I think relationships are very low on the totem pole for her. But I think that financial success is something that gives her a sense of worth, so I would write that down.

PD: So she defines herself by her financial status?

YB: Absolutely. Financial status is important to her. I think that gives her a sense of worth because I think that's also something that she's come from. Sometimes people feel that way because they haven't come from means, but I think she's someone who's determined to stay on par with where her parents raised her. But, also, I would try to think of where is she politically, in terms of her position. I think she's a little bit of a conservative, which is also not that popular to be right now. But I think she's secure enough in herself that she would kind of go against the grain. She's still young, but I think she has very firm opinions.

She's going to protect her money. And as I said, I think her relationships are going to be secondary. She's going to climb up the ladder as quickly as she can and secure her spot there. And then, whenever *he* fits in, she'll fit him into the picture. What else? Let's see.

PD: You're dimensionalizing the character first.

"If you have multidimensional characters, then the situations will come . . ."

YB: That's what I do. If you have multidimensional characters, then the situations will come, because you always know what they will do in whatever scenario you give them. There are only a certain number of plots and certain curves that you can throw at these people, but if you know what they'll do, that's the thing that makes them unique. That's why we can have a hundred different family sitcoms, but they each have their own point of view. But the point of view comes from who those individual characters are, who their kids are, who their parents are, who their grandparents are.

PD: What other dimensions do you look at?

YB: Those are the main ones. And then I usually do a list of quirks. Do they have any quirks? Are they superstitious? Are they kind of guided by their horoscopes? I also look at where they are spiritually.

PD: So where do you place her?

YB: [Spoken with a hint of sarcasm.] Oh, this is so fun! You know, that's an interesting question. I'm not really sure. I don't have an immediate vibe on her. I think she'd like to live right. I'm sure she believes in God, but I'm not really sure if she follows the tenets of the Bible. How about that? Yeah, I think there's temptation, there's compromise, but her spiritual growth keeps her on the right path, which would create more comedic fodder. I think it creates more comedic conflict if you have that groundedness that's pulling you back, even though you want to do the wrong thing, even though you might want to do what's best for you.

PD: So when she's faced with a spiritual conflict, like, whether to move ahead but screw your friend over, what does she do?

YB: I think she tries to move ahead, without screwing the friend over, which may not be entirely possible.

PD: You end up with some great conflicts.

YB: Exactly, exactly. So that's kind of my model.

PD: What other quirks would you look for?

YB: I think she probably has a really bad sense of direction. There are people who are incredibly charming, or book smart, who just have no sense of direction. I know some of those people. There are a lot of them. There's a saying: "God does not give with both hands." And so I try to apply that pretty much to every character: Where they're strong in one area, I try to give them a weakness, like a real crutch, in the other.

JD (JEFFREY DAVIS): What about the mother?

YB: Molly's a mess, because Molly's been spoiled. She's never had to do anything on her own. She's that character who would probably in many ways be very quickly labeled the "breakout," because she knows nothing. She knows nothing about taking care of herself. She doesn't know much about being a mom, because I think she's really been just about herself and her possessions and her lifestyle and her social status. So, in a way, the mother becomes the child, which is a very common dynamic. I'm not unfamiliar with that.

My mother's certainly not spoiled, but very often the children kind of rise above the parents, in terms of responsibility. Maybe that's really the way it should be. But again, you've got to find those things that are also universal about the dynamics, so I'm saying even though we might not all have a very pampered and privileged mother, we would have a mother who needs us more than we ever thought our mother would need us. So that would be the universal dynamic. And then we'd get the comedy from the fact that there's this woman who's in her early fifties.

PD: That's universal, and really pulls any kind of audience in and says, "I resonate with that. I get that."

YB: Right, right. Because that's what you've got to find. You've got to find your specifics for your situation, and know all the dimensions of all the characters, and then find what's universal in that. Why is it going to entertain anybody other than myself? That's the key. Why is what I'm doing going to be of interest to anyone but me and my family? "Here, everyone, read my script. Everybody in the kitchen—do you like it?"

JD: Where do you think that comes from?

YB: I try to put my degree to use. I have a degree in psychology and political science from Stanford. Life is very political, and how we deal with people is all very psychological and sociological, so I really try to observe people. Most people in my life circle are like, "Careful what you say around Yvette," because I always change the names to protect the guilty. So I don't really create that much. I just take from life and put it down on paper. It's kind of my own admission to the world that I don't make that much up. I just take my own observations and funnel it into concepts and story lines.

It's actually the only way I know how to do it. And certainly the way I've succeeded, when I've succeeded. When I haven't succeeded, I actually can look at it and say, "You know what, there was something in here . . ." Well, there's always the politics of it, and who wants a certain star in their show. But I think that where the concepts haven't totally stood up, it's because there was something that tried to be too quirky for its own good, or some central character who just wasn't relatable enough.

PD: Would you do a little more with Molly the way you did with Sarah?

YB: Molly is very much about the money. She also came from money and from privilege, and thought she married into it, and kind of did, but then only to discover that there wasn't enough of it to sustain her after her husband's passing. I think her ethical and moral lines are very fuzzy. I think there's very little she wouldn't do to get ahead, or put herself in a better financial or social position.

PD: So she's not really as spiritually grounded as her daughter.

YB: Right. I think her daughter's just more aware. Sarah's just grown up at a different time, and just has developed her own set of values from perhaps her college experience, and who her friends became then, and how she met different people from different socioeconomic backgrounds. And I think that influenced Sarah, where Molly was kind of isolated, perhaps, more in the higher socioeconomic background. So she's fifty and she's broke.

Okay, I think it's really interesting, given her former social status, that she decides that her daughter's apartment is the perfect place for her. So, again, that's one of the reasons I made Sarah place a certain measure of value on her finances and her career, because that is where she came from. But her apartment's got to be nice enough so that Molly would say, "I'm setting up camp here." Sarah's not living in some tenement somewhere. She's living in a really nice place. Otherwise, Molly would find a friend, a socialite, or someone who might take her in 'til she could figure out what she was going to do, how she was going to, say, rewrite the will, or come up with something to turn around her financial circumstances. I think clearly, to a certain degree, she was in love with her husband, so when we talk about romance now, I think she was in love with her husband, but maybe she was more in love with his money. And now she'd like to find someone else so she could love his money, and maybe love him, too. Which I think is very different from her daughter's approach: Sarah would like to have her own money and then find real love, and if he happens to have money, then that can work out as well. I suggest it's easy to love a rich man . . . it really is.

JD: When you go in to pitch a show, do they want you to talk about the arc of the first season? Do they want you to go past the pilot and really talk to them about what you think people will be watching a year from now?

"I don't want to advance someone's social or financial status that far in the first season."

YB: I always do. Again, I start out very simply with what is it that I want to examine, or talk about in this series, and then what are the best group of characters to approach that topic through, I don't go on a pitch unless I have twenty story areas. Now, every show that I've sold thus far I probably have used, on average, six or seven of those twenty that I have when I go into the pitch. I've used six or seven of them in the first season. By the time the series has come to its end, four or five years later, I probably have used all of them at some point. You can come up with a really funny story that you know already in your gut is a great episode, but it's not a Season 1 episode.

But when you're pitching a series and you're trying to sell it, just for them to know that you have a multitude of stories and places to go beyond Episode 1, you don't really have to draw that line so hard for yourself because you also have to know where to go beyond Season 2. When you're working in production, that's what you figure out: What are all the Season 1 episodes? And I do a lot of talking to the staff about giving them feedback when they're pitching me something. I'll be very clear about whether or not I feel that's actually a Season 1, or a Season 2 episode, because sometimes people will pitch something, and you go, "That's like Season 5. We don't know these characters well enough yet." I don't want to advance someone's social or financial status that far in the first season, because there are so many baby steps we can take to get great episodes out of. And I don't like to go in and pitch without those, because the worst thing I think that can happen to someone is that you sell an idea and you don't know what Episodes 2, 3, 4, 5, and 6 are. That, to me, would be the scariest thing ever.

I hear people talk about it all the time: "I wrote this really phenomenal pilot." We see lots of great pilots, but somebody goes, "You know what? This is so bizarre. It's so quirky, it's so funny, it's a live-action cartoon—wow. It made me laugh so hard." But now what? I just saw a pilot last week and thought, "This is a cute pilot, but I don't see this for five years," and I'm really intrigued to watch subsequent episodes, because I don't think they're going to do it. But if they pull it off, they're brilliant. But nine times out of ten, they won't pull it off. There really won't be a series. There are series that are developed and they have these great devices, and I can actually watch it and tell that the writers were getting very tired by Episode 3 or 4, in trying to incorporate that device of telling the story backwards and sideways, and trying to manipulate the form. There's a reason why a certain story structure has worked since the beginning of time. And it's not like it shouldn't be broken. But I really do feel as if you need to know the structure in order to break the structure in a way that works, like the antistructure.

JD: What would make us want to watch this as a series?

YB: I think this show could be an interesting exploration of where women are in the millennium, now trying to be executives in the ranks with men, as well as balance these multigenerational issues with our mothers, and perhaps our younger siblings. I might even give Sarah a younger sibling, who is different from her, in terms of her desires and wants—maybe more like her mother—so she finds herself in this sandwich. And just have it be a show about where we are as women, and where we've taken on too much, and where we need to take on more. Again, that would be like the seed of it.

And then there's also the grandmother, correct? There are the grandparents. So the grandmother, obviously, was probably a very fifties housewife, so she did what she was supposed to do in her little cubby, and they provided very well for this daughter, who had a very comfortable life, and then she married this man, and she had a comfortable, fabulous life, and never really learned to do much of anything for herself. But now Sarah's coming up at this time when women are really doing it for themselves. I mean, we can't have the "movement" be in vain. So we're trying to do it all. And then the question is, Have we taken on too much, as individuals, and then also as members of our family? Because I think the family element is a really interesting element.

JD: If you didn't have to worry about any constraints from networks and you could do anything you wanted to give it the Bowser touch, what would you do?

YB: I'd give Sarah more dimension, and make her represent women like me as much as possible, in as many different facets of her life—that would really be it. I wouldn't say, "You know what, I just want to make it a cable show," and suddenly she's naked. I once pitched a show to cable and when I left I really wondered, "When they want to have these sex scenes, or certain kinds of things that go against my personal, spiritual grain, I don't know that I'm really ready to do this." I think maybe there'll be a time and a place, but I kept thinking you know when I'm ready to tell the secrets and stories yet untold. I've told so many stories on network TV, and then I pitched this idea to cable, and then I just thought, "Am I really ready for them to be naked?" I don't know. Or same-sex scenes or rough sex scenes or any of the stuff that cable might impose on an idea. I don't know that that's really who I am.

To me, there's a challenge in keeping it clean and knowing where those lines are for network television, and that makes it harder. I curse like a sailor sometimes, but I don't necessarily know that it's what I want to put in a show.

JD: So what problems do you find with the networks?

YB: Executives like to try to guide your vision too much. This recent process that I've been involved in has been really pretty good. There's been very little tampering. But I do find that executives have a sensibility that leads toward either the extremely quirky or the extremely conventional. If you give them a story that just goes to the left of what they've seen before, they will almost always try to bring you back to that one story that they've seen a thousand times. And it worked twenty-five of those thousand times. But it's not fresh. For myself, having been in the business now nineteen years—I've been a show creator and show runner for the last thirteen years—I probably challenge myself more than executives do, because I just have a strong desire to keep it fresh, to make the material somehow new for myself. You have to go and sit in a room all by yourself and face your pad of paper, or face your computer, and it's like, *Blue Sky.* I don't want to feel like I'm just writing the same thing I wrote and succeeded with thirteen years ago. I have to contribute to my own evolution, as a person and as a writer. So I have certainly done the pilot that focused on a young woman and her mother and the relationship ended in the pilot. We've seen it a thousand times, haven't we? So when I'm writing another show that focuses on a young woman, I'm not opposed to making the story have something to do with her romantic life and the conflict there, but I just don't want to do it like this: She's in a relationship, he breaks up with her, or he cheats on her, she discovers the pictures on the Internet, she discovers a text message, or something. I barely want to see it again, let alone write it. So it is mostly about keeping it fresh for myself, and thinking that, quite frankly, that's what the audience wants. The audience doesn't want to see the same old pilot again. It's not 1970, when we've only had twenty years of television. Now the audience has higher expectations. And they don't just want whacky, single-camera comedies that look like live-action cartoons, where people suspend each other from the tops of buildings. We still crave the basic humor and premise of *I Love Lucy*. Characters—we know so purely what their motivation is, and we have our own expectations, and we're humored by our expectations of what they'll do, and we're also humored by their violation of our expectations of what they'll do.

PD: As a female writer—the "f" word—you've worked with lots of male writers. How was that experience?

YB: Well, let's see, I'm not only the "f" word, I'm the "b" word, which is black. So my experience is, again, as the double minority. I decided to take what could be a double negative and make it into a double positive, and have very much made a career out of that. I have certainly experienced sexism along the way and racism along the way. And it wasn't necessarily covert racism. But the inequities that I experienced really drove me to create my own show.

I was on one show, and I called my agent. I said, "Get me off this plantation." They didn't know what they were doing. And they were treating me badly (a) because I was a girl, and

(b) because I was black. I had come from a very nurturing environment, where what I had to say as a woman and, particularly, as a black woman was very relevant to the show that I was working on, which was *A Different World*. I spent the first five years of my career in this very insulated and unique situation. Bill Cosby was at the helm, and it was female-friendly, and it was African-American friendly, and it was also a situation where it welcomed people who were intelligent.

PD: When you became a show runner and then a creator, was it sometimes difficult to be the boss?

YB: I've always tried to be a really good mentor to people, and I think there's been a fine line between *teacher* and *mentor*, but I think mentor is a little bit more like, "I'm trying to help you be my equal," as opposed to "I'm teaching you something that you need to know, little person." So I think that's probably the difference.

PD: You got out of college as a psych major. How did you make this transition into comedy?

YB: I lived somewhere right around these parts in a building where our neighbor was a really good friend of Mr. Cosby's. So during my senior year of college, I was having a "pity party" with my best friend, and we were watching *The Cosby Show*, and I saw the name of that person on the credits, and I tracked him down. And it just so happened that he was on his way to the Bay Area to do some music for a movie that Cosby was shooting in Oakland, and we met up on the set and I begged Cosby for a job. "I'll get coffee, I'll get sandwiches, I'll do whatever I have to do," just to see what it is, because I didn't even know what writing for TV was.

PD: Have you always had a good sense of humor?

YB: I wasn't voted Class Clown, but yeah, I think so. I think people have found me amusing, so I just decided, "Oh, then I must be." But I don't hold myself out as the funniest person, and I try to have a diversified staff when I'm staffing a show, and I try to make myself *not* the funniest person in the room, because that's a lot of pressure. I try to find people who I think are actually funnier than I am, smarter than I am. I try to always find someone who knows TV history better than I do, because I like to have people in the room who can say, "You know what—they did that on *The Mary Tyler Moore Show*," "You know that was in an *I Love Lucy* episode, and let me tell you how it went," so we can go, "Oh, OK, how do we make this situation work for us?" There are staffs where they'll sit around and talk about, "OK, what retread can we do this week?" And that just drives me nuts.

PD: Did you learn all your comedy writing craft OJT?

YB: Yeah, on the job, just watching other people do it, seeing how they did it. Again, part of that hazing process that first year of being an apprentice was contributing ideas for characters and story lines and actual episodes that other people ended up writing and putting their names on, that had actually been generated by me. So once I saw that I could do it, that I was actually doing it—I was saying it, the writer's assistant was writing it down, and then the actors were saying it—I realized, "Oh, I have a gift for this." And basically, again, I went back and spoke at the Stanford graduation, and I realized, "I'm sorry, gang, I've told all your stories on my show." It was a hugely popular show back at Stanford, because, particularly, the black community had seen a lot of their stories told. We had some black sorority and fraternity stories, and things like that, and people were like, "We know who was doing that."

PD: I get the sense that when you say you're strong, it doesn't come from a place of ego. You approached it with reason and said, "And here's why."

YB: Absolutely. I don't respond to people who try to shove their agenda down my throat, so I wouldn't imagine that someone would respond well to that being my approach.

JD: Have you ever backed down on a piece of writing, something you felt should go into a show, and then later said, "Shouldn't have done that."

YB: Maybe where the network was concerned, but I don't really think so. Well, they're the people paying the bills, and at the end of the day, particularly when you're doing a pilot, if you don't take the notes, find a way to make them your own, and convince them that you're giving them what they've asked for, you'll be sitting at home watching your pilot in your robe.

PD: Some of the writers we spoke to haven't shared your eagerness to work with networks. Some came right out and said, "I will never write something again if I can't produce or direct it." And still others have said, "I'm just so tired of having to have my outline approved, and then my story approved, and the characters approved. And you were saying that's part of the challenge.

YB: I think people forget the salesman part of the job—that's part of it. Unless you're paying for it yourself, when someone else is paying for it, you have an obligation to sell it to them. And you just continue to sell them on your point of view, on your approach to a given story, on your approach to a particular scene.

They're really separate skills. And I do feel I've been blessed with both. I'm a pretty good writer. And I feel like I'm a really, really good manager. And I don't know if I'm better at one than the other, but I know that once the writing really gets started, the production really gets started, there's a lot more to manage. My approach has also changed over the years. The first year of *Living Single* I took home every script, and every script went through my typewriter, which was a computer at the time. It's evolved, but we still say that.

JD: Stephen Sondheim suggests that the more specific something is the more universal it will be. Do you find that in your work?

YB: I do. I completely find that to be true. Unless it gets to be so inside some specific dynamic. There was a show on TV recently, which I actually thought had an interesting pilot, and it dealt with people who were in therapy, but as the series developed, the people who were in therapy—their issues or their neuroses—became so unrelatable to me that I disconnected. But what was relatable to me initially was that here was a group of human beings who had very different circumstances, but who were somehow bound together and looking to each other for help, and then it just went in a different direction. So I saw a tremendous potential from the pilot, but it wasn't really fleshed out in the series.

PD: You take a story and make it pass a litmus test of universality.

YB: Right. It's like the core values have to be universal, so that you're not just writing it for yourself. It can come in so many ways. The show *24* is a show that everybody from its inception was saying, "Ohmigosh, we can't miss an episode." And I kept saying, "I refuse to watch it, because it sounds really good, and I'm going to get addicted, and I can't afford another hour of TV." And this year I watched Seasons 1 to 5, and I am a complete junky, even though the situations are ridiculous, they're preposterous, and yet on an emotional level they pull me in every week. I can see myself in that set of circumstances. I get passionate about what's going on. And there's a formula. I know when Jack Bauer's going to say, "You're lying." I know it. I know when it's coming, and yet it still grips me.

PD: Talking about formulas . . . You have a very precise paradigm for how you go about writing, dimensionalizing the characters. Has that evolved much over the years? Has it been pretty constant or do you keep adding wrinkles and changing it?

YB: I say, "If it ain't broke, don't fix it." So, no, I haven't changed it much. I start out with my list of things: I go beyond the romantic and the spiritual and the financial and the political. What do the characters think of holidays? Any topic. Sometimes I'll take headlines from the news and say, "How does this character feel about this? How would this news article play out in this situation? Just to see if I have enough different points of view in a series idea.

For example, I like to dress down when I go shopping in Beverly Hills, just to see how the salespeople treat me. And the ones who treat me right I give them my business with my black American Express card, and those who don't, I don't patronize them. It's my little game. And I wrote an episode about it on *A Different World*, and we got a Humanitas Award for that one.

MY MOTHER THE SOCIOPATH

 An Interview with David Breckman

A partial list of David Breckman's credits as a writer
and executive producer includes *Monk*, *Saturday Night Live*,
Pic Six, *Underfunded*, and *Pulled Over*.

U nlike some of the other writers featured in this book, David
Breckman never had to worry about showing up at the
breakfast table with a zinger. He grew up in a supportive
environment, where books were treasured and humor was gold. He
spent "forty-five minutes" attending college and then began his real
education. He signed up for courses with Mark Twain, Woody Allen,
Monty Python, and his older brother, Andy Breckman, who preceded
him on *Saturday Night Live* by ten years, and who he calls "the funniest
man alive." He funded his education by earning as he was learning.

David Breckman has an innate sense of what's funny, but is
uncompromising in his pursuit of what makes a story work. As he
develops this premise, he moves from a wide view to something
very specific that tips toward the dark side of the spectrum without
diminishing the commercial aspects of his project.

✦ ✦ ✦

DB: (David Breckman) Well, my first-blush reaction is that it's
clearly a sitcom. The premise is great for a sitcom because it's

loose. Sitcoms are primarily about the characters, and then each individual episode can be very tightly written, and very premise-driven. But the premise of the show itself is typically very loose. *Seinfeld* is just a bunch of neurotic New Yorkers hanging out and having adventures. I don't agree that the show was about nothing, because, particularly in the later years, it was the most plot-driven show of all time. Often, there were three plots going on simultaneously and they would all dovetail at the end. The whole thing about the show about nothing—that was true for the first year or two.

I would want to do Molly and Sarah's story as a feature. Molly, who's lost her husband, and perhaps lost her anchor, is, to some degree, rudderless now and also struggling with the idea of being middle-aged. Maybe she starts competing with her daughter, Sarah, who she's just moved in with, for the attentions of a guy. I don't know who that would be, but that's another way to go with it. And that's something that a lot of people, myself included, can relate to—the fact that we're trying to hold on to our youth and we're feeling threatened by every succeeding generation.

You could do it as a feature, where Molly, the mother, was the heavy and doing it from Sarah's point of view. Sarah would be faced with the prospect of having her own mother competing with her, and indeed, trying to undermine her, as they're competing for the attentions of a guy. And it could be funny, but there's also something heartbreaking about it—knowing that your own mother is sabotaging your efforts at seducing or romancing this guy. And there could be scenes with Sarah as this realization first dawns on her, as it's first sinking in: "Holy crap, the tires on my car were slashed. I couldn't imagine who would do that. I thought it was my creepy neighbor, Jack, but I'm seeing evidence now that it was my mother."

That kind of dawning realization would be harrowing. Your "frenemy" is your mother, of all things. So that's another way to go. But one problem, one of the recurring flaws of that premise, is that although mothers and daughters traditionally are at odds with each other, I don't think this situation I'm describing happens very often. So I don't know if there's a lot of relatability there. You can talk about a mother being stifling, you can talk about a mother being smothering or intrusive, but a mother sabotaging you—and whatever the female equivalent of "cockblocking" is—in your efforts to romance a guy. Well, God forbid, if it happened. But I do think it's a funny way of going.

PD (PETER DESBERG): It's a funny idea. I'm just thinking that Molly has convinced herself this guy's not really right for her daughter.

DB: That's great. She could be rationalizing these atrocious things she's doing. Because even people who do the most dastardly things don't ever think of themselves as evil. No one thinks that what they're doing is malicious. They're always rationalizing everything they do, even Stalin, Hitler. So I guess both parties would feel justified in what they're doing, although, Sarah, I think, with a lot more justice.

If this is a feature, the central character is Sarah coming to terms with the fact that she is competing with her mother for the attentions of a guy, or a job. Her mother moves to town and throws her hat in the ring for the same job Sarah's going for. Molly starts sabotaging her. And then there could be a guy at the company they can both be competing for. This is an easy way. What if it's the boss? I guess the basis of the story would be realizing that you have to compete with your mother, which is alternately funny and harrowing.

At a certain point, Sarah could say to her best friend,

"Ohmigod, my mother's sabotaging me," which is a bitter pill
to swallow because your psyche is denying this the whole time.
"Okay, she's going out with Ted. I love Ted, but she's dating him
and she's spending the night at his chalet—I'm sure with the best
of intentions. Just wait a minute, I'm sure she had a reason, but she
slashed my tires. But I'm sure it was with the best of intentions." At
a certain point, all her defenses would be down; the firewalls have
been penetrated, and there's just no conclusion left except, "My
mother might be a c-nt." Which, in a sense, makes this almost a
horror movie.

Yeah, I think that might be the way to go with it, and it would
just be sort of this slowly dawning realization. I don't quite have a
resolution for that. There's any number of ways to go with it. Focus
groups would probably want a comeuppance for the mother, but
then it also depends on what studio you're doing it for. There might
be a reconciliation of sorts.

PD: You can also come up with three or four endings.

DB: Right, which is sort of how it's being done now. They ultimately
end up with three or four. The focus audiences will reject the first
ending, and the studio will very hastily demand a new ending, and
they'll reshoot the last ten or fifteen minutes. And typically, the new
ending is much blander and more by the numbers and unsatisfying.

PD: Composers have false cadences, where you think you're going
to the ending, but they're setting the audience up for a different
ending.

DB: That's my favorite kind of storytelling. It should be the goal
of any ending. It should be satisfying, but it should be surprising
at the same time. That's a difficult nexus to find. But you're right;
ideally, you're going for something like that. What you end up

with is something usually much more unsurprising, unfortunately, and clichéd.

PD: How would you handle the question of the mother's likability?

DB: You'd have to decide if you want the mother to have a tenable argument. You'd have to decide if the audience would be called upon to sympathize with Molly. I don't know if that would make for as entertaining a movie. If it was more from Sarah's point of view, the mother could be more of a heavy, and you wouldn't have to make her as likable. As a writer, I'm inclined to make it about Sarah, and to make the mother this villain, which I think is just more interesting. But maybe if you wanted to attract Jessica Lange, or some really talented fifty-something actress, you'd have to end up making the mom more sympathetic, which, frankly, I'll say, for me, just won't be as much fun. If you're talking about a fun ninety minutes, this should be a perverse sort of horror movie. But instead of, "Oh my God, my mother is a werewolf," it's, "Oh my God, my mother is a bitch!" And so to keep this as entertaining as it can be, I would not feel obligated to make Molly sympathetic.

The other thing is this: Sarah we like. She's your protagonist. You would like her. I'm not a marketing person, but I suspect that young women, twenty-something girls, would really relate to the idea of a woman who is at odds with and fighting for her life against her mother. Of course, we'd be pandering, but . . .

PD: You've come up with some very good, film "noirish," dark-comedy elements. Is that something that interests you?

DB: It's funny you should say that. One spec I wrote a long time ago and I'm retooling is actually a dark comedy. It's a riff on the Hitchcockian premise of the innocent man falsely accused, and then having to go on the run and establish his innocence. *North by*

Northwest is a classic example of that, but Hitchcock did that a lot. He did it in a movie called *Saboteur*. He remade that movie at least three or four times.

I tried to think of what would be the most horrible thing you could be accused of, something that you would then have to establish you were innocent of, but still maintain a comedic tone. And here's what occurred to me: a spate of killing of grandmothers. In America we love mothers, but we *really* love grandmothers. So if you were accused of that crime, and the people who were framing you—in my story this guy is being meticulously framed—it looks for all the world like he's doing it. The cops show up at his apartment when he's not there and they find five dead old women on the floor. And the police were summoned there because of a phone call that he apparently made. The cops had his voice coming from his apartment. They come in and find five dead grandmothers on his carpet. It looks very incriminating. Think David Schwimmer in the first couple of seasons of *Friends*. "I did *not* do this. I am *not* the granny killer." But no one believes him. And this guy would never survive eleven minutes in prison because a lot of convicts were raised by their grandmothers. So he escapes his captors and he goes on the run, and he's trying to find out who's doing this, who's setting him up, who framed him. So that, I think falls under the heading of *dark comedy*.

But like we do with *Monk*, I want the mystery elements to make sense. It shouldn't just be an excuse to have gags; hopefully, the comedy works. But the mystery should make sense. One of my favorite movies is *Silver Streak*, which is a really good comedy thriller.

PD: How would you take those elements and integrate them into Sarah and Molly's story?

"The more perverse part of me, which is the dominant part of me, thinks you can't go far enough."

DB: Well, this is not a thriller. Hopefully, there'd be moments of suspense. It has that sort of *Enemy Within* feel. You don't know how far the mother will go. You'd have to decide how far you'd want this mother to go, and exactly what she's willing to do. The more perverse part of me, which is the dominant part of me, thinks you can't go far enough. Molly would *literally* end up ruining Sarah's life to get what she wants. But then you are limiting yourself, as far as your wrap-up or resolution is concerned. You can't have reconciliation at the end, having them hugging as if everything's forgotten, as you roll the credits.

But if you were to explore that aspect, you could have the mother ruining her daughter's life. Near the end of the film, the end of the second act, where the main character is typically at a low point, God forgive me for breaking out the Robert McKee algebra, because you can't reduce it to calculus. But one problem is every executive has taken these courses and believes this stuff, like it's the Talmud. So they talk in these terms. At these meetings they say, "Tell me your inciting incident. What's your page 30 incident?" And you just want to say, "It's not algebra!" Thank God, because I failed algebra. But if you were to borrow that template, Sarah's low point would have to be where she's completely undone. She would have to be out of work. Her relationship with the guy—we'll make him Dermot Mulroney—is in shambles.

Let's just say it's Reese Witherspoon, Dermot Mulroney, and Jessica Lange. So what if Dermot Mulroney has a Schnauzer. Dermot Mulroney hates Reese because it looks for all the world like she backed over the dog in her car and killed it. Of course, it was Jessica Lange who did it. Jessica Lange undermined

Reese Witherspoon at work and took credit for her work. She's the one who came up with the new account at the advertising firm where they both work.

PD: Would Reese figure out it was Jessica?

DB: Oh, yeah, absolutely, by the end of Act II. Without question. She knows, but there's nothing she can do about it. She's impotent at that point. She knows. And then in Act III, she strikes back. And in Act III, the wrap-up is some kind of public comeuppance. I don't know what that would be yet. The easier way, almost a cliché, is some kind of a videotape of Mom being thrown up on a jumbotron in a public place. We would see this compromising thing that would undo the mother entirely. It would expose her as a fraud . . . the monster that she is. And it would vindicate Reese [Sarah]. And of course it would reestablish Reese in Dermot Mulroney's good graces and allow her to get her job back. But that's kind of a cliché, but maybe for commercial purposes it's the best way to go. I don't know what that footage of Mom on the jumbotron would look like.

PD: Given the expression on your face when you say that [a grimace], where would you take it instead?

DB: I'm not sure that the public comeuppance scene is necessarily awful, if it was clever and surprising. If it was just entertaining, that could be great. I guess we'd have some fun lunches just trying to talk about what that climax would involve.

PD: You alluded to something before. You could try to find a resolution in this idea: Jessica turns out to be okay. It was all a huge misunderstanding.

DB: Right. But you'd have to soften all her actions preceding that moment. She can't, at least intentionally, completely ruin her daughter's life that way. The problem with that is if she does it unintentionally, and she's aware of it, and doesn't do anything to make restitution or to put the pieces back together, then she's a monster. So what you have to do then, if she's doing it intentionally—and that's the only way it's interesting to me, if she's doing it intentionally—and you want some kind of reconciliation, then you've got to soften the actions and whatever she's doing prior to that. It just can't be as extreme. It's more of a subtler, nuanced James L. Brooks kind of comedy. Your way is less broad, which may not be the worst thing.

I think my taste, probably because of my background as a sketch writer, tends to run toward broad comedy and I tend to take things to extremes. I think there's less of an appetite for that, at least among executives. Most people, certainly directors like Mike Nichols and James L. Brooks, would want something that's more grounded in reality.

PD: What if Molly did the wrong thing, thinking it was the right thing, and then was reeducated?

DB: Then you're imposing constraints on your character's behavior. You can talk about reeducation, but, again, that only works if the mother's behavior is more moderate. And I don't know what she'd be doing, unwittingly or half-unwittingly. I think doing intentional harm is less commercial, but I think it might be funnier and more satisfying.

PD: Maybe it is commercial. Earlier you mentioned this twenty-something demographic. "My parents are my antagonists."

DB: I wish you guys were running Warner Bros. Yeah, it's relatable to some degree. But, again, the overriding questions are still these: How restrained is the behavior of the mother? Is her behavior moderate? Is she unwitting in her behavior or is this calculated? Does she know what she's doing and is she truly trying to sabotage her daughter's life?

PD: If you said, okay, the things she did were a little more on the benign side, what would that be?

DB: Well, if you want benign, you want to talk to someone else. Where do you go from tire slasher and dog killer? But some of the more outrageous things might be, if Jessica Lange is trying to undermine Reese Witherspoon's nascent relationship with Dermot Mulroney, she could, à la Iago, place things in Dermot's line of vision. It's far more persuasive if the person you're trying to con or dupe appears to discover them for himself. If I tell you that something is amiss, you might believe me; you might not. But if you seem to uncover that on your own, you're more apt to believe it. So I would have Jessica Lange leaving evidence for Dermot Mulroney to discover that Reese Witherspoon has chlamydia.

JD (JEFFREY DAVIS): Do you think Molly is insane?

DB: That almost meets the definition of a sociopath. "My mother is a sociopath. The wrong parent died."

PD: The new term for it is *antisocial personality.*

DB: That just doesn't have the same ring to it as, "My mother is David Berkowitz." The movie would be a continuous campaign of undermining Reese Witherspoon.

So the other person is convinced of it. Like the handkerchief in *Othello.* If you haven't read anything by this guy—Shakespeare— you should. He's really good. What's so great about Iago? What's great is that Iago is brilliant. He sticks up for Cassio a little bit. He sticks up for the guy he's undermining. He's saying, "I'm telling you,

Cassio is a great guy. He would never have done what you say. He would never have done that." And, of course, this raises Othello's suspicions. "What are you talking about? What did he do?" Iago says, "It doesn't matter. He's a great guy. Forget I said anything. Let's play cards." "No, go back to what you said about Cassio." And so, what would be very insidious would be if Jessica Lange were pretending to stick up for her daughter vociferously, just saying to Dermot, "My daughter is great. This thing about this positive lab slip she got, tear it up. It means nothing." "What positive lab slip?" "You didn't hear?" "No, I didn't hear that." "Doesn't even matter. Nothing. No positive lab slip. My daughter is great." That's always more interesting to me. So not only is she undermining her, she's pretending to stick up for her.

This makes her evil, and, to me, interesting. That would be the mother's campaign. A campaign of terror.

JD: Tell us a little bit about how you started.

DB: I went to Wagner College for forty-five minutes. I guess I was kind of a depressive sort. So I was just knocking around doing odd jobs and minimum-wage jobs throughout my twenties. But I always wanted to write and I always loved film and was working in the kitchen at a South Jersey bistro, making salads and mopping the floor and writing as much as I could in my spare time. I was just trying to learn how to do it, teaching myself the craft.

My brother wrote for *Saturday Night Live* in the '80s and introduced me to Jim Downey. He liked what I gave him and he asked for more. He recommended me to a couple of the producers there who wanted to see more work, and then there was a round of interviews. After several months, I ended up on staff there in '96.

Dennis Miller has compared *SNL* to Gladiator School. And if you've ever worked there, you'll know that's an understatement.

It's fiercely competitive. It's twenty writers competing for a certain number of slots every week. When I was there, it was even harder because, of those eight or nine sketches that were available, most of them were being filled with sketches that featured recurring characters. The Cheerleader, the Ladies' Man, and Mary Catherine Gallagher. Because Lorne Michaels had been spinning these characters off into feature films, and it was lucrative for a while.

But as far as sketches are concerned, I like Pythonesque, premise-driven sketches. That's just what I've always loved and what I've always written. But there was only room for one or two of those per week.

PD: Did people work together?

DB: Yes, a lot of times they did. I was kind of writing on my own, which, on reflection, may have been a mistake. But I don't regret it because the kind of sketches I was writing are the only kind of sketches I like to watch.

PD: Once you came in with a sketch that they liked, would other people work on it with you?

DB: The sketches were rewritten collectively, usually on Thursdays around the big table.

PD: How was the rewriting process for you on *SNL*?

DB: Frustrating, of course, but generally the sketches got better. But you did lose the singular voice that you had going in, which is always unfortunate, I think. But there were very talented people there, so the sketches got better.

PD: Were you a funny kid growing up?

DB: I always tried to be. It was sort of my default setting. I wasn't always successful. I don't know, you hear these stories. When you were sitting around the table, you were jockeying for attention and you always hear the same story. If you weren't fast with a zinger, boy, you were in trouble. It wasn't like that; it really wasn't. Thank God. It would've been terrifying, just waking up in the morning, "Do I have a zinger for breakfast? Holy f--k, I'm a dead man." That would've been terrifying. But I wasn't a very happy kid, and I think that's almost a prerequisite for getting into this business.

JD: Were you mentored?

DB: By my brother, Andy Breckman, who was and remains the funniest guy I've ever met. He is eleven years older than me. Certainly, he's mentored me during the eight years I've been on *Monk*. We never worked together before the show. But he's the show runner, he created the show, and I've learned as much about writing from him as from anyone, particularly comedy writing. He didn't set out to do that. It wasn't like a tutorial, but just through osmosis, just watching him work.

JD: How do you work in the room? Do you break out stories?

DB: Here's how it works: Andy [Andy Breckman, *Monk* creator] will approve a story nugget. They're called *nuggets*, a kernel of an idea. Typically, we start with the mystery kernel. And Andy generates some of the ideas, but just as often, if not more often, he's approving ideas; usually they're shot down. For every idea that he approves, there are ninety-nine more that are shot down. And a mystery nugget might be this: A man is murdered twelve hours before he is due to be executed in the electric chair. Someone killed the guy on death row twelve hours before he was going to die anyway. Why on earth would anyone want to do that? What could possibly be a motive for that killing? That's an intriguing question. So we would just break our ass trying to come up with a satisfying answer. That's intriguing, and it also gets Monk in a prison, which is, we hope, fun. This guy is very uptight, and a nervous guy, a persnickety guy, finding himself dropped in the middle of San Quentin. We thought it was a funny notion, so we ran with it. We had a solution that was a little more surprising, but, hopefully, logical. That's typically how we begin a story, with a premise like that, and then the question is this: How does Monk get into this? And is it fun? It might be a great mystery, but it may not be fun. It has to be a fun ride for the viewer. And what's Monk doing?

And then there's another question that has become more important to my brother over the years. What is the emotional core of the episode? What's Monk going through in this episode? We've had episodes where, in the course of the story, Monk is coming to terms with his own mortality; or Monk has to overcome a specific fear; or Monk starts to date again . . . that kind of thing. And Monk is very faithful to the memory of his late wife, but in an episode we did, he's feeling a romantic yearning for a woman who might be guilty of murder. And so we have a clever mystery going on, but we are also addressing Monk having these feelings.

PD: Do you develop these ideas around the table?

DB: Yes, absolutely. When Andy approves a story, we typically spend five or six workdays outlining these stories, and putting note cards up. It's five cards per act. Four acts, roughly twenty sequences. And you've got to bring the funny, but you've got to also bring the heart, although *heart* is a word I despise when it's bandied around writers' rooms and executives' offices because there's something almost calculated about it. "Where's the heart?" If you have to impose it like that, if it's artificial, like you're talking about a bottle of Excedrin, you're talking about an artificial heart. But you have to bring comedic and emotional elements and hopefully, it works as a mystery. So there are all these things that have to work together.

PD: Is it collaborative rather than competitive?

DB: People who have worked in other rooms, who end up in ours, say it's one of the best environments they've ever been in. Obviously, it's competitive to the extent that everybody wants to shine and we all have egos. But it's mostly supportive. We love the comedy and we love writing it, but we break our asses getting the mysteries right. Because we all have comedy backgrounds, it's easier for us to do that than it is to write the mysteries, which we're really proud of. Mysteries are very hard to structure: They're very intricate if you're going to do them right. They have to have a tantalizing puzzle at the beginning, and then a satisfying solution. But before we're through, everything goes through Andy's typewriter. Andy's antiquated writing software . . . *Word Star,* actually. Think Hoover administration.

DON'T THROW AWAY YOUR
10 PERCENTERS

 An Interview with Peter Casey

A partial list of Peter Casey's credits as creator/show
runner and writer include *Frasier*, *Wings*, *Cheers*,
The Jeffersons, and *Encore! Encore!*

Peter Casey is insightful, demanding, and nice. Some of the writers we've interviewed would say that's an unlikely blend of characteristics to be found in the co-creator of two of television's most successful situation comedies. But it's Peter's work experience that tells the story. He and his partner, David Lee, started out on a show where writers were encouraged to compete with each other in unproductive ways. Where there was little camaraderie. Where very often second best was good enough. Then Peter and David had the good fortune to move to *Cheers*, where they were mentored by the Charles Brothers, two guys who are poster children for toughness, never settling for second best and . . . nice. The staff on *Cheers* worked hard, because they were treated well and their ideas mattered. Even working into the early hours of the morning and not settling for the first joke or story idea that came along became an opportunity for celebration. It was all about esprit de corps.

Peter saw firsthand the success this approach created. Following in his mentors' footsteps, he ran with this idea and, judging by the fruit it bore, he made a good call. His shows have won Golden Globes, Peabodys, Humanitas Awards, and Emmys—over thirty in all. Spending time with Peter Casey, you realize that Leo Durocher was wrong. Nice guys can finish first.

❉ ❉ ❉

PC (PETER CASEY): This premise does have elements of *Frasier* in it. You have this daughter, Sarah, who is on her own, and she's got this independent life, and she's on the opposite coast from her parents. *Frasier* started that way, with Frasier being in Boston at *Cheers* and the rest of his family in Seattle. Now it happens that he's the oldest one and he moved west, where in this case, the mother moves in. But when Frasier did get out west, he was starting this brand new life, where he says, "I'm going to have it the way I always wanted it. I have my apartment the way I want it. I have this new, exciting career." Everything is perfectly set in place and then the dad moves in, and the dad brings the dog, and because of his condition, the health care worker moves in. And suddenly, this sort of idyllic life that Frasier had set up for himself is kaput.

PD (PETER DESBERG): And the chair . . .

PC: The chair was a character. When our set designer came in, we said we wanted a Barcalounger and it's got to be pretty hideous. We want some duct tape on it. And he comes in with this book of fabrics, and I swear the book was this thick [holds hands about six inches apart], and it was that pattern of fabric just in various colors. It was literally that same striped pattern, but with different hideous combinations of color, which he obviously thought were great. I can't imagine somebody actively going out to make an ugly chair. So we just picked the worst one in the book and there we go.

"The more different they are, the more chance you have of disagreements and conflict . . ."

But, yes, this premise has certain elements that are reminiscent of *Frasier*. It could benefit from Molly and Sarah being a little more different from each other. The more different they are, the more chance you have of disagreements and conflict, and that's where you get fun in the family. Molly might be trying to get Sarah involved with someone while I could see Sarah thinking, "If I can get Mom hooked up with someone, I don't have to have her in the house anymore." So I think you have a whole array of stories that can work that back-and-forth way.

If Sarah had a confidante, she could express her frustration over whatever's going on with Molly, whatever difficulty she's having with her mom. Then you could really state them very clearly to the audience. It could be a girlfriend, it could be a guy friend. You could make it a guy at work, and maybe the mother's always thinking, "Well, he's such a nice guy, you should go out with him." And Sarah's always going, "No, he's just a friend." "Oh, honey, that's the way your dad and I started out."

Molly is fifty-ish and broke and probably constantly telling Sarah, "Your father, God rest his soul, I loved him so much, but the bastard left me dead broke." And it also seems like you have the possibility of a lot of stories where you're trying to get Molly work-ready. Sarah might say, "Oh, maybe you need to look for a little job." And Molly answers, "Well, what am I skilled at?" "Well, you're not really skilled at anything, but let's find something for you, even if it's volunteer work." Or Molly's decided to take some classes at night school and is trying to expand and explore her life. So those could be stories. In fact, it might be funny if Sarah's decided to take a class, and when her mom hears about that, she says, "That's a great idea." And then, the next thing you know, Molly shows up at the class, too.

This sets up conflict of another kind. Sarah's feelings are, "My dad's just died. My mom's got issues. I've got to be pretty sensitive toward her." And maybe Molly, in turn, is being very insensitive to Sarah. So those strike me as some possibilities that you could do a lot with. That's just stuff off the top of my head. Short interview, huh?

PD: You've set up a whole bunch of potentially interesting conflicts.

PC: But that's always the thing. You want as many types of conflict as you can find. If you look at any comedy, that's ultimately what you end up having. That's what I think makes any story funny.

Molly being a little older, and being a mother, may look at certain things in Sarah's lifestyle that she may not agree with. Maybe that's the way kids are dating now. She also could be one of those clichéd and traditional moms who keep asking, "Why do you have this career going? You really need to settle down and have a family." And maybe there's something funny in the idea that Sarah just can't bring herself to tell her mother, "You're the reason why I don't want to have children because I saw what you did to me." So those are the kinds of differences you'd want.

There could easily be feelings of resentment on Sarah's part, in the sense that, "You've not only invaded my life, but I've been doing something very nice for you, and you don't seem to look at it that way. You can be completely insensitive to me, and I have to take it because you're the one mourning the loss of your husband."

There's also something I was thinking about. I remember sometimes when we'd have my mom down here from the Bay Area, after my dad died, and we'd go out to some place in public, and my mother would just strike up conversations with strangers, and I'd start thinking, "Oh, God, I didn't come to this restaurant to sort of chat with these people." And it may be the kind of thing where Molly's trying to make friends. "Well, you told me I need to go out and make friends." And every time Sarah's coming home, somebody else from the apartment building is in the apartment. It's like, "Well, who's this?" It seems like you could have some fun with that, too.

There is an issue here. It's not just the character of Molly, who's old. It's me who's old. So it might be tough getting networks interested in me. But the obvious solution is this: You've got to make Sarah incredibly hot, and it doesn't hurt if she starts wearing some hot clothes—the least amount of clothes she can get away with.

It's tough. It's interesting when you stop and look at something as great as *Everybody Loves Raymond*. This show had two older actors in very prominent roles, but they were great, they were gold. The younger the network executives get, the harder it is to convince them that there's fun to be had there. We had John Mahoney on our show, and, interestingly enough, people didn't realize John's only about ten years older than Kelsey—that's all. Yet he played his dad. But we never had a problem with that. I think that problem has started coming up of late. Look, it all boils down to demographics. They keep wanting this eighteen- to thirty-five age group. The thirty-five to fifty-five age group doesn't matter that much to them, which is very sad, because they're the people who have the money to spend. But when you ask the executives about that, they say, "Well, that's not what we're looking at. The advertisers are looking at future buyers. Eighteen to thirty-five is where they're forming their buying habits, and if they decide they want to buy Crest toothpaste, they're going to buy Crest toothpaste until they're fifty-five, so we don't have to worry about selling Crest to the forty-five-year-old people. Their buying habits are set." It's not every eighteen-year-old who can buy a BMW. "Buying habits—we're looking to get those, as soon as they have that money to buy things. At about twenty-eight maybe."

I think some of it also has to do with casting. If you get somebody who's really terrific as Molly, that'll make a difference. And it also has to be how good the character is. If you look at Peter Boyle's character, he was a fun character because he was so cantankerous. If he was sort of warm and cuddly, I don't know how particularly interesting that would have been to the network and advertisers. So I think it's a matter of how you make this work. And you really are kind of treading a fine line, too, because you don't have a lot of room between making them interesting as an older person, and making them unlikable. If you make them too soft and fuzzy, they're probably not that interesting. So you try to put a little more edge into them. But you can also make that go over the line into, "I really don't like watching this." So you don't have a lot of room for error, I think, with an older character like Molly.

JD (JEFFREY DAVIS): If you could do anything to this premise you wanted, what would it be?

PC: I'd change it to two men. First of all, I know that better than I know women. I also think that viewing audiences are more apt to watch a show with men in the lead than women. That isn't to say that you can't have great shows that feature women in the lead. *The Mary Tyler Moore Show* was a pretty good show, but I just think that, if not both of them, certainly Sarah should be a man. Part of the reason is that, in my experience, the only thing harder to find than a really attractive, young, funny guy, is a really young, attractive, funny woman. It's just really hard casting. When we were doing *Wings*, we had lots and lots of casting sessions out here that were unsuccessful, and we finally had to go back to New York, and we found both Tim Daly and Stephen Weber in

New York casting sessions. But finding attractive, funny women? Really hard.

For *Wings*, we were going crazy trying to cast the lead part of Helen, and finally the network called and said Crystal Bernard. Well, the character was originally Greek . . . so when Crystal finally came in and read for us—and she was far and away the best person we'd seen—we said, "Look, we'll rewrite it to Texas." So long Greece, hello Texas. Just had to do that because the casting was so hard. And then, she had already had a pilot that she had shot, so we were in second position. And we were just sitting there praying that her pilot fell through so we could get her to do ours. And it did.

Well, again, to me, it feels like you have sort of a classic *Odd Couple* situation set up here. That's in a way what we did with *Wings*. We had this sort of buttoned-down brother who owned the business, Tim Daly, and then the completely wild-haired other brother. And they had a long history of animosity in dealing with each other. But as their father's dying wish, he wanted them to work together. And that's how that came about. So if we changed Molly and Sarah to a father having to move in with his son, you could even do the kind thing where the father doesn't necessarily want to be there with the son, and each believes this is all going to be a very temporary thing. In fact, maybe the father has not let the son know that there's any kind of financial problems, or that he's broke. He's just too proud to let his son know that. And the son thinks, "Okay, he's going to come for a visit. Let's just put up with this for a few days, and then he'll be gone." And then it comes out that they could have had a strained relationship. That's one way of doing it.

PD (PETER DESBERG): If you had a chance to play with this and you didn't have to worry about networks and oversight and you could take this anywhere you wanted, and make it as outrageous as you wanted, what would you do with it?

PC: I've come to really enjoy edgy. We didn't always do a lot of edgy on *Frasier*. I thought we did very smart humor. I remember how we used to talk about the difference between us and the Charles Brothers. Besides their being just incredibly brilliant writers. But with *Cheers* they never came off the cynical end of the show, and we usually would. We'd usually show a little heart at the end of our episodes. So that was a difference we had. But I like shows that are a little darker, that have darker humor. My favorite show on the air right now is *The Office*. I'm so in love with that show. I can't wait to watch it. It really is the best show I've seen in years. And those characters, as quirky as they are, they're so real to me. And I like "real."

When we created *Frasier*, we spoke with our writers, especially during that first season, and we said, "We'd rather have a page of good dialogue without jokes, than to have two or three mediocre jokes on the page." And we said, "Look, we've got the horses here in the stable. If you want to write a good, dramatic scene between Kelsey Grammer, David Hyde Pierce, and John Mahoney, you've really got the capacity to do that. So let's try to be real about this sort of dysfunctional family we have here. And don't feel like you have to cram jokes in."

There's nothing worse than having worked out a story, and then given it to a writer, and you wait for a week and a half or two weeks for that first draft, and you go, "This is a train wreck. We've got to push this whole thing." And that happened a couple of times in the first season, because you're feeling your way.

**"Almost always, a train wreck is a story problem.
It's a structure problem. And that's our fault.
We're the ones who came up with the stories . . ."**

JD: How do you fix a train wreck?

PC: Almost always, a train wreck is a story problem. It's a structure problem. And that's our fault. We're the ones who came up with the stories and then we would try to construct them, and then farm them out to the writer. And it's the same thing, even when sometimes you'd get the drafts and you'd think, "Oh, this should be great." And you'd have a bad reading. It wasn't the actors' fault. You'd have to go back to the story. You can't just go back to the script and say, "Oh, well, we just need to punch it up and make it funnier." No. You've got to go back to the story, to the structure of this thing, and why are we having problems with it? I always hate to use that phrase, "Somebody has to have something at stake." That's the phrase that sends chills down a writer's spine because it's what every network executive says. But the fact of the matter is that you do. In *Frasier*, even when a story was built around Niles, you had to go back and say, "Well, what does Frasier have at stake in this thing? What is he looking for out of this?" Because even if it was Niles's story or a story about the dad, you had to bring your star into it.

The show's called *Frasier*, so he's got to have some very strong point of view in any given situation. And it's always great if every character has a point of view. You can't have everybody meandering along, and reacting to one person talking. Give them all a point of view. When David and I were creating the show, we really made a conscious effort not only to show how Frasier related to the other four characters in there; we made sure that every single character had specific feelings toward each of the other characters. So that if you needed to do a little side scene with Niles and Roz, there was a relationship that was set up there. They happened to have a very antagonistic relationship early in the show, got better as they grew, but that's how it should be. There are many people you meet who you may not particularly like when you first meet them, and then over time you begin to get along. But very early on? Oh, they couldn't stand each other.

What I'd try to do with this premise is this: I'd look for little, quirky things that you can play between the father and son, again and again. One of the things that we did the entire first season, which I always loved, was every time Niles would come into the coffee shop, or over to Frasier's house, and Roz was there, he'd walk over and say, "Oh, hi, I'm Niles." And she'd go, "We've met!" "We have?" It's like she made so little an impression on him that he completely forgot her when he left, and then every time he'd see her, he'd reintroduce himself, and it would just piss her off. And that gives you an attitude, right there. It gives you something to play all the time. And she had no problem calling him an "uptight prig," and he would make constant comments about the fact that she'd slept with everybody in Seattle.

You want to have those things, and on *Frasier*, what we wanted to do was isolate Frasier. The dog irritated him; his father irritated him; Daphne irritated him. And Daphne and the father got along great. She's the one person who really brought out the sunshine in the father. And yet, that just irritated the hell out of Frasier, too. You also look for the things that your actors can do well, and Kelsey explodes well. He's just very funny when he does that. So I'd look for qualities like this in the father and son who are stuck together.

I remember when Kirstie Alley first came onto *Cheers*. Shelley Long was brilliant, and it was very hard to see her go because it was such a well-established relationship. When Kirstie first came on the show, we were having trouble finding what makes her funny. And for the first few episodes after the episode that introduced her, we were doing stuff where she would walk in, say a couple of lines, and go out into the office. And it was like, "Okay, now we've got our other guys that we're comfortable with." Then we did a story where she'd asked Norm to paint her office. Norm was out of work as an accountant, so he'd started doing house painting to make money. So while he's in there painting, she comes in and starts kind of opening up a little to Norm, and what you find out, what you realize, is that this very hard exterior of hers is a façade. She's a completely insecure person underneath, and she's very frightened about taking over this job, and during this conversation, she breaks down and cries. Kirstie was really funny when she cried, and we said, "Okay, now we have something that can play." And so anytime we could get her to get all sniffle-y and cry, we would. So once we cast this father and son show we're talking about, it might take some time to discover what's funny. What the actors can do.

With Shelley, it was the total-opposites-attract kind of thing. But with Kirstie, it was all about, "This woman's incredibly hot and she doesn't seem to be attracted to me. Aren't all hot women attracted to me?" You see this guy, the guy who usually is the cocksman of Boston, and he's suddenly doubting himself.

PD: Was that a conscious decision to say, "This can no longer be a boy/girl show?"

PC: We were there when this transition was made, but it was the Charles Brothers who created Kirstie's character, and they wrote the episode where she was introduced. I think they still wanted to have this sexual attraction going on, but they didn't want it to be in the same way, the same configuration as with Shelley. I mean, in a way, you lost a certain amount of intellectual aspect of the character when Shelley left, because she was just really book-smart. And that's not necessarily Rebecca's character, but they were just trying to find a different way of making sure they still had the sexual tension. And they still had Sam being able to be Sam.

I remember one of the things that used to make us crazy on *Cheers*, when we'd be sitting in story sessions with the Charles Brothers, and you're sitting there thinking, thinking, and somebody would pitch something, and they'd go, "That was an episode of *Phyllis*." And I'd go, "*Phyllis*? Can't we just change it?" To their credit, I tip my hat to them, they would not do something they had seen before. But that made it tougher. They raised the bar incredibly for David Lee and myself, because we had started out on *The Jeffersons*, and *The Jeffersons* was just a very different type of show, and the jokes were easier, and the jokes were a little more on the nose and in your face.

In the room with *The Jeffersons*, there was almost a sense of panic if it got quiet when all the writers were together. So people were constantly talking, even if there wasn't something funny on story, you just made sure you had some noise in the room, and pencils going in the ceiling. And there always had to be activity and noise going on, and I remember when we got *Cheers*, and we sat in the room with the Charles Brothers when they brought David and me in to pitch story ideas. We pitched our first idea, and they'd sit there and they'd just be very silent. It was like going to confession and watching the priest. Glen Charles would sit over in his chair, and he'd have his hand out the window with the cigar, and he'd be looking out the window, and you're just going, "Oh my God, what's going on here? Is anybody going to talk?" And there'd be like five, ten minutes of silence, and then they'd start talking about story. But they gave themselves time, a lot of time to just think, and kind of put it together. There never seemed to be any urgency.

"... when you create a television series, you're creating an open-ended movie."

PD: What's fascinating for us as you were doing it was watching the procedure that you had. You're really interested in people's relationships. That's the first thing that you went for.

PC: Okay, how can I take these people who like each other and make them collide? Or, how can you get another twenty more episodes here? Okay, well let's look at Sarah. We'll get Molly to get socially involved.

I remember somebody once said, "When you write a movie, it's two hours from a beginning, to a middle, to an end. And when you create a television series, you're creating an open-ended movie." When you create it, you have no idea when it's going to end. And if you're lucky, you get to end it, as we did. You don't get a call at the end of the season and they say, "You're not coming back." And you're kind of left up in the air. And you don't know if that's going to be three seasons, or six seasons, or, in our case, eleven seasons that you're going to be on the air, but you want to make sure that you've given yourself enough possibilities to keep generating stories.

PD: How did you get into comedy?

PC: The first script we ever tried to write was a *M*A*S*H*. That didn't get us any work. We actually wasted a year writing a pilot, thinking, "Well, let's create our own show," and that was just this really stupid mistake, because when you're unsold, and unknown, the last thing a network's going to do is trust you with doing your own show. They want you to run a show. You'd better have experience to do that. So after we wasted that year, our agent said, "Look, write an episode for the show that you like the best, that's on the air right now. It should be a really popular show, so that other producers will know the show." So we did a *Barney Miller*. And the *Barney Miller* was rejected, but it got us into *The Jeffersons*. So it took three-and-a-half years to finally get our first pitch session.

PD: There's a lot of craft to writing comedy. How did you pick this up?

PC: I spent six years on *The Jeffersons*. When I started, it was the only way I knew that this is how things were done. Mike Milligan and Jay Moriarity were there for the first year or two years I was there. And then Ron Levitt [co-creator of *Married . . . with Children*] came in to run the show, and he had been over at Garry Marshall's company doing some of the shows over at Paramount. Mike and Jay were more the Norman Lear style, and when Ron came in, he kind of changed the way we did things. The way Mike and Jay did things was to have David Lee and myself go in to work on a story with Mike and Jay. There would just be the four of us in a room. And we would work and work and work, until we got a story.

Once we got a story, we would go out and we would write the story outline, then we would meet with the two of them, and they would give us notes. Next, we would do our draft, and then we'd get notes on the first draft, and do a second draft. When the show was on the stage being produced, we'd watch rehearsals. Their style—and it's a style now that I think was really counterproductive—meant we wouldn't go down to the stage. Instead, we would sit in their office and watch it on the monitor because the show was done on tape. When the show was over, with all the writing staff in the room, they'd say, "We need a new joke on page 8. We need another new joke on 13." They'd point out where all the new jokes were, and they'd say, "All right, come back when you've got something." And you would see the writers go out of the room, everybody would go to their separate offices. The last thing you wanted to hear was a door open and close down the hall, and hear people walking by your door, because it's like, "Oh, sh-t, they're going to get their jokes into the show; we're going to be left out," and it really became a cannibalistic thing.

And so what Ron did was have everybody in the room working on the story. Before you figured out the story, they would've decided, "Okay, it's going to be your assignment." So then everybody starts working on the story. And they would literally work on it almost line for line, so you're just sitting there writing stuff out, making sure that you're getting everything down, and there's obviously places where you're going to get your material in, too. They can't have everything; you've got to cobble it all together. When you walked out of those meetings, you would have 70 percent of the script written already. So we tended to work more as a group under Ron, but there was still some of that pitting elements of the writing staff against each other.

When we went over to *Cheers*, what we found from the Charles Brothers was, first of all, they didn't settle for the first thing that was pitched, even if it was funny. They'd say, "Well, let's see if we can do better than that." That was never the case at *The Jeffersons*. If somebody pitched something that got a laugh, "Okay, let's move on to the next thing." And then the other thing is, they always had the staff work together as a staff. No matter whose story it was, they had everybody come in for a story session. The Charles Brothers' philosophy was, "Get as many minds working on one problem as you can." They gave you much more of a chance as a writer to do your thing. When they would pitch the story, they'd pitch the beats of the story. When they'd start cobbling a story together, you'd get the beats of the story and you'd get the occasional joke they'd toss you like a shiny, gold coin; and you'd make sure you caught that, get that written down.

The other thing about Ron Levitt was that you'd never do a story outline. You turned in your first draft and that was it. Then they'd do some brushup on it and then they'd send it off to the stage. But with the Charles Brothers, they had you do a story

outline, a very clear, concise story outline, then gave you notes.
Once the story was accepted and it was your assignment, then they
worked with you—just you, the writer, and the Charles Brothers.
But then when it came time during the week of production, we
would be down on the stage with the actors. At the end of every
scene, the director, James Burrows, would stop and the actors and
the writers would talk about the scene. And we would say, "What
works for you? What doesn't work for you? Are you comfortable
with this? Do you feel this isn't like your character?" And there
was a wonderful exchange of ideas, and then you'd move on to the
next scene. And when you were finished with the rehearsal, the
whole staff would go back to the Charles Brothers' office, and we
would all work as a group on the rewrite. So it just became sort of
a community banquet. And that was the style the Charles Brothers
learned from James L. Brooks, when they were on *Taxi*. That's the
style we took with us to *Wings* and to *Frasier*. That's the way we
wanted it to be. We said, "Let's all pull in the same direction. We're
all in this together."

JD: What are your feelings about jokes? How do they best fit into a
script?

PC: What we used to say was, there are certain jokes that we call
10 percenters. You figure, look, it's a little sophisticated, who knows,
maybe only 10 percent of the audience gets it, but we don't care.
Let's put it in there. And inevitably, when you'd do it in front of the
live audience, almost everybody got it anyway. So what it basically
told us, very early in, was don't write down to your audience; give
them credit. If it happens to be something they don't get, that's
okay. If you really love the line, leave it in for your own pleasure. If
it happens to be something they don't get, you go, "You know what?
We were wrong. That shouldn't be in there." Take it out or rewrite

it. But don't dismiss something before you even give it a chance, because you think they're not going to get it. One of the things that we felt was a solution to a lot of problems, is simply, "I'm trimming it down; it's too long. Cut, cut, cut, and then clarify."

I got a very early baptism of fire on *Cheers*. We were staying for three, four nights in a row until one or two in the morning, doing rewrites, because the Charles Brothers were very exacting and demanding and perfectionists. Their whole thing was, "We stay until we get it done." We would never change the story in midweek at *The Jeffersons*. With the Charles Brothers, after the table reading, if the second act didn't work, you threw out the whole second act, and you rewrote it that afternoon and evening and early into the morning. I ate more dinners at *Cheers* my first year than I ate in six years at *The Jeffersons*.

PD: You had a long and successful collaboration with David Lee. What is the nature of a good partnership?

PC: Comradeship. I'll tell you what it isn't. I can't remember who these two writers were, but they walked in to pitch an idea to the Charles Brothers and when one partner is pitching the story, he makes a story point and one of the Charles Brothers says, "I don't think our characters would ever do that." And the other partner turns to the first guy and he says, "See?" Oh, man! That's not the best partner you want to be with.

THERE'S SOMETHING ABOUT ED

  An Interview with Ed Decter

A partial list of Ed Decter's credits as a screen and television writer include *There's Something About Mary, The Lizzie McGuire Movie, The Santa Clause 2, The Santa Clause 3, Senior Class, Boy Meets World,* and *The Closer.*

We taped this interview; otherwise, we would have been like students frantically taking notes on the fine points of comedy writing. If there was a PhD in comedy, Ed Decter would not only have one, he'd be the chair of the department that granted it. As he effortlessly takes us through premise development, he cites movies and sitcoms that reflect his ideas, or identifies the comedy principles behind them. Two interviews in this book—this one and Charlie Peters'—stand out as great teaching interviews as well as brilliant comedy creations. In Ed's hands, industry terms like *middle-slice pilots, four-box demographics,* and *pipes* become as understandable as if you'd spent your life around the writers' table. He can give you the rationale for every setup he creates, but instead of making it sound academic, he makes it sound funny.

ED (ED DECTER): The first thing is, for me, it's not a feature because these days, a feature needs to be played out on a bigger palette. It could be an independent feature, a really well done independent feature for a small market. But these days the criteria that they have for movies, at least the kind that I work on for the studios, is what they call *four-box movies*. That means that it has to have almost every demographic; the studios want them to be huge. And this would make sort of a delightful small feature, something the British do very well. But it does seem to be a television premise. I come from sitcom, and it lends itself to sitcom.

"... a pilot is different than anything else on earth because in a pilot you have to think forward and backward ..."

I don't like sitcom any longer. I don't believe in it anymore, but I do believe in the half-hour film comedy. An executive would tell you that this is one of the premises that lends itself well to three-camera because it's not like Sarah's a private eye or something that has to be taken out of her home and out of her apartment a lot. So, assuming that you're going to do it this way, the first thing you have to say to yourself is, "Why is it funny? Why do we care about these women?" And then you have to go about conceiving a pilot. And a pilot is different than anything else on earth because in a pilot you have to think forward and backward at all times. You have to think, "What's a good story? What's a good story for the pilot?" And, "What would make a very good episode?" And plus, it is the trend these days to do what they call a *middle-slice pilot*, meaning that it's a run-of-the-mill episode that could be aired any week, and yet, it still has to set up all the characters, and all the story you need to know to set up the show, so that people understand what they are seeing. Even more importantly, it's what the advertisers are going to see at the upfront and decide to support. So that means that your pilot has to be burdened with an enormous amount of what they call backstory, or *pipe*, we call it, which is information about why these women are living together, who they are, and what their relationship is.

Then you need to tell that story in 23½ minutes. You have to tell a story that entertains you and teases you, so you say, "Oh I would really like to see next week's episode." And it has to also say that these people have known each other a long time. What's more, it also has to say this will be a good, long-enduring franchise. That's why pilots are so, so, so difficult. And that's why those of us who do a lot of pilots get hired to think backwards and forwards at all times. What's really difficult is that a pilot should really be two episodes. It should be the backstory episode about how these women came together, and it should also be the episode that we wanted to watch, but they won't produce that. They won't make that. They believe that it should exist, that it should be like any episode. So you have to do it in a half-hour, or exactly 23½ minutes.

Now, say you did this as a single-camera pilot. You could show the scenes where Molly's grieving, or start at the funeral and set up what's the lock of the situation. The other thing is that with every show that has a concept you have to present to the audience what the lock is of the concept, or else the audience isn't going to buy it over the length of time.

The lock means, Why does Molly have no other option but to live with her daughter? You have to show it, right? You have to show why she has no other option but to live with her daughter. If the audience feels she wasn't that bad off, as with what we've got here, it seems to me she has many other options. They're not going to buy the fabric of the series. And so the first thing you would do is develop a pilot episode that shows that somehow, some way these women can't live without each other, even though Sarah was doing well [Ed makes quote marks in the air around the word *well*] in her life before this. But something about Molly's arrival would have to point out to Sarah immediately that by the end of the episode—not at the top because there has to be conflict, but at the end—that there's something about having Molly there that is incredibly helpful to her, or needed in her life at this point.

So you have to design the story backwards from that point. You would say, "What is that moment that Sarah realizes that it's not just a burden to have Molly?" because that would be like hitting someone over the head with an ax every week, if it's the same joke. So there's got to be something that Sarah gets out of this relationship with Molly, and if it's that moment of humanity where she realizes that it's sometimes good to have a mother around, then the audience will say, "Oh, that's very sweet. I understand what's funny about it, but I also understand what's fulfilling about it." The next thing you have to do is try to find what will hook the audience into what's relatable about this premise, because most people—maybe just the people I know—wouldn't want to have their mother living with them. And if Sarah's successful enough, there's a whole bunch of situations in which I would imagine she might suggest, "Let me rent you an apartment." See, again, you have to think backwards and forwards. If Sarah's rich enough, or successful enough, to rent her mom an apartment, well then the show is over, right?

So it occurs to me that one of the ways you can do this show is to have the mother-in-law apartment, or the mother-in-law guesthouse behind the main house that you often see advertised, so that the Mom is there, but you understand that it's an adult relationship where they're trying to keep their separate spaces. Because, otherwise, it's an incredibly old-fashioned premise. Then again, maybe Sarah isn't successful enough to have a place like that, where she could have her mom. Like, for instance, in *Frasier* where the dad lived with him, and the first thing that they did was made him injured and he had a cane, so there was never a question of why he lived there. So here you have a fairly successful young woman on a good career track, why is this her only option? So the first thing I would do is build in a lock where maybe she has that little converted garage in the back of her house, so that Mom is always around, always watching what's going on.

There was a show called *The In-Laws*. It was about two families living next door to each other. They had converted a garage for their kids, and you understood that beautifully. It was a good lock because the kids couldn't afford to have their own place, so they converted a garage for them. Now they had both sets of parents meddling in their lives. So this could work the same way. There's the little house in the back and then, of course, you could do a whole bunch of things where in getting that house ready for her mom, it's disaster after disaster after disaster, and the mom has to stay in the main house. That would be a good thing for the pilot because then they'd be smashed together, in really close quarters. And then the other thing is, if the father had left a lot of debts, not just no money, but debt, that now was burdening Molly, so that she really had a pressing need to take care of this or else somehow it would crush her. And in some way, if Sarah were impacted by this, Molly could be homeless, or worse, then it builds in the lock. However, everything I described to you takes pages and pages of exposition.

Now, if you did it single camera, you could help yourself visually. You could see the funeral. You would show the funeral, then you'd show the meeting with Molly and her husband's CPA. The CPA would say, "I've got to tell you, you're in a volcano of badness, a sucking abyss of badness." So Molly finds out all this, and then she comes to stay with Sarah temporarily and she's looking for a job, and trying to get her life back on track, and that's how she would ingratiate herself. And there's another thing that they do now where they have a *hybrid pilot*. In a hybrid pilot, there are certain scenes that are filmed out of the studio, and certain scenes that are on a soundstage. The most famous of these would be *Seinfeld*. So assume you could accomplish that lock very quickly now, again, that lock of why she's there, and why she has to be there, and what their prior relationship was. Again, it takes pages, and those pages eat away from your present story of what's going to be entertaining about that thing, which would be, obviously, something about Sarah and her love life, or her professional life, or her lack of love life because of her professional life.

And the problem with that is, it's a story we've seen ten million times. It's the woman who's got a career, and her love life interferes with the career. I mean, it is the fodder for almost every show on television. Look at *Grey's Anatomy*, which is a fantastic show, but it's about that every week. It's about how much sacrifice do we make for our dreams, and our professional careers, and how much time do we set aside for love. So the first thing you would do in the writers' room, or when you sit down to write this, would be, How do you flip that story so it's fresh and interesting? And then all of that has to service the bigger issue, which is that how, at the end of this, with all the funny conflict that's going to happen and all the intrusion into Sarah's life, how, at the end of that do you make it where they almost discover that they really need each other? But, of course, they can't really discover that or else your show's over. I mean, so that discovery of the fact that they need each other has to be fought over a long time if you're going to do a comedy, because if they both say, "I really need you. It's really great that you're here," there's not a lot of conflict after that, if they're in accord.

"Writing a comedy pilot is a little bit closer to poetry. I'm not talking about the highfalutin' concept of poetry, but every single word makes a difference because it's taking away from another word."

Here's the classic example: If you made Archie Bunker say, "You know I've been wrong about so many things, and people are all the same. I've made a lot of mistakes, and I really love all races," that would be the end of the show. So in a sitcom, and in any comedy, or in any good drama, you have to leave a lot there for the show to explore. And then, we haven't even discussed what other characters are populating the show, and those people eat up pages, and you have to service those people so everybody in there has to be very important. Writing a comedy pilot is a little bit closer to poetry. I'm not talking about the highfalutin' concept of poetry, but every single word makes a difference because it's taking away from another word. I do drama pilots as well, and I'm not saying it's easier to do a drama pilot, but you can have a scene that adds a lot of character, or suggests something else, but you can't in a comedy pilot. In a comedy pilot, you need every single thing to work for you in a certain way, and you can't have a little dangling edge, except for maybe the last scene that sort of suggests what next week's episode is going to be. So the tenets of what you need are a really great beginning that hooks you about why Molly's coming to live with her daughter, quickly get into the current story about Sarah's life and what she's actually lacking in her life. Show how, in a funny way, her mother tries to solve it, makes it worse, and how then they come to some partial truce at the end that suggests many funny things to happen later in the series. And again, not being critical of the premise, but the problem is this treads on a lot of familiar ground that you have to find a very fresh way to turn over.

So the first thing I would do is look at that classic story of Sarah's spending so much time at work, and she is not devoting herself even a little bit to this very good guy in her life. I would try to find a way to flip that. That, in fact, Sarah is distracted by some very hot guy at work, and her work is actually suffering. I'd do anything that flips what you'd expect to see. Or the fact that her dual pursuits of a love life and a career leave her ignoring her mother at this very difficult time, and her mother is vying for her attention. Her mother needs someone, and maybe they've never had that relationship before where the mother seems needy, and of course, the thing that's relatable to everyone is that when you become an adult, ultimately your parents become your kids. That is something that I think an audience will relate to.

Now the other big question is about the audience. In other words, is the audience relating to that idea, the people who you want to be watching this comedy? Because you'll find that a network will say, we want the *Heroes* crowd, the people who are watching *Heroes* to be watching these comedies, and not the *Everybody Loves Raymond* crowd, because maybe the *Raymond* crowd doesn't spend a lot of money. So one of the things that you would imagine when you're doing these shows is what's best for the show. It's not always that. A lot of times you'll be sitting in the room, saying, "How do we make this demographic younger and younger and younger?" So it's very possible that a network would not buy this show because there's a middle-aged woman in the show. Now, one of the most successful sitcoms of all times was *Everybody Loves Raymond* and it was all about middle-aged people and older people. But it's not necessarily true that the current network wants that demographic. For instance, the only successful sitcom on the air right now is *Two and a Half Men*. It's the only successful sitcom in the top twenty. No one even talks about it. No one mentions it. It's not hip in any way, although it's a very solid, very good show. But no one talks about it. It's not water-cooler stuff.

They're talking about all the other shows—*Grey's Anatomy*, *American Idol, Lost*—shows that cover much fresher territory. That's not to say that the people who would do this show aren't going to reap tremendous rewards, or the network's not going to reap tremendous rewards, but you'll notice that there's no sitcom up in that area, so that's why the networks, and everybody else, are searching desperately to find a way to freshen that genre. And *The Office*, for all its acclaim and for all its brilliance, is still not doing that well.

PD (PETER DESBERG): Why do you think that is?

ED: I think that in this cycle, they want to do something like *Ugly Betty*. *Ugly Betty* gives you the soap aspects that people like, but it also gives you a fresh, energetic, fast-paced comedy, and it's an hour, and that's fantastic. Now what syndicators like is *Seinfeld*. So everybody's still looking for that half-hour that really works. *30 Rock* is a brilliant, fantastic, half-hour comedy. It's incredibly low-rated and it's just barely hanging on, but it couldn't be better, it couldn't be funnier. And that's all fresh and new and applies to a younger demographic, a hipper demographic, and all the things that they want. So not only are you writing a show and telling the best possible story for that show and trying to find a fresh way to do it and trying to find a way to set up all the pipe at the beginning, and the story in the middle, and the teaser at the end—not only are you doing that, but then, you're also being asked to think like a marketing strategist.

So all that fear and business stuff creeps into what you need to do for a pilot. Your show doesn't exist without it.

The best example I can give you is that if you have a show that's running and working, you don't have to do anything to set up a joke. I can go back to Jack Benny to describe this, but the best way is with *Friends,* which people know much better. You could start the series after it had been going for a while, and if you just showed the apartment and showed a horrible mess on the table—things dripping and glue and something had fallen and it's disgusting—and you started the episode with no characters there and you saw the apartment you'd start to laugh. You'd know that Monica was coming in the door, that Courtney Cox was coming in the door, and as soon as the door opened, you'd get another laugh in anticipation of the fact that it was incredibly messy—she's so anal and neat— and then you'd get a laugh on the setup, you'd get a laugh on the anticipation, and then you'd get a laugh on whatever brilliant line David Crane would put in for her to say at that moment.

So that's really great comedy writing. But that's an up-and-running show. That same situation with a new show with friends and the same character—she's very anal—but now you've lost everything when it opens and there's a mess, you don't know who's walking in, you don't know whose apartment it is, you don't know why that's funny, or not funny. And then when the character walks in and sees it and reacts to it, and is anal about it, you go, "Well, that's bad storytelling," because you've set up a joke that really isn't happening. You don't know the character who's coming in. You would only set up a scene that way when you know Monica's coming in, and you know how her character's going to react, and it's going to be a mess. So then you get that anticipation. In this other one, you'd have to show Monica's character through a conflict that shows how anal she is. There was a great episode where she was describing folding the ends of the toilet paper, and how it makes everything so neat in the bathroom. That's very funny just in description, right?

So getting back to this premise. I say, "Okay, who is Molly and how is she this outside force in the life of Sarah?" And, "Who is Sarah?" And then again, the whole thing would be to *not* make

Sarah that stock character who nobody wants to play, which is just the career woman who misses out on love. That's the first thing I would work on because my brain goes blank thinking about that, because I've seen it so often. And the other thing is, How do you make that fresh? How do make the summer breeze of Molly be irritating, funny, and sustaining, so that you're looking forward to seeing what she does every week? And then, thinking businesswise, you have to say, "Well, who wants to play Sarah? Is she the straight person for love?" And nobody wants to be the straight person. The greatest straight person in the history of comedy was Bob Newhart. Bob had no problem with other people being funny, and he knew that his face, when you cut to it, would get a laugh at his disbelief, and his beleaguered expression would get a laugh. And that's why he was able to do the phone bits in his stand-up routines.

Okay, so, who's Sarah, and what makes her funny? Why is she funny, even if Molly never came into the story? So you might do it that she was the hypertensive, neurotic, organization person. The first thing that comes to mind is that she's the ultra, ultra organized one, and Molly comes in and she's Bohemian, and you would think, "Well, that's a switch because Molly's older." But we've seen that, too. So you'd have to come up with a fresh way to do that, and maybe Molly, for all her Bohemian ways, kept a tidy house. And Sarah, for all her organization and killer instincts at work, is a slob. You're treading right on *The Odd Couple*. And so that's inherently relatable, because *The Odd Couple*'s the ultimate, relatable story: Everybody has that friend. Everybody has that opposite. And then again, how do you make that fresh, how do you make *The Odd Couple* fresh when Neil Simon did it better than anybody's ever going to do it? And Garry Marshall did it better than anybody's going to do it. How do you make that *Odd Couple* thing fresh? And yet, it still can work. If you find the two characters appealing, it is an infinitely renewable premise. *The Odd Couple. Two and a Half Men.* It is the central theme of a bulk of stories. I'm not an expert on that Joseph Campbell guy, but one of the archetypes of comedy is that *Odd Couple* thing. And even before Neil Simon did it, somebody did it.

JD (JEFFREY DAVIS): You mentioned Jack Benny. Were you going to do the *Your Money or Your Life* routine?

ED: It's not the *Your Money or Your Life* joke, but the classic Jack Benny joke that fits here would be the one where somebody would say to Jack Benny, "Well, we could fix your car, but it's going to be $400." So that's a straight line. You'd laugh at the straight line, at the anticipation of Jack Benny thinking, because he would take this long pause, and you'd be thinking, "What can he possibly say?" Or "How is he going to try to get it done for less than $400?" And then he would say the joke. Then the amazing thing is, he would say the funny line about how maybe there's something that he could do . . . he'd offer to perform at a benefit for this guy . . . to not pay that $400. And then there'd be a wait while that guy was thinking, and it would be funny, because you'd be thinking about how Jack would respond. That's the classic melding of what's best about comedy, which is surprise, and then great character. A character that is inherently comic, which means a character that inherently causes conflict. And that's what you'd have to find with both Molly and Sarah to make it work. And also, you'll find that almost everybody who's doing comedy has a good sense of the history of back-and-forth, because everybody, usually, who's in comedy started the same way. In my era it was the Carl Reiner/Mel Brooks record *The Two Thousand Year Old Man.* And among the people who work for me now—young people who work for me who come from shows like *South Park*, which is also unbelievably, enormously funny—there's usually a sense of the past. There's some reason that you didn't become a hedge-fund manager. The only smart thing to have done in the last twenty years. And any of us who didn't had to have some crazy reason why we didn't do that. So, anyway, that's what I would do with this.

JD: You've done both. What's the difference between working in television and features?

ED: I had a friend who made a beautiful distinction. He said, "Features are like war, and television shows are like government." The Marty Scorseses, the Clint Eastwoods, the Steven Spielbergs— they have well-established, creative freedoms, and then there's everyone else. And it's completely changed. A maverick filmmaker like John Ford said, "Oh, we're behind in the script . . . you're worried because we're behind in the script. We'll just take the script and rip four pages out and throw them out. Now we're caught up." That guy does not really exist anymore.

To be a show runner, you have to be very present because it's a lot of work. Your day gets divided. Only 10 percent of your day is necessarily working on the script for the show, and 80 percent of the day is dealing with the network and studio. Say Warner Bros. is the studio making the show and is paying your salary. They will often partner with a network, say NBC Productions, or CBS Productions, their production arm, because those shows get picked up a little bit easier by the networks. So then you have two production companies involved. That means two companies who are writing the checks for the show, and have creative input. So now you've got NBC or CBS or ABC. That means there's a lot of sitcom writers for the show runner to deal with. You can say what you want, but they're fast and funny, and can do stuff really quickly. It's amazing, when I do a feature rewrite now, I sort of laugh. I mean, people think it's going to be weeks, and it doesn't have to be. But, when you're in that room, most of the time you're going, "Okay, CBS Productions—which is not CBS, the network—CBS Productions wants the woman to enter first, and Warner Bros., who's paying most of the money, wants the guy to enter. And the network doesn't think anyone should enter but the dog. You know what I mean?

So I have a writing partner and he's very patient. He'll get on the phone and say, "Well, you know, the network was thinking the dog could enter first, and that could work and get you what you want. I think the same thing. If the next person to enter was the wife, quickly followed by the husband, and then it seems like they all enter together, but . . ." and not a lot of funny comes out of that. And that is what your day-to-day life is. So people always say, "Why is there so much bad stuff on television?" And then, one time I went to the upfronts [sponsors] and met a lot of people from Coca-Cola and Chevrolet, and all those people who advertise and who write our checks. And, to them, the show was the gray thing that happened in between the commercials. So that gray thing just had to provide the right people to sit there looking at the TV until that commercial came on, and the really important thing happened. So it depends on what your point of view is.

"Good storytelling is looking the truth in the face and sometimes taking a little step to the left."

JD: If you didn't have to think about the networks, is there anything in this premise that speaks to you?

ED: Well, unfettered, I mean . . . to me, there is a relatable part. My mom passed away, but before she passed away, my dad had passed away. So for twenty years, even though she was technically my mom, I felt like I was her dad. My mom didn't know how to write checks, she had never written a check in forty-five years. To me, those types of things are interesting. But again, my showbiz, entertainment senses are saying, "Well my mom was much older than Molly is and she was not out there dating, and everything like that, but to me, that interests me, and I know a lot of people go through that when one of their parents dies. And now that person is sort of newly revealed to you as who they are. So that's what I connect to, and relate to this, and that's what I would bring to this. I once had a fiction teacher in college who said, "Good storytelling is looking the truth in the face and sometimes taking a little step to the left." So the truth of this is there's a tremendous sadness, which a lot of times runs under good comedy. There's a sadness, because obviously her father's passed away. I would connect with the parenting of the parent. How do you launch that person back into the world after she's been sheltered inside a long-term relationship?

This would be a scene between Molly and Sarah in one of the episodes. I remember that my mom couldn't watch movies I had done because they're not making videotapes anymore, and she had a videotape machine, and so I would send her the DVDs of the movies I had written. She didn't have a DVD player. So I sent her, through Amazon, a DVD player. And then I got the call, "Okay, it's here, it's in a box. I'm never going to hook it up." "Well, why not?" "Because I don't know how to." I say, "It's the easiest thing in the world." And then on the phone, like in one of those movies where the pilot dies, and somebody has to land the plane, I say, "See, there's a yellow, red, and white plug." "I don't see it." "It's in the back there. It's yellow, red, and white, and there's three things, and all you have to do is take the yellow, red, and white plugs and put them in the yellow, red, and white spaces." And so that could be a scene. Now the funny thing is, I immediately would flip it and make it that

Sarah's been so focused on her career, and all that kind of stuff, that she doesn't work with things technical, and that her BlackBerry, and everything technological confuses her. I mean, something to make that fresh, so that she's not Ms. BlackBerry, and all that kind of stuff. And maybe somehow Molly, who had more leisure time when she was with her husband, was able to have all those gadgets, and when he died, they were all taken away from her.

JD: How many pilots do you do a year?

ED: We're doing a drama pilot this summer, and this will be my eleventh produced pilot, and I've had four series. The thing you get very quick and good at is how to get the people into the room because all sitcoms, all television shows, are family shows, whether they take place in the workplace, or they take place on an island, as in *Seinfeld* and *Lost*. Or they take place on *American Idol*. Our four main characters are our judges, and Ryan, and they're there every week. We like them, we get to know about them, our family, through their interaction, and then we get to know our contestants. They're our new characters, and then we go to their hometowns.

The reason why *American Idol* is better and more popular than current sitcoms is because it's real, and even though it's *created* real. We go to their hometowns, and we go to Alabama, and we see somebody delivering mail, and it turns out that that person can sing, and there's our backstory. That's an episode of the television show. And so, what we would have is somebody from Alabama as our lead character. Then, somebody comes to visit her from her hometown, and she says, "Hey, how come you don't sing anymore? You used to be such a good singer." And then we would come up with some sort of phony set piece where she would sing at some club, and reconnect with something that she used to do in their past. Well, that's really phony, and really stagey, and that's a bad example, but when you go and you see Vonzelle, the woman post office worker delivering mail, and then singing with a beautiful gown on and all dressed up, that's a better story than anything you could tell in a sitcom.

And that's why, in things like *Ugly Betty*, they said, "You know what, we could do this differently and better." And they did. And so it delivers you all the punch of a sitcom without the laugh track, gives you all that good serial drama, and has fresh, high-stakes stories.

We're asked to make multiethnic casts. That's very important, obviously, but that's not why people turn it on. They turn it on because, very simply, everyone has had a job, and everyone has been beleaguered in their job, and she is a "working girl." She's the girl who's smarter, more sensitive, and better than the people she works for, but she's hidden by the fact that she's a nobody. And then the other lovely complication is she's not as physically appealing as the people she works around on the surface. But, of course, after two episodes, you want to see Betty more than you want to see all the glamorous supermodels. But nevertheless, it's everyone's story; everyone's had a job. And what you do when you create a show—you find that thing.

You asked what I would do with Molly and Sarah were I not concerned about demographics. I went through raising my mom after my father died, and so I connect with that very deeply, and it is an *Odd Couple* situation. When my mom would come to visit me, I would only have about a ten-minute patience level. And from that point on, it was kind of hellish. But nevertheless, that could be done very funny. And the way I dealt with it with my mom was to keep her moving. Playing golf, activity, so we wouldn't have to just sit and talk. And I think that the reason why you laugh is because it's very relatable. Because people deal with their parents that way.

PD: Listening to you talk, I get the image of the plate-spinner on the *Ed Sullivan Show.* You're saying, "Okay, got to get the lock here, a good grasp of the characters there . . ."

ED: My partner and I use this example. We use the saber dance song—Da-da-da-da-da-da-da—we use that in the room all the time, that exact example. You always want to throw up your hands and give up, because you go, "Well, if we can't have any character older than fifty years old . . ." And you want to say, "Hey, did you see "*Raymond?*" It was a phenomenal show, but it was an old-fashioned show. They only had six scenes, maybe four scenes. It was as old-fashioned as *The Dick Van Dyke Show,* which is the highest compliment you could ever give it, but it was the same structure as *The Dick Van Dyke Show.* You sit with these long scenes in the living room, and yet it was brilliant, because all the characters crackled.

They had the exact same thing. Raymond's wife, Patricia Heaton, would be cooking and you'd see her struggling and just getting a little frustrated, throw some spice in, and at that moment, at the door, you would see Raymond's mother looking through the door at Patricia. And then, there'd be this huge, anticipatory laugh, and friends of mine who worked on that show told me that scripts were very short, much shorter than your average sitcom, because the spread of the laughs was so great on every episode. They couldn't fit in more story. So the less successful your sitcom is, the longer your scripts have to be, and the more successful it is, the shorter your scripts have to be.

JD: Can you elaborate a little more on the four-box demographic idea the studios operate on?

ED: There's eleven to eighteen, and eighteen to twenty-five, and then twenty-five to forty-nine, and then forty-nine to . . . And so, there're these boxes of demographics. They are obsessed with which

box the movie's in. Now, you can make a movie for one box, but
it'd have to be at a certain price, you know what I mean? You can't
make Shrek just to appeal to kids two to eleven. If you did that,
you would fail miserably, because somebody has to take those kids
to the movies, so there has to be something entertaining for the
parents, and then when everything's working, like Shrek, it appeals
to everybody. Teenagers will go to that movie. It became hip to go
see an animated movie because of Shrek. So that's when it hits all the
boxes. So, obviously, if you're going to do a $100 million movie, it
has to hit as many boxes as it can. You can't just make a movie, like
you'd think, for teenage boys. It has to appeal to other people. You
can make a movie for teenage boys if you make it for $20 million,
or $30 million. You can make a movie, and if it returns $80 million,
you're a big hero. But you can't make a $100 million movie for one
sector of the population, because, like Indiana Jones, it'd have to hit
everybody. A movie that you make for $100 million, the theaters
keep half the money.

So to get that $100 million back, you have to make
$200 million at the movie theater. But then you've spent $35 or
$40 million promoting it, so you need to get that money back,
too. So that's another $100 million you need to get back, because
you have to split it with the theaters. And as you go, you have to
make more and more and more money. So obviously, to cover costs,
that's why somebody like Tom Hanks—who is one of those Jimmy
Stewart, Henry Fonda guys—gets paid so much money to be in a
movie. It gives them a guaranteed lock on a certain audience. But,
occasionally, Tom Hanks's movies fail. Even Tom Cruise movies
sometimes fail—not often, but they do. So that's why you have to
care about those boxes.

In television, it's the oddest thing in the world. The second you
finish your pilot, they start to test it. You can go and see your pilot

and they put it in a room in front of people, and the people have dials, and girls have dials and guys have dials and everybody has dials, and when something's funny, they turn the dial, like that, and when somebody's not funny, when there's something that they don't like, they turn it the other way. And the guys are blue lines and the girls are pink lines, and you see an average of those lines as the show is being projected to you in your little secret room. As it's being projected to you, you see a graph being projected of the pink and blue lines.

Obviously, what you'd like to see is a very happy line that goes infinitely up to the top of this band of funny. That means they turned the dials all the way, and you'd like to see it not go to the top early, but you'd like to see it go higher, higher, higher, higher, and end in a beautiful two lines at the top of the chart. But you never see that. And then the funny thing is, you'll do a joke and you would think that guys would like that joke, and the guys go up, and the girls don't like that joke, and then the guys plummet. The whole process of testing is being influenced by various notes to "service this" and "service that" about things that aren't necessarily what's funniest, or what's best for the show. Because of that, what you get is a very tepid little line going back and forth like that. And then they say, "Well, it didn't test very strongly." And then they'll say, "Let's do a reshoot, or let's add some things to the editing to make it spike." People who are experienced know how to make it spike at the end a little bit. If you have somebody dancing at the end of your show, dancing and singing, dancing to a piece of music, people like that and it spikes.

There are embarrassed laughs . . . In *Something about Mary*, you'd go to the theater and it looked like a revival meeting. People were laughing so hard that their hands were going down and coming up, almost like a horror film. The audience moved around a lot. Then you'd hear people come out, now most people were, luckily, very pleased with it. But you'd hear people say, "That was disgusting," and you would see that they had laughed from beginning to middle and end—they laughed the whole time—but when they came out, they felt that they should say it was disgusting.

JD: What was the germ of *There's Something about Mary?*

ED: Well, my partner John Strauss lived in an apartment that overlooked a condo, and his apartment faced the bedrooms of all these condos. There was this one really, really attractive girl who would come home each night. It sounds like I'm making this up, but it's true. She was an aerobics instructor, and she would come home and she would get undressed, take a shower, and then stand naked in front of her mirror. She'd try on various outfits that she was going to go out to clubs in. This was a long time ago, and I was a very young man, so it was way before I was married. Nevertheless, when she would come home, we didn't want to get caught staring at her, so if it was night out, we would turn off the lights in the apartment and we would watch. And, of course, I think it was my partner, John, who said, "We're stalkers at this point. This is bad. We can't do this." And I said, "No, maybe we're not stalkers, maybe we're detectives, thinking about what women do in their private moments, and we could bring this knowledge to bear on all our lives and the lives of our friends." This is the rationalization for being creepy. So then we said, "Well, what if some guy couldn't find somebody and they sent a private eye to do that. The private eye would fall in love with her, and the first thing the private eye would say was, "Oh, she's horrible, she's fat, she's ugly, you don't want to have anything to do with her." Then he'd take that woman for himself. And then the next thing we thought was, "Well, by having followed her, he'd know everything about her so it's the perfect setup to get her. He would know everything she was interested in and everything she did wrong and everything, so you'd have all this information." So that's how it was born.

And then came the Farrelly Brothers, who were the single greatest guys. They're like the Irish brothers that you would want to have. So we start the script with the Ben Stiller character endlessly talking to his friends about this girl, Mary, that he knew in high school. One of the Farrelly Brothers said, "We need to see that." But we said, "The problem is that Ben's going to be in his thirties, so are you going to have another actor play the young Ben?" And he says, "No, no, no, we're going to have Ben play Ben when he's in high school." And we said, "That could look really goofy." And he says, "Yeah, it's going to be hilarious." And, in fact, I think that single thing was why the movie was successful. Because as soon as you saw Ben with his braces, and being clearly a thirty-year-old guy playing a high school kid, the audience relaxed and said, "Oh, all these funny things are going to happen." And you had a guy up in a tree singing. Of course, the studio absolutely was going to cut the guy singing in the tree and the troubadour thing, and they were going to cut the hair gel scene and the dog—the dog was clearly an animal activist's nightmare—and they didn't want the mentally challenged brother and they didn't want Cameron Diaz.

In retrospect, it all worked right. Cameron Diaz had been in *The Mask,* so she had been the hot girl in *The Mask.* And Ben had a television show and wasn't that well known, and Matt Dillon was at that time the boyfriend of Cameron, and was a bigger star than either of the other two. So they didn't want any of those people.

PD: How did you prevail?

ED: Well, I didn't do anything. It's the Farrelly Brothers. They engage in The-Raiders-of-the-Lost-Ark School of Production. They get this huge ball rolling, and they get it rolling so fast nobody can stop it. That's what they do and they agree and they're jovial, so they always say, "Oh, absolutely, yeah, we're changing that. We're getting on that." And they don't. And they do *exactly* what they think is funny. And the greatest thing about the Farrelly Brothers is that the other alternatives that most of us agonize over that are not the funny things you ultimately settle on, what you hope is the funny thing—those other not-funny things don't occur to them. They're incredibly efficient, and they only shoot things one way. They always choose the funniest one.

Peter Farrelly said to me, "Whatever happened to *There's Something about Mary?* I said, "That's so weird that you brought that up after all these years, because I just today got the rights back." He says, "We'll do it!" He says, "When I teach screenwriting, I teach that script." I say, "That's very kind of you, but you haven't seen it in many years, so I'll give it to you." He called me the next day after he read it, and he said, "We'll set it up at Fox, and we're going to do it." And he says, "And here's the eight things that we're going to do." And from that point on, it just rolled. So no project ever really dies.

SIT DOWN AND WRITE . . . BUT FIRST, STAND UP

An Interview with Michael Elias

A partial list of Michael Elias's credits as a television writer and screenwriter include *The Jerk, The Frisco Kid, Head of the Class, The Cosby Show, Mary Tyler Moore, The Dick Van Dyke Show,* and *Lush Life.*

Michael Elias wanted to wear a tweed jacket with leather elbow patches, which means he wanted to be a serious writer. His first writing job was creating the material for his own comedy duo. After success in clubs and television, including *The Tonight Show,* he was called out to the West Coast by William Morris and began earning a living as a writer. His stand-up comedy background served as his training ground. It's where he honed his instincts about what was funny and what he wouldn't want to face an audience with.

ME (MICHAEL ELIAS): It's kind of old-fashioned. A parent moving in with the daughter, and she wants to start a new life. This has been done before, I suppose with some success, more or less. But I'll stay within the parameters of this premise. I don't want to turn it into a war movie.

So you've got Sarah, who seems to be like a personal assistant. She's creative, but she's not going to go anywhere in her life or on the job. She's so focused on her work she's unaware that she's relationship-challenged as far as men are concerned. I don't know how you're unaware of that, so she's gotta be aware of it, or it's not true, so let's try to think what would work better. Anyway, let's see if we can make a movie out of this. And how can we make it more contemporary? And who's going to be a star? So it's the mother and the daughter.

✥ ✥ ✥

"That might be an interesting thing for this striving young woman who finds herself saddled with a sexually active mother."

Actually, the mother interests me more than the daughter. They come together at the same point in their lives. That is, they're both single, sharing an apartment, and relationship-challenged, so dating should be a big thing. How do a mother and daughter date together and search the Internet or the world for men? It might be interesting if the mother is actually much more successful than the daughter at dating men. Cast her kind of sexy, still attractive, a woman who rediscovers her sexuality in middle age and is just going to do nothing but have sex and sex and sex, and is having a great time at it. That might be an interesting thing for this striving young woman who finds herself saddled with a sexually active mother.

So I think the mother would embarrass Sarah. Molly's got a guy she met online who's crazy about her. It's about her relationship with this guy. At the beginning it's about how this relationship develops, and then she's living with a guy. I mean, the daughter is living with her mother, who's dating a guy who might be a no-goodnik, or he might be younger than she is, or he might be a criminal. That might be interesting, if he's some sort of criminal. And not only does the mother want to have a real relationship with him, maybe she wants to rehabilitate him and get him out of his life of crime.

So Sarah's watching all this going on around her. Her mother is having an incredible time; Sarah's embarrassed. The mother's trying to get the daughter's life turned around. Maybe the daughter is very conservative, so there's real conflict there. Say the daughter works as a librarian in a private library, a medical library, in New York City, and she's got a very settled life, and she expects her mother to come in and have a very settled life with her. And they would do all kinds of cultural things. Instead, her mother is now hanging out with a Dominican dope dealer. She's got a Brooklyn-Haitian boyfriend.

Her grandparents, Molly's parents, can come in and complicate things. Give Sarah a guy. They've had this long sexless relationship, where they do all these terrific things. Go to lectures and it's all very fine and nonsexual and the mother is telling her daughter, "Get rid of this guy," and she keeps bringing Hector the dope dealer's friends and cousins to meet Sarah and take her out. Maybe that's the beginning.

Or maybe Sarah could be a writer, like the Kathleen Turner character in *Romancing the Stone*. She stays home and writes her books. So the mother is an interruption at home. Yeah, if Sarah's a writer and she works at home, then having this mother who's bringing all this fancy life and fun into her apartment is a drag. What Sarah writes could be a reflection on her life. I mean, maybe she writes spinster-detective stories, where she's got this alter ego. Oh, yeah, she's got an alter ego who she writes about, who is nothing like her. That would be better. And her mother keeps saying, "Why can't you be more like the person you write about instead of the person you are?" "I can write about her because I'm not her." "Well, if you can write about her, why don't you just be her?" "It's not easy." So she's not afraid, she's not shy. She's all those things. So that could be interesting. Yeah, and maybe her boyfriend is her editor. It's kind of skewing old. I'm thinking of the commercialism of it. Now you've got a fifty-year-old mother but there are a lot of actresses who could play this and be sexy and funny. And the daughter—she wouldn't be Lindsey Lohan, but she would be of age and I think you could have a lot of fun with that.

What else about mothers and daughters? Molly is a widow, so there's a lot for Sarah to learn about what her parents' marriage was like. "Your father didn't touch me for the last ten years of our marriage." And "I didn't know what I was missing. I forgot what an animal I was." You can do a nice thing here, where the mother talks to the father. She's got a picture of him, and she says, "George, I know you don't approve of this, but he's a great dancer, he's this, and this . . ." and she turns the picture to the wall every time Hector comes in, and Hector says, "Who is that?" and she says, "It was a guy who sold me insurance a long time ago." She won't admit to her past.

Yeah, so you could have parallel love stories—what's going on in the mother's life, what's going on in the daughter's life. If it's an apartment, you've got a neighbor across the hall—4F, 4G—Sarah's never seen. Life in New York. It might be funny to bring in a character who's a lawyer, who deals with the father's estate. It's going to be one of those Dickensian estates that's going to be tied up in probate for the next fifty years and every once in a while this guy comes in and says, "We've made some progress. Turns out your sister-in-law, if we can give her X amount of dollars, she won't sue for this . . ." It's like the guy died, and their inheritance is basically trouble . . . and lawyers.

JD (JEFFREY DAVIS): If you didn't have to think about commercial constraints, what would you do?

ME: What fascinates me is that Molly is young—she's fifty. If I went out with her, I'd be scoring a young chick. I think the age is interesting. How a person can be really hip. How people can be old in age, but their heads are young, and deep down we're all sixteen. And we all just keep going through the same stuff, whatever it is.

Would I really want to develop a show about a mother and daughter living together? Even if I could do whatever I wanted with it, I'm not sure that's something I'd want to develop. That's what I'm saying. But, as a member of the writing community, that's what you're asked to do a lot of times. So you come up with something and say, "This could be it." But I have to say, people on the edge of criminality, in a way, interests me. Maybe because I've lived here so long.

PD: How do executives change your writing?

ME: I once had an executive say to me, "If I can find a way not to screw you on this deal, I won't." Another thing about television executives. These guys would say, "Okay, that's the pilot. Tell me what happens in the twenty-second episode." "I don't know. You got me." I remember when my partner, Rich Eustis, and I taped the pilot of *Head of the Class* and afterwards, one of the network executives came by and said, "This was great. You're going to get picked up. You're going to get it on the air. Don't worry." Later, I said, "Rich, I can't think up another story. Can you?" and he said, "No." So we just went, "What are we going to do if they pick us up? I can't do it." He said, "I'm not going to do 100 episodes." We did 150 episodes.

I think they're all scared now. I think they're all terrified. And the stakes are high for everybody. But I don't want to be one of those guys

who says, "In the old days . . ." Because if I said, "In the old days . . . ,"
one of these guys is going to say, "No, no, in the old, old days . . ." and
then another guy would say, "No, in the old, old, old days . . ."

"On sitcoms, [the writers' room is] three jobs: this week's show, next week's show, and last week's show."

JD: What was your experience in the writers' room?

ME: Well, I gave up on them, at some point. In the last one I ran, Rich
and I were on *Head of the Class*. On sitcoms, it's three jobs: this week's
show, next week's show, and last week's show. Rich was very good on
postproduction. He liked it; I hated it. So, he would take care of last
week's show, and together we would work on this week's show, and
then I would work on the writers' room. But writers' rooms used to
be different. If I go back a long time, the writers' room, for instance,
on *The Cosby Show*, was myself and Ed Weinberger. That was the
writers' room. It was because you hired a lot of freelance writers, and
they delivered a script, and you only needed one person, who was
called the story editor then, which was a really big job. There were
two people to work out a script, an outline, whatever it was to break
a story. And that writer would go away, write the script, and come
back, and you'd have a draft. So the writers' room was now you and
the story editor. I was assistant story editor and we would rewrite the
script. Simply to make it conform with all the previous scripts and
characters that we had. That's the job, basically, of the story editor, is
to make sure that each chapter in the novel of a sitcom resembles the
previous one, and is consistent with it.

So then they stopped giving out scripts to freelance writers and
you had all the writers on your staff. And now the staff is eight,

ten, twelve, and the deal was each writer, or team, would get a job as a story editor or associate producer and write one or two scripts, and then the show runner used to rewrite all the others. But what it evolved into is writing scripts with a bunch of writers. Or one of the writers on the staff comes in and the script is not finished, or it's not good, so everybody would pitch in and rewrite it line-by-line. And I hated it! I hated it because it wasn't writing; it was writing by committee. There was no personality, no voice. It was talking, it wasn't writing. And then you have this assistant who has a computer, and his monitor is the television screen. So everybody can look up and say, "Change this, change that, or here's a better line," and so forth. And I said to Rich, "I don't want to do it anymore. I'm not going in there." "So I'll rewrite with you," he said, which we used to do anyway. We would take the script on Sunday and rewrite it so we would have it on Monday. But I hated it. I hated it. It could be funny, because you've got funny guys and women, you know, throwing ideas around. But, in terms of actually being a writer, it doesn't resemble writing as far as I'm concerned. How do you write a monologue for a character who wants to pour his heart out? How can five or six people write that?

JD: Was *The Jerk* written on spec?

ME: No, no. *The Jerk* was written first for Paramount, and they turned it down. Carl Gottlieb and Steve Martin wrote a first draft. They gave it to Paramount. Paramount rejected it, said, "We don't want to make this." They took it to Universal. Universal said, "Yeah, but it needs a rewrite." Carl said, "I don't want to work on it." He went on to do other things. Steve called me up and said, "I've got to rewrite *The Jerk*. At that time it was called *Easy Money*. "Would you come and write it with me?" And I said, "Yeah, sure." So we rewrote the whole thing. Universal liked it, and made it. I said to Steve, "You know, you can write novels, and get Pulitzer Prizes for plays, and you can be a great art collector, and everything, but still, on your tombstone they're going to write, 'Here Lies the Jerk.'"

PD: You come from a creative family. How did you get started in comedy writing?

ME: I wanted to be a writer, a serious writer with leather elbow patches on a tweed jacket and a pipe. And then I decided in my last year of college that I wanted to be an actor. So I went to New York and I tried to be an actor. And they had all these improv classes and I took one and I met this guy, Frank Shaw, and we were very funny together. And I said, "Okay, let's be a comedy act." We started doing a comedy act, and we had some success. We toured the country, mostly nightclubs, and we had a kind of smart, Nichols and May act that went over some places and didn't go over in others.

PD: Was it a big part of growing up in your family?

ME: My father liked to really turn things on their head. It's like this Jack Benny writer I once worked with. He said, "Just for argument's sake, what if we make him a chimpanzee?" And that was always great. It would start you thinking completely differently. My father made fun of everything, including us, and we learned to be funny. My whole family has a good, ironic sense of humor. Nobody's allowed to take anything too seriously.

JD: Do you think you carried that into the improv and the writing?

ME: What I didn't like when I became a writer and director was people improvising any of my words. And I would say, as a director, "I want to hear it the way I wrote it. Then we'll talk." But I want to hear it first the way I wrote it. Television is the writer's medium, because in television you're in charge. They need you more than they need the director, and you can say to the actors, "This is the way you say it" or "This is what you say." Then, at a certain point, the actor gets a lot of power.

PD: How can you tell when something you create is funny?

"For me, [comedy writing is] always the mark of a really professional writer."

ME: You mean before it's tried out by an actor? It's experience. Comedy writing is a schizophrenic occupation because you make something, and then on the other hand you have to make it better, and in order to make it better you have to realize that it's not good enough yet. For me, that's always the mark of a really professional writer. He's skeptical of his work. And it's also the reason why comedy writers do better as teams, because either you can make the other partner laugh or he says, "Not so funny."

PD: Do you think that writers with a stand-up or an acting background develop a survival skill for what's funny?

ME: That's absolutely true. My years as a comedian and thinking something's funny and staring out into two hundred faces—you'd better make sure it's funny. Or, this is what not being funny feels like. So I don't mind telling actors, "Don't worry, it's funny. Just do it. It's funny, you'll see." I want to have the confidence, know that the actor's going to help make it funny. My experience as a comedian, I think, really helped me, because people would say, "This is going to be funny." And I'd say, "No, it's not; I'm telling you it's not." The hidden part of that sentence is: "because if I had to go up onstage, I couldn't make people laugh at this piece of crap, so don't tell me it's funny."

PD: We did an interview with a joke writer for Bob Hope, who said, "Hope is so infallible. When you give him ten jokes, he says, "These four are funny. I can get laughs with these two." He knew. And he was right.

ME: Right. But then there are guys like Cosby, for instance. when I wrote on *The Cosby Show*, this is the first one when he was a teacher, and then I did his variety show. Cosby was different. You couldn't make Cosby say a line anyway. He would never say exactly what you wrote. That's why you had to write situationally. You had to give him an attitude; you had to give him a situation that was funny, and he would approximate the line. It didn't matter—he would make it funny. So you knew going in, he's not going to hit the word to make it funny. He's not going to take a beat and say the word—whatever it was. But he knew how to make it funny in his own style. So that was a different kind of comedian.

PD: How did you pick up skills like how to write a setup, how to pause a beat, when to do that . . .?

ME: Well, I had teachers. And through experience being a comedian, writing our own material, and doing it all the time and finding out, "This didn't work, this didn't work. Hey, if you take a beat here, it'll work." So I got a pretty good experiential grounding, but I never took a writing course, which I regret.

JD: Are you ever in conflict when you direct something you've written?

ME: Something happens when you're the writer and the director with actors who are really good, like Forrest Whitaker, Jeff Goldblum, and Kathy Baker. I mean, writers have inhibition levels that go to here [Michael holds his hand at chest level]. Actors have them up here [he holds his hand at forehead level]. They leave you in the dust, so when they read something you wrote, you're like, "Wow, did I even write that?" I have no memory of that because I didn't think about the guy shouting or acting or whatever. So that's one thing. The other thing is, you have to look and say, "The scene doesn't work." If the scene doesn't work, you can't say, "As a writer I love the scene," you have to say as the director, "Hey, this scene doesn't work." Now you have to call on the writer—yourself—and say, "How do I fix this?" If you can't be self-critical, not to the point that you're indecisive, or completely negative, but you have to be self-critical so you can repair what has to be repaired. And that's the good thing about television. You don't have to do it on the spot because you've got five days. So if the scene isn't working, I guess that's a place where the writers' room could be effective. Sometimes you just need more jokes; it has to be funnier. So group writing can help there.

A writer, a producer, a director, an actor—they're all different personalities. I became aware of this when I wrote the screenplay for *Lush Life*. When I started out talking to people who were interested in producing it, I was going to be the director. And at one point I realized that I was going to meetings with the writer's personality, not the director's personality, because they would say, "We really love the script." "Oh, thank you, thanks." "But we're a little unsure about maybe the ending, or whatever it is," and I said, "Yeah, sure, we can talk about that" or "No, that has to be the way it is." And I came out of these meetings, and I said, "Something's wrong here. I know what it is. I'm going there as a writer." Because a director would go in and say, "You know I really love the script. Let's talk about schedule, casting . . ." Then the writer in me says, "But you said you love the script?" And then the director in me says, "It doesn't matter. We're getting another writer to rewrite it anyway."

BLONDE WITH DARK ROOTS

 An Interview with Heather Hach

A partial list of Heather Hach's credits as a writer includes *Freaky Friday*, *Legally Blonde: The Musical*, and *Freaky Monday*.

Heather Hach's sensibility in comedy was shaped by milestone events like her father insisting that the entire family walk out on *Cannonball Run*. Her taste runs toward the dark side, which is a surprise, since she looks like a cheerleader and got her big break as a Disney Fellow. Despite her pull toward the dark side, she is versatile enough to have written *Freaky Friday* and the book for the stage version of *Legally Blonde*.

❌ ❌ ❌

HH (HEATHER HACH): I think there is something interesting about this idea of the delaying of aging. People are telling themselves that sixty is the new forty and forty is the new thirty. It seems as if women, in particular, are looking younger. I think about what my grandma looked like at sixty. She was what we think of as a classic grandmother. My mom won't be called "Grandma." She's glamorous and she's fabulous and she looks forty. There could be a really interesting relationship here between the mother and daughter, especially if the mother is reverting more to a daughterlike persona, especially if she's a free spirit. But you have the restraint of not having any money. I might get rid of that aspect of the premise.

Sarah's a workaholic with a guesthouse above her garage that's unused. What if Molly comes to live there? I think the fun of it is Sarah thinks that her mother is in a really bad place. She tells someone at work, "My dad died a year ago, she's totally destroyed. I've had to talk to her on the phone every day." So she goes to pick her up at the airport, thinking she's going to find a grief-stricken woman in a shawl, but instead, Molly steps out and she just happens to mention she's into Pilates. She looks fabulous. And maybe she says, "Everything I thought I needed, I don't need. I'm starting over."

The fun is the shock Sarah feels when she finds out that her mother isn't like who she was expecting. She was prepared to help her grief-stricken mother, when in actuality the mother could be helping her daughter find her sense of fun. Since Molly looks fantastic and is into Pilates, what if she opens up a Pilates studio that's really successful and fabulous and fuels her kind of craziness. Here's an idea for that kind of craziness. She's having an affair with the pool guy. I think that's a funny juxtaposition, especially if you have it in your mind that it's going to be one way, but it's so completely the opposite.

It's funny if tunnel-vision Sarah is freaked out that her mother is way hotter than she is, and has a much better social life than she does. Molly's the one on Match.com, and she's the one setting Sarah up on dates, and she's the one with a second lease on life. She tells her daughter, "I'm not going to apologize for being sexual." Automatic conflict.

It could be a series, but frankly, there is so little TV that I respond to that I always go toward film. The first act would be the revelation that Molly is not in this grief-stricken, devastated place. She's been so busy that she just kind of hears what she wants to hear. And maybe the movie is also about destroying the myth surrounding Sarah's father. And maybe it's Molly who does the destroying. He was supposed to be this stallion when it came to finances. But it was a complete lie, and he invested all his money with a Madoff-like guy. So where's the truth? "Mom isn't living for a man, as I always assumed she was." We've seen workaholic women like Sarah ad nauseam, but if you have it playing off her mother as a free spirit, I think it can be fun.

PD (PETER DESBERG): She's a free spirit, but is she also smart?

HH: Not in a traditional way. I think she's clever. She's always lived her life for other people, and now suddenly, for the first time, she says, "Well, what about me? Someone forgot to put me on the checklist." And Sarah says, "Oh my God, my mother has gone crazy." It would be funny if Sarah works herself past exhaustion, and her mother comes home and says, "The Pilates studio has taken off."

Maybe at the same time, Sarah fumbles in her own career. She screwed up at work. Made a bad decision. Maybe they join up and the solution is that Sarah becomes the CEO of Molly's company. Together they open up this really successful juice bar/Pilates workout studio. And what happens is that Sarah realizes she needed a time-out from the corporate fast track. She needed a rejigger of her own life as well. Fun. It's a really fun movie!

JD (JEFFREY DAVIS): What personal element would you add to this story?

HH: Honestly, my taste for film is always much darker than what people expect of Heather Hach. Everyone thinks I must watch *Sleeping Beauty.*

PD: How would you darken this?

HH: I would give it a more *Flirting with Disaster* edge, as opposed to the Goldie Hawn route. You know, make Molly more Mary Tyler Moore with a drinking problem. Because there are a lot of people who are healthy and yet they drink a bottle of chardonnay at night. There is some fun to be had with that kind of mom, someone who is completely obsessed with her appearance. She pretends it's all about health, when health has nothing to do with it. It's all about vanity. I can't watch ten minutes of TV without seeing wrinkle remover and injectable face-lifts. There's so much comedy in that world and in that reality. Let's be honest, there's comedy in how much pressure there is on women not to age. I'd like to explore that aspect of the story.

PD: What ends up happening to Molly as a consequence of her drinking?

HH: She bottoms out. She has to face the drinking. Or does she? This is a part of the problem with movies. You always have to have everything completely fixed at the end. Not every movie, but commercial, studio-driven movies. I always loved the end of *Election*. It's just stunningly perfect. I think *Election* is also one of the best political movies ever made. It's also very human. At the end, when Matthew Broderick is at the museum and there is the new little Tracy Flick, Reese Witherspoon's character, with her hand in the air, it says that nothing changes, which I love, because nothing does really change.

I like a happy ending, too. I don't want to walk out of the theater absolutely, morbidly depressed. But I like movies that have a darker edge and feel more real. If her mom is an alcoholic, at some point Sarah has to find out about it and confront it.

Maybe Molly agrees to cut down on her drinking. She says, "I'll only drink on the weekends." And even then her drinking is completely out of control. I'll tell you what I wouldn't want to see in this story. I don't want dialogue from Molly like, "You're right. Thank you for illuminating the truth. I do need to stop drinking." You want it to be real. Of course, we go to the movies to see people who look better than we do and have better romantic lives. But what is so satisfying is when a film also reflects what we feel and didn't know we felt.

Frankly, I had much darker impulses earlier on in my career. What really started my career was this script like *Heathers* about a sorority where they kill a lesbian and they cover it up. But then I got *Freaky Friday*, and that's not exactly a sad day at Auschwitz. They always want you to make it sweet and happy. But one of my friends said, "You are a very dark blonde." I would like to see Molly still drinking at the end.

JD: Would the audience find this out at the same time as Sarah?

HH: Probably as Sarah discovers it. How about this? No one ever talks about the fact that people who drink tend to be more fun. I'm sorry, I'll take the drinkers over the nondrinkers almost any day. I'll find the people who like wine, like I do, at the party. So what if Molly does stop drinking, and she becomes a complete pain in the ass? And then Sarah is begging her, "Please start drinking again!" I think that could be really fun. I do like the lesson in moderation. It's a valuable lesson when there is a happy medium where you still get to be a little bit bad, but it's still kind of satisfying at the same time.

PD: So she goes from drunk to sober to moderately sober?

HH: Moderate to occasionally sloppy. Because isn't that more interesting and real?

JD: Where would you take their relationship?

HH: I think it's got to be tied to the business because everything starts to collapse for Sarah at the time that everything's going really well for Molly's new Pilates studio. So they start to work together and you can have this wonderful montage of everything going so great and then the drinking and all the other things start to snowball and drive it all down. Maybe that's what makes Sarah say, "I gave up my job for your Pilates studio, and you're more focused on guys and dates than work, and you're still a booze-hound."

Sarah has been on this delusional path of working, working, working and that's why she didn't see the truth about her father. Maybe Sarah is so driven because her father was so driven. She's modeled herself on him. She didn't see the truth about her mother, either, and says, "I'm not seeing the truth about myself." She's putting everything into it and it collapses.

PD: Does Sarah change as she goes through this experience with Molly?

HH: I think she's got to wake up and face the fact that she's been on this hamster wheel. She's got to be honest about herself, and her mom and her dad. She's got to realize that her life is passing her by. She sees clearly that her mom has a better social life than she does. She's never made time for it. This could be a fun movie, especially if it was done with a little bit of a subversive edge. You need a little complication. What if Molly starts dating Sarah's boyfriend from high school? That's creepy, right? This is the guy Sarah always pined for.

PD: Did he dump her?

HH: Yeah, in high school. But this is about how Molly and Sarah don't communicate, so Molly doesn't know the truth about anything. Sarah never told her mom how much he meant to her. And her mom doesn't even remember this guy, and he comes to the Pilates studio. They start dating. Sarah finds out about it and reverts to the high school girl who had a crush on this guy.

"... the only satire that works is satire that has a soft heart toward what it's satirizing."

No matter how sophisticated you are, or what you accomplish in your life, you're always just two emotional beats away from being the girl who didn't get asked to dance. It never goes away.

I would do this as satire, but I think the only satire that works is satire that has a soft heart toward what it's satirizing. You can't do it with malicious intent. There has to be a little bit of empathy and emotion.

PD: It has that feeling, especially if neither the ex-boyfriend nor Molly has such a great memory. She innocently stumbles on it.

HH: Sarah never confided in her, but she's enraged anyway. "You don't remember my prom date?" That's kind of funny. "No, I don't. It was a long time ago." "There were pictures. More than one." You thought your mom was so checked in and completely there for you. She had no job, but she was just out to lunch, and Sarah didn't see the drinking growing up.

PD: So she starts dating him. Where does that go? That's going to bring up a huge conflict.

HH: He doesn't know that this is Sarah's mother. So when he sees Sarah at the Pilates studio, he says, "Oh my God, it's Sarah." Suddenly he's in the middle of a crisis. "You're mom is so hot." "Stop saying that!"

PD: Who does he end up with?

HH: Maybe neither one. It's too loaded. Once you've made out with Mom, you can't date the daughter anymore. I think he should just go away. He could be the catalyst to bring them to a greater disclosure about the drinking and all the other secrets they've kept over the years.

PD: Who are the secondary characters in the movie?

HH: I think you've got to populate the world with the Pilates clients and the other instructors. It's such a funny, self-centered world. "We're really going to focus on those glutes." There's just so much fun to be had in that world. It's therapy. We don't talk to the closest people in our lives about the truth of what's going on. And you end up sitting next to someone on a plane and they know more about your life than your parents do. It's the same thing with Pilates. It's a weird dynamic. It's intimate. People spill things to Molly they'd never tell their husbands.

PD: Were you always a funny kid?

HH: I was always a liar. I would tell horrible lies. My best friend's mother in preschool thought my parents weren't married for a year. "That's not my real dad." Now my three-year-old daughter is doing it. Her teacher pulled me aside and said, "Harper's been telling everyone at school she's pregnant and she's going to name the baby Drake." And the kids believe her. Here we go again! And my daughter is so cute. I'm hoping to God that her teeth come in crooked. I had glasses and I had horrible teeth. I'm so glad I did because if I had been the cute girl in class, I don't think I would have had to be the funny one. The best thing that happened to me was bad vision and bad teeth.

PD: What did you study in college?

HH: Journalism. I didn't think I could write movies. This was beyond the scope of my imagination. I was always a writer, but I just thought I had to be practical about it, and make a living. I didn't know anyone in Hollywood. Even though movies and comedy were my passion, it just seemed abstract.

> **"I really think that studios should pick five top candidates and pay them at least a couple thousand for the amount of work they do . . ."**

JD: You've spent time in development?

HH: There are things that are so great about what we do as writers, but the thing that is so frustrating is the amount of work you do for nothing. I put in hours and hours and hours figuring out a whole movie. Rehearsing it, really thinking about it. It's not easy to come up with a movie. And then you go into a studio. I really think that studios should pick five top candidates and pay them at least a couple thousand for the amount of work they do, because the amount of work we do for free is just absurd.

Then you pitch and they always come back with, "We want it like this." It's like everything is another movie that reminds them of something else. "Okay, yes, we know you've seen that great film." Or "Yes, we all love *Tootsie*, but this is a different movie." It's just frustrating that there seems to be no other headspace beyond, "It's *like* this." I have a movie right now, *French Women Don't Get Fat*, that's trying to get a director. And people have said, "Oh, it's kind of similar to *Julie & Julia*."

JD: Were your parents funny?

HH: My dad is very subversive and very funny. My mom is "Miss Show Tunes." I didn't think she was as funny as I've come to see. She's a big personality and always singing. My dad was always like David Letterman, always at the expense of someone else, which most comedy is. We'll drive by somebody running really slow and he'll say, "There's somebody I could beat in a race!" Just that kind of mean comedy. They have great taste. They showed me great comedy.

JD: For example?

HH: People think I'm making this story up but, before *Plan 9: From Outer Space* was a huge cult favorite—Ed Wood's worst film ever— they saw it and they thought it was so hilarious. My first night back from college, they were so excited to be together and said, "We have *Plan 9: From Outer Space* to watch!" I just don't think that's a really common back-from-college, reunion-for-the-whole-family story. They have good taste in film. As a young kid I watched *Harold and Maude*. I remember we went to *Cannonball Run*. It was such a hit. Everyone loves *Cannonball Run*. So we're in the middle of a packed theater in Colorado and my dad says, "I can't take it! I gotta get out of here! Everyone's dying of laughter, and we had to creep over everybody and I was like, "This is funny, I think. I don't know what's going on." My dad's like, "Get outta there. My God, it was awful." So I was always aware of good comedy versus cheap laughs.

JOKE, JOKE, STORY, JOKE, JOKE

 An Interview with Mitch Klebanoff

A partial list of Mitch Klebanoff's screenwriting credits includes *Disorderlies, Beverly Hills Ninja, The Jersey,* and *Swap Meet.*

Mitch is a study in contrasts—by turns screwy, off-the-wall, and adolescent as he comes up with original jokes, and then morphing into an adult who makes use of his math/science background through his attention to story structure and detail. This rare balance of oddball comedy associations layered onto well-crafted stories that have a strong cause-and-effect relationship, makes the most "outside" or outlandish situation become plausible, and produces some extraordinarily original work. Mitch's placement of a mother-daughter relationship against the backdrop of punk rock is one of the most unusual stories we've seen in these interviews.

❖ ❖ ❖

MK (MITCH KLEBANOFF): The first thing I would do to make this premise seem different is do it single camera. It would change the whole nature of how you'd go about it because I would be bored with the idea that you have a living room with a whacky mother and daughter. I'd find a way to make it more like a movie. In the movie world, you're following the action and you're going to watch and see everything that's relevant. In the sitcom world, a lot of things are going to happen offscreen and you're then going to see everyone's reaction to it. I like those shows where you're using the visual medium much more than just doing some dialogue-based comedy.

So what are the visuals of this show? Where's Molly? Molly being in a living room is not a particularly visual idea. The visual would be how we get her into a place where she's trying to work or trying to do something. Each week I would probably try to do a new task of figuring out what she wants. And we'd be following her, going with her, whether it was an interview or starting a new job. And they would be silly or visual or something like that as opposed to having her go off and do those things and then come home and tell Sarah about them. I'd like to see her do all those things and if that means she sells lemonade in the mall with one of those funny hats, that's what she's doing. I don't know if that's the best of all jokes. The wackier, the more it would grate on Sarah's nerves. Because Sarah's very officious. The more lowbrow Molly's job is, the more it would grate on Sarah because she's a VP, so she's not going to want to see her mom working at a lemonade stand at the mall. I would probably do a bunch of different shows where the mom's not working at a level that the daughter would find satisfying. At some point you might want to do the reverse—have the mother get a job that the daughter would be jealous of. Working with male models?

If Molly got a job as a photographer, or an assistant to a photographer, now, she's working with all these hot male models, who are not gay. But I wouldn't want that one joke to define the show, because it could end up throwing the whole show off in a direction that wouldn't be worthwhile.

Another thought is that Molly starts a dating service, but not just a regular dating service, but like eHarmony, where she's actually really successful at it and all her friends now look up to her. The oldest way of telling that joke is she's a matchmaker. The modern way of telling that joke is she's working at eHarmony. And the goal is to set her daughter up. One could start a whole, multimillion-dollar business just simply trying to get her daughter laid.

Molly's going to be the person who fuels the comedy every week. There are a lot of great fifty-year-old comediennes. Probably very underused and really hysterical.

PD (PETER DESBERG): How do you go about defining the characters?

"I know everyone says you start from the character, right? I start with whatever comes to mind."

MK: I know everyone says you start from the character, right? I start with whatever comes to mind. And so in trying to solve logic problems, ideas emerge. Like anyone else, no matter how creative, I'll get hung up on the logic of it and I won't be able to think of anything until I understand the premise and make sure that it's really solid. Everything has to be believable within some world you're creating. Even with *Beverly Hills Ninja,* something has to ground it enough to say, "Okay, yes, he washed ashore on a Japanese island, he was brought up by ninjas, so obviously he wanted to be one of them." Well, that defined who he was. If all your brothers and sisters are running around throwing nunchucks, you're going to want to throw one, too.

So we start fleshing out Molly and Sarah because we wanted to know why Molly wants Sarah to date. Molly works around male models. Maybe she sees how desperate Sarah is to get ahead. Maybe she's an ass-kisser. Now, that's not very heroic, so that's a tough call. You have to decide right there. Would I be willing to make Sarah an ass-kisser? That means she's not attractive. She could be beautiful, but she could be an ass-kisser and that's going to be funny, but usually you would give that role to some other character. You wouldn't give that to your hero or your heroine. She has a reason to be an ass-kisser on this.

This brings back four billion conversations they had when Sarah was sixteen and when Molly was 40. All teenagers do is pick out all the possibilities for hypocrisy, which we all are filled with. It brings up this issue: If you do that episode, which is the *hypocrisy* show, which, of course, would be really attractive to all our teenage viewers, is it like *Rashomon?* Do you go back and retell the story. And do you go into a flashback? And you have to try to make Sarah look like she's 16 and Mom look like she's 40, which is a casting problem. That would define the problem with that episode, which is that you probably couldn't do that show. Or you'd have to come up with a funny way to do it so that we could buy the fact that Sarah's going to play herself at 16. Because do we really want to bring another actress in to play that role that day? Not likely. But it would be funny to do *Rashomon.* You always want to show how nobody remembers anything the way it's supposed to be. And the hypocrisy is certainly going to be an issue that is going to come up over and over again. It's not just going to be one show, it's going to be many shows and it's going to flip back and forth between them.

PD: They're dealing with each other as adults, but the same conflicts have been there all through their history.

MK: Yeah, that doesn't change. It's possible that they may flip, so Sarah is acting like the adult and Molly is actually the child, but the truth is that it might have been true when they were 16 and 40. In terms of fleshing out the characters, she might have been born adult. She always knew. Molly may have always been the wayward mom, if she was a hippie.

Actually at this point, she wouldn't have to be a hippie. She could actually be a punk rocker. In other words Mom was a punk rocker, but she's now a mom. Okay, I think we've gotten enough years past punk rock, which probably started as early as 1974. That's thirty-two years ago, and she would have been 8 then. Yeah, Molly could have been a punk rocker. So that's funnier. That's better than being a hippie because that's already too old. And we've seen that idea. But I'm not sure we've seen the idea of a mom who used to be a punk rocker.

PD: Would you ever play around with the idea that in business situations, Sarah is mature, but when it comes to relationships they would change roles?

MK: Anybody who's going to be as protected as Sarah is going to have her vulnerable side. And the question is, How often does she let you see it? What button gets pushed? And how often do you want to push it? I mean it would be repetitive if you constantly played it that way, where she has this veneer that's really tough. She's officious, but she's got this other thing going on. It wouldn't be repetitive if it was there all the time. But it would be repetitive if you were making a point of the series showing this.

PD: You'd have to work really hard to not make it a one-joke series.

MK: What show is not a one-joke series? Let's talk about *Seinfeld*. It's four jokes. One for each character and they get repeated every time. I didn't watch it every season for that reason. I got bored with it at some point. The safety of the formula is also its potential downfall. Some people don't have that problem with it. There's this theory out there that audiences want to see the joke repeated.

JD (JEFFREY DAVIS): What would you do if this was a comedic movie?

MK: It could be an indie movie if you made it really quirky and you didn't try to make it mainstream. Then it would make more sense to me. The punk rock idea not played cheesy could quirk it up. If you did it in the comedy vein of *Office Space*, which I don't see as a mainstream movie. If you found really offbeat comedy having to do with some of these places Molly worked at, and odd characters that were quirky and bizarre, and you were able to have her meet a lot of people along the way.

PD: The people in the punk rock movement believed in what that movement was about. They were intense social critics and they expressed themselves in really shocking ways.

MK: I don't know if I've thought it through that far. Now that I think about it, it would be an interesting thing to do with this mom, because she may have already dampened all her intensity. That may not be what she's been doing for the last twenty years and then her husband dies and she's out on her own. All of a sudden, maybe the real Molly suddenly starts to reappear. And that person is not just a person who has punk rock in her background, she has punk rock in her spirit. And that's different.

PD: I remember walking through the streets of New York in the 1970s with them yelling "Die Yuppie Scum."

MK: I remember that phrase.

PD: And here's Sarah, who is Yuppie scum, and Molly raised her.

MK: I tell you what wouldn't make it quirky is if she picked up a guitar. Then it would be like *Freaky Friday* or *My Mom is a Rockstar*. That's not what I meant.

Think of how embarrassing the political activism would be for Sarah. The punk rockers were kind of nihilistic; they weren't even trying to make the world a better place. "Die Yuppie Scum" was purely a gut reaction. I don't think there was a "Let's do this" part. They didn't care about what people thought of them. If people walked out and said this is horrible music, they could give a sh-t. Molly, fifty years old, all of a sudden gets back in touch with that music. That's not even a comedy anymore necessarily.

PD: Especially if it was done suddenly where she's not going to pierce her lip with a safety pin. It's more the attitude than the accoutrements.

MK: But with that attitude she would probably start to hate her daughter. All of a sudden she's watching Sarah and she's basically saying, "Die Yuppie Scum" and her daughter is the yuppie scum she's going to end up hating. Or, I guess there's a comedic form of that hate. But if it played real, it wouldn't be a comedy anymore. We're going into drama now. Molly is a mom who is bitter about her husband's death. She actually blames all the institutions that have caused it. And then you start to explore that part of it, which is Sarah asking, "Why did Dad die?" Then it would be like a French film, or German. There's got to be a conflict, there's got to be something at the core of it. The question is how close you cut to feeling like it's a drama as opposed to masking it and really holding it together with the dramatic push of the movie. I run into this problem all the time. "I fall in love with a joke so I go, joke, joke, joke, joke, story's gone. So now I go joke, joke, story, joke, joke."

JD: Is this something you do when you're writing a rough draft?

MK: I do that in my fiftieth draft. It comes up all the time. Lately, what I do is scene lists. I pretty much write down every scene prior to writing the script. That doesn't mean I do those scenes if something new happens. But I've found that if I don't do that usually the story goes awry. Probably my logical mind is working on the scene list, and then my right brain mind takes over when I'm writing the scenes. Then, instead of ending the scene where I expected to end it, I get some new idea and then the next four scenes go off in another direction. Then all of a sudden, I have to pull it back somehow. And if I love those four scenes, that's worse. Because then I have to figure out a way to make them work and then I'm retooling everything. And that's really the problem.

JD: You talked about *joke, joke, story, joke, joke.* What does that mean?

MK: When I'm writing a comedy, I'm always insecure about how funny it is, so I'm always pushing to see where I can find humor. But sometimes that's a mistake. You just can't push. I'm not saying they're not funny, but I am saying that, at least in the reading process, not everybody is going to get the joke. So you'd better get the story working well because if they don't get two of those four jokes, they've really lost the story. If they get all four of those jokes, they'll wait for the story to come back around, but that's a risk. You know the reading process of Hollywood. The linearity of the plot is relative to the short attention span of the reader. You don't know that those four jokes will work for everybody.

PD: How do you know if your writing is funny?

MK: I don't. I make judgments for the moment and then basically it's a consensus operation. I used to say, when I was writing with my partner, that if one person were writing alone he would have no idea if it was funny. The fact that we were working together meant we had twice as good a chance at thinking it might be funny. We all know that until you go and give it to other people, it's just like a vacuum—you just can't tell. I tend historically to write or come up with comedy that has a wide range of appeal. So I tend to think it might be funny because I have been able to make a larger group of people laugh. But on any one given joke? No. There's no way of knowing. My intuition is probably ultimately pretty good, but I've written plenty of clunky scripts. Sometimes you find yourself in the middle of a script and it's like finding your way out of a paper bag.

JD: How soon do you think you should show a draft?

MK: I'll show it right away, as long as it makes sense. Especially if I think there's enough for a person to be able to help me judge it, and tell me what's good and what's working and what's not good. Show it to your agent? I'd wait quite a long time. Show it to your studio? I'd wait even longer. I won't show a draft to a studio that's not at least the sixth draft, and that's only if I was lucky.

PD: When it comes down to actual joke construction, how did you learn to build a good setup, a payoff?

MK: It's all mimicry. Ultimately, it's like learning how to speak English. You're experiencing it and you absorb it through some form of osmosis and then eventually you regurgitate it. Here's just a little thing. I'm watching your eyes, what you're responding to, the things that get you excited. I'm like a dog. I'll put in more of those. I think that's really what it is. It's like a behavior modification concept. I guess I have a humor gene. And somehow in my youth it started and then I just fed it more.

PD: As a kid did you tell a lot of jokes?

MK: I was voted class chatterbox. I wanted to look at it as a positive thing, that I was a joke teller, but it could have meant that I was extremely talkative. Partially, it's self-entertainment. We entertain ourselves. And then we try to entertain other people by being clever or witty and then you get accused of not being engaged in the reality of what's going on in the moment because you're trying to be funny.

The first thing I ever did was copy *Raiders of the Lost Ark*. I loved the movie. Basically, I tried to write a new version of it and with completely different characters and completely different situations, but really I tried to mimic it.

PD: You're analytic in the way you approach things.

MK: I was a much better math student than I was an English student. I mean I was a decent student in both, but math was my thing and especially visual math—geometry. That's why having partners is good. Because when you lose track of story and structure, there's somebody to reel you in and tell you that you've gone off the deep end. I've been in comedy rooms and some people don't have that piece. There's just that freewheeling thing. And you become like the cop, where you have to bring it in and say, "Well, could you help me with the context of this material? Could you tell me how I would possibly throw it into this scene?" But sometimes you really want that freewheeling thing because it's brilliant. If they had five people to choose, they will get two people who are completely off the wall, no logic, but brilliantly funny and two logic people. And then somebody who actually has a heart. Somebody throws out the gem and then somebody else has to be smart enough to know how to catch it. And I don't know that it would matter if they worked off each other in terms of the moment. Like improv.

PD: How do you deal with people in a room one-upping one another?

MK: Well, in some shows I'm sure gold came out of that competition.

I don't think that would be the best motivator. The way it works in improv is people really have to give themselves up for the moment to their partners. One way of working in the room is to have people improvising off each other. Here's another way. People take role positions. The person who's nutty and off the wall needs the logic person to throw out the logic situation to start them off. It may not be something that would have ever occurred to them that the logic of the situation is that Sarah would act one way and Molly would act another. That's the given.

JD: Were people in your family interested in the arts?

MK: Nobody in my family comes from an artistic background. No, I shouldn't say that. I'm going to totally contradict myself. My mother and father did *Guys and Dolls*. They did a little bit of theater. They acted. I was an audience. It was Temple Theater.

PD: Where did you go to high school?

MK: I grew up in Queens until I was thirteen and then by the time I got to high school, I had moved farther out, onto Long Island, which was completely the opposite. It was a completely white community. The junior high I went to was 95 percent black and so between that school and my dad being an attorney, I probably picked up a lot of ethnic humor beyond just Jewish humor. And it's actually the cornerstone of my life right now.

PD: Is it difficult for you if the character is unlike you? What about a really quirky character?

MK: No. It's not all a difficult. It's probably easier, actually. Obviously, Chris Farley in *Beverly Hills Ninja* is nothing like me. But there came a time where I knew his language pattern. I knew his sense of being orphaned, or what he felt like. I knew who he wanted to please and who he didn't want to please. Who he wanted to boast to and who he didn't want to boast to. And once I answer those basic questions, I'm there. Or if you were writing for Inspector Clouseau, how deep does that have to cut? There's a certain amount of things that you know you want to do. Yes, if it gets repetitive you might have to add and rethink that. But mostly it's being a chameleon. Where you're just being able to place yourself in another person's body and think the way they think. Specificity is crucial, *absolutely* crucial. In a movie like *Ninja*, the givens are limited. Not limited, but the concept is so high concept that you don't know how much detail you'll need. Like did the ninjas pick on him and that kind of thing?

PD: You didn't use any of those details in your screenplay?

MK: No. It just helped me understand Chris Farley's character.

PD: How is writing alone different from writing with a partner?

MK: For years I wrote with a partner, but that eventually played itself out and I started writing by myself which was very, very difficult. One reason was the reason you brought up, which was not knowing what's funny.

And then I went onto a television show and I didn't have to solve that problem right away because I had a bunch of partners again in a room. When that ended, it took me a while to figure out what I could do by myself. And partially it was by going back and doing the sequel to *Beverly Hills Ninja* because it was familiar territory. The character was different in the new one, but it was a joke I knew how to tell really well. It helped me in a sense gain more confidence and go back and be really funny again.

PD: Do you have a preference between writing alone or with a partner?

MK: Now I really like working by myself, but I need a lot of support so I use a lot of people in different ways for help. Here's an example. I have a student who was really funny and I used him to polish dialogue. He'd tell me what he thought was funny when he'd give me fairly immediate feedback.

PD: You set things up so logically, even though the ideas you come up with are really funny, off-the-wall ideas.

MK: I certainly feel at this stage of my career that I've come to accept myself more. I trust wherever my mind is going to go and that eventually most problems will get solved. And they will probably be kind of funny in the end. Will they match up with what Hollywood wants at the moment to put out on a Friday night? I don't know. Most of the time, probably not. I focus on Friday night because that's what screenwriters do—movies that we do. It's all like what will they sell on a Friday night and will it match up?

And that's just matching up. I mean you could try to match that purposefully. There are people who are probably really good at that. And there are probably times in my life when it was all a big contrivance and I was good at that when I was selling things. But it's the way I approach it now. I just happen to have very adolescent taste. But that is part of the sell. The stuff that I've been able to get people to get behind is the stuff that matches with that boy energy, that adolescent thing that I can still tap into. When I try to do a genre thriller, they're very competently done. They're pretty good scripts, too. Have I been able to get someone to match that up with what is happening moviewise? No. Not always. It brings up a really interesting question. Is something genuine at the core of everything that gets made? And I would say that's probably not true.

GUNFIGHT AT THE KLEIN CORRAL

 An Interview with Dennis Klein

A partial list of Dennis Klein's credits as a creator, show runner, and writer include *The Larry Sanders Show*, *The Bill Cosby Show*, *Grace Under Fire*, *Buffalo Bill*, *The Odd Couple*, *Laverne & Shirley*, *Beverly Hills Cop II*, and *Love American Style*.

In the other interviews in this book, we asked questions, the writers gave answers. Sometimes we discussed things. They developed the premise. They left the conflict on paper. From the moment we walked into Dennis Klein's house and began setting up, we knew this interview would be different. In our other interviews, we asked the writers where they would be comfortable sitting, and they told us. Dennis took charge, arranging the pillows, the lighting, the backdrop, and he kept moving the camera around until he liked what he saw. And he hadn't even looked at the premise yet.

Good writing is all about showing not telling. It's what makes for great drama and great drama is what you get with Dennis Klein. If you've seen *The Larry Sanders Show*, you know it had a unique edge to it. Characters clash and always show strong emotions. Dennis hates bland comedy. He likes things to be unpredictable and uncomfortable in the extreme. More than anything else, he's got to feel passion for an idea. To prove this point as no other writer in this book has done, as he develops the premise he points out that he doesn't like doing it, and that it's an irrelevant task anyway. When that doesn't get the intense reaction he's looking for, he goes after us—directly. He creates the climate that others only talk about. It is a brilliant example of theater within an interview. You will not just see what Dennis believes, you will feel it.

⊠ ⊠ ⊠

DK (DENNIS KLEIN): By the way, profanity? You wish I didn't use it?

JD (JEFFREY DAVIS): Absolutely not. Use it. Use it to your heart's content.

DK: This premise is really written like a television show. It seems that it all takes place in Sarah's apartment, and there isn't anything about it that says, "movie."

PD (PETER DESBERG): You can immediately buy a trailer and have them start going across the country.

DK: That's true. That's very, very true. Well, gee, immediately, there's nothing about this that is at all interesting to me. To some extent, I have it, but I'm trying to see if there is anything that I kind of like, or could kind of like in it.

PD: A good place to start would be, What elements would you change to like it more?

DK: But to like it more, I mean, that is sort of the same as to dislike it less. There's something that's really exciting to me, and if this works, you could go on the air with this tomorrow.

I'll tell you something. At some cost to me in terms of money and friends, I have chosen to never, never work on anything that

I don't have an excitement about. So this falls into that category so far. When I started in television, people were still doing a show imitating *Sergeant Bilko*. And even when I was working with your father on *The Odd Couple*, there were writers who had done *The Honeymooners* maybe a decade before, and they were still working.

What I noticed about them was that they weren't excited about writing. They only wanted to be producers, not writers. They wanted to supervise writing, but they didn't want to do any writing themselves. And they were bitter and cynical and they hated everything, and they weren't even available to be turned on by an idea. Not that they didn't think it was possible; they just weren't looking for that. They were really burned out. I thought, "Well, gee, these guys are in their late thirties, some of them, some of them in their forties, and I want to be doing this for a long, long time." I didn't want to be bitter. They were unhappy people. And I realized that the shows I was excited to be writing on—*The Partridge Family* and *Love American Style*, that kind of stuff—were a comedown for them. And for me it was great. I had just been writing jokes for comedians. It was really actually exciting, even beyond just the paycheck.

PD: Imagine if we said to you, "We bought the rights to this thing, but what we really want is you, so you can change any aspect of it."

DK: I understand the rules to this thing. All right, so I'm going to see if there's something about this that I can actually love.

JD: If you can get to like . . .

DK: . . . no, no, no, has to be love. I won't get to like. I don't care about like. The only thing that's sort of exciting is the thing about where Sarah is. "There's only room for one woman vice president, and the vice president is a woman," and I guess that's for television or a movie. I don't know where that goes, but I love that. I must say I like the idea that this Sarah character is confused. She's not confused actually; I like the idea that she's torn in all these different worlds. I don't like any of the different worlds—even the woman vice president. Then we're into feminism stuff and the politics of that, which is okay, but it's more head stuff. But emotionally, Sarah is a person who is trying to be alive in the world and be herself. And she's being crushed by this other woman. I don't consider it so much like the focus of the thing, but it's constantly happening to her. And she can't do anything about it, as long as she wants to stay at that company, she's stuck.

So I don't think that's a fun thing to explore, but as a small other character in the show, which is how you have it, I like it. And then she has a mother who's a pain in the ass. And she has a father who is dead and has f--ked them by not taking care of them properly, and now he's dead. I guess Molly's better off with him dead, isn't she? Was she better off when he was alive, fiscally speaking?

PD: Molly thought she'd be taken care of, and was stunned to find out . . .

DK: Are you going to finish every sentence? So when he died, then the income stream stopped and it wasn't replaced by anything. So when he was still alive, the income stream would go because he was actually earning money. So that's the problem: He had nothing but an income stream going, and that was enough for them. They didn't need more than that, right? They were living fine. Now he has left nothing to replace it with. It's too bad there isn't more happening. The grandparents are just in this one sentence, and so they are whatever you want to make them. See, that's the problem with this thing. It's wafer-thin. There's nothing here, really, for me, anyway, or possibly for others. So the question is what can be added to this or changed? Boy, it's amazingly uninspiring. With all due respect to whoever came up with it. You know, my daughter started using that phrase, *All due respect* . . . and she realized what an insult it was. For a couple of weeks she was saying, "Now, Dad, with all due respect . . ." and it just was always kind of a knife into my heart. And that made her want to do it more.

JD: I love the thing you came up with about what's going on at the office with the female boss. We never see that. It's been mostly ignored.

DK: I would throw away the whole lifestyle thing, and the mother living with the daughter. Jesus Christ, that is dull and boring, and there's no way that I can think of that becoming interesting or fun. And then, I keep trying *not* to cast Diane Keaton as the mother. There's a possibility that I could like it and that Gyllenhaal girl as the daughter.

I just keep thinking that somewhere there will be a word or a syllable that will pop out at me that will suggest comedy, or drama. Even if it's drama, the comedy will be easy. That's just the icing on the cake, but the drama has to be there. It seems to me there has to be something that's interesting. So Sarah is working for a woman who's envious of her. If that were a series, then the problem would be to stay with the mother. Then, there'd just have to be more because either the boss/employee relationship would have to be richer. But it couldn't really happen without sort of destroying the fun, or the premise that they're in competition. Because at a certain point you say, "Well, why doesn't the boss fire her or why doesn't she quit?" You really have to say, "What is she doing there?" She has to be doing something else that doesn't have anything to do with the boss, because that's a questionable relationship.

So the problem is, if you really examine that relationship— Sarah and her boss—it doesn't make any sense in a continuing way for her to stay there. See, if it's a series then it has to be five years' worth of somebody staying somewhere where they shouldn't be. Then if it breaks up, you don't have a series anymore. So you really want to have that be a meaningful part, and I'm trying to make it be a meaningful part of the story, because that's the only sliver that's there. Otherwise, I have to leave your premise behind completely. But part of this is a challenge. I mean it's easy to just throw it away and start over again. The challenge is not to make this work, or to make it palatable, to make it okay, to make it not horrible. The challenge would be to make it great and still maintain some semblance of what you have there.

So it seems like you're talking about a movie at that point. It's a contained amount of time, and you would think that, at the end of it, something would be done about this relationship: Either Sarah would quit, Sarah would be fired, Sarah would be hired by a higher-up to replace the woman who's jealous of her. Whatever it is, that could happen in a movie. It couldn't really happen in a series without destroying the integrity of the series. But still, I don't like it as a central premise, but as one of many things that are happening to Sarah. So then, I would have to invent a lot of things that are happening to Sarah, and then I would have to actually figure out, which your premise has not done, Why do I give a sh-t about Sarah at all? So that's what your premise has done. If I may, with all due respect, your premise has come up with all the unfunny, uninteresting, uncompelling things about Sarah and her life and the people around her. Leaving the, hopefully, funny and compelling things for somebody else to come up with. But if you come up with funny and compelling things about somebody, why do you need all the unfunny, uncompelling things anyway?

JD: What's funny to you?

DK: In general? We're not talking about this project?

JD: If you didn't have to take any of this, or just take that one little sliver.

DK: I'm interested in the troubles that people can get into that are not containable, and are not usually where people get their entertainment from. There's something on the air about a sleeper cell, or something, but I remember somebody told me the premise, and it seems like they've made it into something more probable. But I'm interested in the horrors of that, not just the horrors of what they do when they blow people up. If your life is your sleeper cell, that means you are sitting around waiting for some order from somebody. But I guess that's how we all spend our life, to some extent. But then, you're just an absolute victim, and what must that be like? Getting up every morning and being at the behest of other people.

I'm just interested in whatever it is that people do that is disgusting and horrible, like that *Woodsman* movie with Kevin Bacon, where he's a child molester, and he's not the bad guy. He is the bad guy, of course—he's a child molester—but he's not the bad guy in the movie. The hero is somebody who's trying to catch him, or stop him, or doctors trying to help him. I like things that make people uncomfortable, make me uncomfortable.

JD: You feel that same way about comedy, right?

DK: I *am* talking about comedy.

PD: When you first came up with the idea of saying, "I like this relationship. That's the one thing that interests me here," I like the way you described it as a constant pressure. It's not huge, it's not overwhelming, but it's ever-present.

DK: Yeah. James Cagney gave a young actor some advice. Cagney was a very self-effacing guy, and his advice was, "Never relax." And the thing about James Cagney was in everything he did, he never was relaxed. And I think that's good advice. And honestly, that's the way I feel about drama and comedy—that there should be some kind of a tension, some kind of issue, even if I were writing about two people who are totally relaxed, two people like, say, just a husband and wife lying in bed, ready to go to sleep. What could be more relaxing? I think some people make a mistake. They put people in conflict, and I think that's easy and contrived. Everybody's kind of in conflict, but I like to see people who aren't in conflict, because the truth is everybody's in conflict all the time. Everybody has conflicting needs with one another, so you don't have to invent conflict, like, "I like chocolate cake" and "I like carrot, so what are we going to order?" "We both like chocolate cake, isn't that great?" And yet, when it comes, there's a problem, because one of them wants to cut it this way, or dig in. If I have a cake, I like to eat it with a fork. I don't want anybody around me. And if somebody wants to eat with me, I'll say, "Well, you order your cake and you can have it any way you want, and I'll just eat my cake with a fork."

PD: So as long as you get your way, it's OK. Should we censure you for that?

DK: That'd be the day, when I could get one of you to say something critical, because honestly there's glad-handing happening.

PD: With all due respect.

DK: The point is, you guys are being as nice as can be, and there's a tremendous amount of conflict here. You have to be thinking critical thoughts and yet you're not expressing them, so there's internal conflict in both of you, unless you're really, literally as bland as you seem, which I don't believe.

PD: It's a harder skill than it looks.

DK: Fine. A young married couple are about to go to sleep, and one says to the other, "I think if we ever do get mad . . ." Such is the lack of conflict in this relationship. "If we ever get really angry and have a problem, then we shouldn't go to sleep angry." And the other person says, "Yeah, I think you're right," and then they start to go to sleep, and the other person says, "Why wouldn't we go to bed angry?" "Well, I just think it's not a good idea," and before you know it, there's a major battle going on, for maybe the first time that they've ever fought, and very early in the relationship. I don't know what they're doing in bed, if it's very early in the relationship, although I actually do know what they're doing in bed, and I don't want my daughter to know that. When I decided to get married and stop dating, one of the last dates I had was this woman I picked up at a bar . . . Okay, this may not have anything to do with comedy, but maybe it does.

We're in bed together, and she gets up to go to the bathroom, and I'd never met her before and we had a great time and all that stuff. I'm glad I own this stuff, this interview you said on the paper. And so, all of a sudden I see a little bit of metal under her pillow, just a glint of metal, and I said, "What is this?" I think it's odd that something got left there. And I lift the pillow up and the biggest hatchet that I've seen is under her pillow, which I thought then, and I still think, is there for self-defense. Understandably, picking up guys in a bar. But what if it wasn't? So as soon as she got out of the bathroom, I said, "You know something, I actually have an appointment. I know it's three in the morning, it's crazy . . ." And I got out of there really, really swiftly.

I told my therapist about this, and she said, "Do you think possibly now, now might be the time in your late thirties that you might actually think about having a stable relationship?" and I said, "Yeah, there's a signal here." So anyway, the point is, conflict is essential, but does not have to be contrived. So if this is a movie, I'm still answering your question, I'm looking for the stuff that isn't overtly thought. This is, by the way, why I have trouble convincing anybody to do my stuff. It isn't overtly thought to be comedic, or thought to be about people in conflict, or even thought to be interesting by people. I'm not searching for it. But I'm saying I want to be discovering that. I want to find out what that is, but not arbitrarily. I want to find out if I'm interested in it. And what interests me a lot of times is the stuff that's underneath the bland realities of life, because I don't think anything is bland—I really don't. I'm excited and interested about a lot of stuff, about almost anything except contrived situations, because they're phony. Like for example, Peter. Now and again, with all due respect, you seem somewhat bland—actually you seem even blander.

PD: Thanks.

DK: You're welcome. But you couldn't be that bland. So I'm wondering, even now, now that I'm talking to you, and I'm theoretically insulting you, but you're smiling and laughing, but underneath that, there's got to be, I'm not saying rage, but there's got to be something happening that you're not revealing to me. But then who are you going to reveal it to?

PD: You've already put your finger on it. You said, "You guys are on polite behavior," which we are. Of course we are. And we're not friends, long-term friends, so it would be very bizarre to start being combative, or pushy.

DK: No, no, it wouldn't be bizarre Peter. It's only bizarre because of your version of the way people should be with each other. Why can't you be combative? Why can't you say, again, with all due respect, why couldn't you say in a nice way, "If you have a problem with something I say," and we could right away leap to a different level of intimacy. So why are you going to wait five years?

PD: Let me answer that question. I think with you I could, but with a lot of people I meet they'd say, "Hey, wait a minute, you come into my house . . ."

DK: That's right, that's right.

PD: ". . . and you're arguing with me. There's the door!" You have made it clear that you're looking for that, which is something more interesting than what we've done here so far.

DK: Fine, exactly.

JD: I understand how you could come up with *Larry Sanders*, because that's what that show is all about. It's all about things that aren't said, even when they're saying it, there's so much under the surface.

DK: It's all about false. Everybody's being false. We've got the camera so we know the truth. We find out the truth, as everybody is being false.

PD: We're saying the conflict in the room is more interesting than the conflict on the paper.

DK: Well, anything's more interesting than the conflict on the paper, and I say that with all due immense amount of respect. But here's the thing. You say, I just want to go back to it, but that's right because I'm interested in what's real, and isn't contrived. Even if this was good, which it isn't—I think it can't even pass for bad, but even if this were exciting to me, which it isn't—I could say that. I do say that. It's still just a piece of paper. There's nothing on here.

Nobody has their heart in this piece of paper. In other words, this was contrived. Even if I say this is great, which I'm not—believe me, I want to make that crystal clear—but even if this were great . . . I'm afraid that we'll never crack that façade with either of you, so I might go back to the hatchet.

Something unsaid, and something unsettlingly horrible beneath our bland affability with each other. So that interests me. Now here, nobody wrote anything on this that their heart was into. I don't know. I'm assuming you guys came up with it, but maybe you didn't. But maybe some retarded person came up with it. I'll bet that there isn't anything in here that anybody can say, "You can take this as a challenge?" There isn't anything on this piece of paper that anybody gives a f--k about. So why are we reading stuff that nobody gives a f--k about, not beyond this moment, but right now I do because you're sitting in front of me.

PD: I'll give you the answer to that one, though it's a little arcane, but an answer, nonetheless.

DK: I would expect nothing less from you.

PD: Since you're on the couch, are you a fan of Freud?

DK: Yeah . . .

PD: Freud believed that the therapist should keep his mouth shut and be a blank screen for the patient to project not just his thoughts, but his relationships as well. That's how the idea of transference came about. Just as a patient can view a therapist as anyone he wants him to be, our intention here was to make a premise as open-ended as possible so that anyone could take it in any direction he wanted. So there's the beginning of conflicts, and it's up to you to do anything you want with it. If the premise was brilliant and funny, there'd be nothing left for anybody to do. Our intention was to leave lots of room for you, as you said, "to do stuff."

DK: Okay, I hear you, I get it, I get it. I got it even when I interrupted you because I was trying to save you from having to say seventeen more sentences. I like using the "f" word. So sometimes a premise is just a premise. Here's the problem. You haven't done it. I agree with what you set out with, but you haven't created a blank screen. It's not blank. It's an idea that exists. It's an idea. It's an ostensible idea.

And that's the problem. If you wanted to get a little closer to what you're saying you want to do, which I think might be an admirable thing to do, then instead of this thing that you've written, you would get an article from a newspaper, or some description of something that actually happened or a picture a photograph. That's where you get into the Rorschach test stuff. A picture of a guy or some photographs of something. Something that is just not made up, that's nonfiction. The minute you put a piece of *fiction* on paper, it is not blank anymore. And now, somebody has to work with *your* piece of fiction. So it already puts the creative person in a bind, in a box. Let me tell you something: I've been presented with horseshit like this and said, "Oh, you can do anything you want with it." Well, I'm already sickened by it. "Oh you can depart from it." Then why did you put it down there? Why'd you put *anything* down there? Why didn't you say, "Start from scratch." So this sinks me. This sinks anybody, anybody in your book is sunk by this. And maybe you mean to sink these people. And maybe that's the anger beneath the blandness, the glad-handing, and all that.

JD: The little piece that you did find interesting was the relationship in the office.

DK: It's the only thing that interested me, yeah. I wouldn't necessarily make it more than a sliver. Well, no, no, let's change that. It could be the whole movie. It could be the whole movie—that whole thing and that relationship. I have no problem with that but, what couldn't be the whole movie is her dilemma, like, "I got the job." That gets boring really fast. But as a piece of the movie, it is, to use your word, "fascinating." If you keep it, then the question is: How small do you make it so it's the right size and it doesn't become boring, and how small do you make it before it doesn't even exist?

Here's a person who's in conflict with the person she depends on and admires. See, I would throw that in. This is a job she's always wanted. And this is a boss she admires and respects. She is saddened somehow, and angered by the fact that her hero has feet of clay. That this woman could be so territorial, because that's what's ugly about the boss. That the boss would do that, and tie it into gender is really unenlightened. If you got Sarah just fighting an unenlightened person, and Sarah is terrific, and the unenlightened person is a devil, and she's fighting her, and it just gets really kind of concocted.

But, for example, what if this woman, the boss, is admirable, and has this problem. And it is even maybe a problem for the boss herself that she didn't even realize. And then you have Sarah fighting the battle. The boss is fighting a battle within herself, and Sarah is fighting a battle within herself, because she wants to maintain her respect for this person, even beyond rising within the organization. But then the question for Sarah becomes, "How much do I want to rise?" In other words, "I can't just be fascinated with this woman and trying to change her, or concerned with my own hero worship at the expense of rising. I'm screwed if I stay here because I can't count on this. How can I count on this person changing?" That's the whole emotion of counting on somebody else changing, or something happening outside myself for me to feel good about myself. Any of that is really disgusting and ugly. Which would be something that Sarah, being a young person, might discover about herself in the process.

She wouldn't be in a television series because characters don't change. But in a movie, she might. She might see through this relationship. How she wastes her time and her energy doing all the stuff, like hero-worshipping this person, if you add that. In other words, what's funny and interesting to me is that Sarah is royally screwed. She is in a job that is hopeless. She wants to rise. And by the very definition that this woman has set up, who is her boss, she can't rise. And yet she's there. Then why would she stay there longer than a precious day of her life? That's something that she has to wrestle with, even beyond the fact that she should quit in the next minute. What actually happens when she's in the office?

I'm interested in Sarah noticing that she's capable of screwing herself, and then looking at every other aspect of her life and questioning it, including her boyfriend and where she lives. "Why did I choose this?" "Why do I dress like this?" But then I'm describing a nervous breakdown and it starts to become a little bit less interesting. What Sarah ultimately would have to find out is that she carries those seeds within herself. There is something about her nature that will force her to always screw herself. So even if she gets out of this situation and quits here, and even if she changes her life and doesn't make the same choices, aren't these new choices something that is encapsulating her "Sarah-ness"? So, it creates a harrowing situation for Sarah because there's no possible way that she can do anything without screwing herself. It makes her paralyzed. But then paralysis is yet another way of screwing herself.

So maybe she does get paralyzed. You know, I worked for a while with John Callahan, the cartoonist. He's a quadriplegic, and he's a very funny guy. He's a very funny cartoonist, and darkly, ruefully funny. He writes books and stuff, and his cartoons are everywhere. In one of his cartoons in the *San Francisco Examiner*, he had Laurel & Hardy in an AIDS ward. Hardy is saying to Laurel, "This is another fine mess you've gotten us into." So John Callahan finds humor in his quadriplegia. In fact, one time I was talking to him on the phone and he said, "Do you hear a buzz?" And I said, "No, I don't." He lives in Seattle, so it was cold, and he said, "I've got a hair dryer on." And I said, "Just wash your hair?" He said, "No, it's just cold, and it's a quad thing." And then I realized that he's a quadriplegic; he doesn't have to turn the heat on in the house. The hair dryer is all he needs. There's a harsh reality to life. I guess that's what I like to write.

"There's a harsh reality to life. I guess that's what I like to write."

But I do want to say something. What you guys have done here to me and the rest of the writers is very telling. You've caged the writer. Everybody has an urge to control writers, and control creative people. I'm not being paranoid here, but there's an impulse to not take what the writer thinks is interesting and funny and put it on the screen, but to somehow control it, shape it, shift it, for good commercial reasons, or bad commercial reasons. Stupid people do it stupidly. Smart people do it amazingly. And then all of a sudden, a writer gets famous off something that I've done a rewrite on. I've seen this stuff. It stinks. And the movie comes out and it's amazing and brilliant, and that writer gets *complete* credit, not just Writers Guild credit. That corrupts the process. So I see that process can work or not work. But it is an attempt to deal a death blow to the sanctity, the singularity of a writer's vision.

You guys couldn't go to a writer—you wouldn't go to a writer—and say, "What's on your mind? Let's see you create. Let's photograph you creating." You didn't trust that, and maybe rightly so. You would've gotten like blank tape. So instead, you've moved down this road, and you tried to make it as tiny a move as possible, but it doesn't matter how tiny or big the road is, you moved down the road toward corralling the writer, and then you said, "Oh, we're corralling you, but you don't have to stay in the corral, you can go graze over here, and graze over there." Well, yeah, try that, then here's a piece of paper. And that's what's made this process and your entire book, in my opinion, with all due respect, bogus.

Now your book is about, with all the taped interviews that you've done, how you can take comedy writers, even comedy writers who have done big things, and turn them into puppets, or sheep. You watch how these sheep manage to have bowel movements that are so interesting, and you're going to photograph those bowel movements of the sheep that we have shorn and . . . I don't know, this metaphor is breaking down as I speak . . . but that's what you've done. Rather than film the creative process of a writer, you've filmed the destruction of a writer's originality.

PD: It's an interesting view. And here's what I think is interesting about this. We've read about studies where people have done what you said. They go to artists and say, "Go and create." And frankly, a lot of what happened is nothing, unless you're willing to do it over a period of weeks and sometimes months.

DK: It doesn't work! That's why writers are corralled. It doesn't work.

PD: There's a wonderful parody that Monty Python did years ago. They're watching Thomas Hardy write a novel and broadcasting it on the radio as sportscasters. There's another way to look at this.

It may be odious to you, but interesting to me. I'm kind of a science guy, and what you do in science is separate and control variables.

What's interesting is that everybody starts off at the *same* place. It's interesting to see how their approaches are different. What's been fascinating about this is that some people have begun, and said, "Yeah, this is easy. I could do this. I would cast this person . . ." And we've had some people say, "This could never be done; I'd have to change this and this and this." And we've had some people say, "Gosh, this just gets me so pissed, this is why I don't write anymore, unless I get either direction or production in my contract, because I don't want people to change what I do." We've had people say, "I love the network system. I really thrive under it. I like the challenge of them giving me something to do." Your response has been the most extreme by far. That's why it's so fascinating.

DK: Mine's been the most extreme?

PD: Yours has been the most extreme view, in terms of not liking the task. And that's great for us, because it's another viewpoint. So this is really valuable for us.

DK: I understand.

PD: You and I clearly don't agree on the nature of the task, and that's okay, because you're not right or wrong.

DK: It's not even that we don't agree—it seems beyond that. We don't even agree on the morality of giving writers this task. But I do want to say that you have corralled these writers. People in charge of all kinds of stuff want it for their own purposes. They don't want to have something be exciting and interesting in and of its own nature. So the first thing they want to do is confine it. And so now you have a premise, you've taken however many writers—twenty or thirty writers—and you've reduced them to little gerbils in your study. So you've got this writer here pulling his pants down, and they're all different, but it's not really creative, even though I might be interested in reading the book.

PD: If I created a show and I hired five writers to help me write it, have I corralled them?

DK: Yeah, so we have to hire the five writers. But you don't have to pretend that you've done a great thing, "Gee, we're all of one mind, and we're all marching . . ." We're getting into an argument now about what's art, which is good. That's always a good argument to have. But the five guys in there you've hired to work on your show—I don't think they're prostitutes, and they're *not* artists, because you've corralled them. They have skills, they have talent. I'm just saying, to whatever extent you've done that, you're destroying their creative output.

PD: You're the one who's saying that if they haven't chosen it, then they're corralled. You're saying there aren't even degrees of corralling.

DK: No, no . . . then I take that back. I'll change that. But to the extent that they haven't chosen it, they're corralled. You know, it's not that black and white.

JD: I'll just disagree with you to this extent. I saw you doing it anyway, and I saw Dennis Klein come out near the end of this, and that was what we got excited about.

DK: Thank you. I was glad to be able to provide that.

JD: I think it just took you a while.

DK: It took me a while because you guys . . .

JD: . . . pissed you off. Dennis, what's the difference between the freedom you have at HBO, and what you have at the networks, which you obviously didn't like? And you've had a lot of freedom at HBO.

DK: Gary had a lot of freedom.

JD: You didn't?

DK: Well, I had the freedom to please Gary. All I care about as a writer, just like in a sex act, is just being turned on. It's like eating. I don't care what I eat in the morning. I have turnips and radishes, and I get into that, because now I try to eat healthy, but I'm not a vegetarian. But when I eat that stuff, I enjoy it. And maybe I dip it into a little bit of that Chinese mustard sauce, give it a little zing.

Early in my life I was confused and mixed up and screwed up, but by the time I reached my late thirties, and to this day, all I care about is being really passionate about what I'm doing, whatever that is. And I don't care what it is. And I learned that from having a daughter and being passionate. Even if I'm not passionate about what we're doing together, I'm passionate about the fact that she's growing and I'm helping, or even just keeping her company. She's got a dad there. That's exciting to me. The same goes for television.

There were some jobs I really loved, like *Buffalo Bill*. That was a show where I was turned on to every aspect of it. Accidentally, I was in complete control of it, but I didn't need to be in complete control. I've been in situations where they needed a joke. I was rewriting *Cocoon*, and Ron Howard needed a joke. Instead of writing a joke for this spot, I wrote forty jokes, and then he picked six and shot them, and ultimately, one found its way into the movie. I had written the scenes and felt ownership of the characters. But basically, the premise wasn't mine. Everything was kind of handed to me, and controlled by the others. Ron was going to pick what he shot, and the producers were going to do focus groups. And so it was completely out of my hands, except for writing those jokes. Writing those jokes was great. And writing jokes is great. Coming up with ideas is great, for me. It's enjoyable, just like everything that I try. I try to make sure that everything that's on the menu of my restaurant, where I'm the only customer, is a tasty, delightful dish for me at that time, at that moment. So that's what I try to do, just keep myself excited, and not do anything that isn't exciting.

At one point Gary Shandling was not sure about the premise of *The Larry Sanders Show*. He was very uncomfortable, and he thought, "Maybe there isn't a series here," and he wanted to discuss how there isn't a series here. I found that tremendously productive, even though he didn't mean it to be productive. That was just his angst, and it didn't really help him. I thought, "Can't we work today?" So I said, "I'll come up with forty ideas, stories for this series—not bland, not clichéd ideas for episodes—tonight. So let's table this discussion. Let's just do work. And tomorrow I promise you, I swear to you, I'll have forty ideas." So the next day I came in and I had written them—handwritten on yellow legal pad—all the ideas. And again, like the forty jokes, I don't know . . . biblical?

So Gary looks at the pages. The first page has eight ideas on it. On the fourth page, he says, "I have to tell you: Number forty-one I don't think is a story. I just really don't . . ."

My mother kept trying to get me to read. She had all these novels. "You need to read novels. You're reading about Nazis and gangsters," and she would hide those books and burn them. I said, "You know, you're burning books about Nazis. Don't you understand? Don't you see the irony of that?" So my mother . . . there was a million times more of my mother in the world than there are Margaret Meads, who wants to go somewhere, do something challenging. Before you know it, you're sitting in an empty movie theater saying, "Hey, this is wonderful, anybody watching it?" This is my most deeply held belief . . . for the moment. People can get mesmerized by crap, and people's reactions to crap, and people who are getting rich doing crap.

I'll see these other movies, or plays, and they're crappy, and people say they're great and I want to kill them. I have those moments. But it's just an important discipline to focus on what's great. I've been saying all kinds of bullshit and you guys are going to cut it down, and you're going to cut it down, and hopefully, you're going to do a good job. There's a couple of minutes there where it was really worth something, and it really worked, and that's nice. That's nice to have that as part of the writing thing and the rewriting. You write a lot and you whittle it down, and that's our job in writing.

Epilogue

A funny thing happened on the way out of our interview. As Peter was putting the recording equipment in the car, Dennis took Jeffrey aside and told him about working with his father, producer Jerry Davis, on *The Odd Couple* in the early 1970s. Dennis remembers that Jerry wore a suit and tie to work every day and there was always a white handkerchief in his breast pocket. Dennis said, "Your dad, regularly invited the writers to lunch. He never left anyone out. Not even the new kids like me." Dennis said he hoped we understood that during the interview he'd been doing "shtick" so it would be more interesting. He wanted to leave no doubt that his interview was theater.

When Peter got home that night, there was a voice mail from Dennis emphasizing how much he enjoyed doing the interview, and thanking him for asking him to be a part of this book. He found the process interesting.

HOW BIG IS MY PAYCHECK?

 An Interview with Bob Myer

A partial list of Bob Myer's credits as a show runner
and writer include *Roseanne, Cybill, The Facts of Life,
Living with Fran, The Gregory Hines Show, Rodney,
My Two Dads,* and *Who's the Boss?*

As a child, Bob Myer caught on to jokes more quickly than other kids his age. By adolescence, he realized that comedy could protect him from being beaten up by bullies, and as an adult he has managed to get big paychecks for writing it. Bob said that he has always had an animated face and mugged constantly. Being in a room with him, we both noticed that what he referred to as mugging was really an expression of the pleasure he gets out of the comedy-creation process.

❖ ❖ ❖

BM (BOB MYER): Well, if you were the network and you came to me with that idea and said, "Do it," or you were pitching it as a pilot or something like that, the first thing I'd say is, "Who's in it? Who've you got?"

PD (PETER DESBERG): And we'd say, "Who would you like?"

BM: Right. This is just the way my mind works. I file back to anything that was similar to it, because, in a comedy room, your first instinct—your first pitch—is something you've probably heard before, or has been derived from something before, so you're always looking for your second and third pitch. This first pitch sounds a little like *Judging Amy*. A driven daughter and a mother who moves in and is trying to get her to settle down. So the first thing you see, when you see a generic idea is, "Who do you have who's going to make this special?" So, failing that, if the casting makes it special, that's the concept. If the casting doesn't make it special, now you have work to do.

"So you have, essentially, a buddy comedy where both of them are having an impact on each other."

Now you have to figure out what it is about. What are viewers buying? What are you going to be up against? What are you going to be compared to? And this is an era of *My Name is Earl*, very high concept shows in which the theme carries from week to week. It's like we just had a family show period, and it's over. Now we're going back to high concepts. So this sounds like a high concept, but it's basically a family show. So now you have to dress it up somehow or other, so that it reads a little bit more like what's contemporary. So those are the things that would go through my head—not necessarily creative thoughts; those are marketing thoughts. So, given those parameters, the first thing you start to pitch is: What does the daughter do? Did the mother have a history of doing anything ever? Whose influence is bigger on whom? It seems to read like a story about the mother coming in and teaching the daughter the values of home life; lay back a little on the job, find a guy, be less driven. And the daughter, getting the mother out there, back in circulation. So you have, essentially, a buddy comedy where both of them are having an impact on each other.

So what does the daughter do? If she's a lawyer, her mother can't be involved in that work. But if she's running a store, a coffee shop, or something like that, that she is trying to franchise, that she's trying to expand, now you can bring the mother into that arena. And that's what I would suggest. I would go to something where Mom is not just at home, because then it's a story about the daughter. So I would suggest that she open something that is growing, something that we can see, something that we can watch, and something that her mother, in getting involved in, can create situations down at the store.

So she's just opened a Starbucks franchise, or, better yet, she's just opened an Ed's Coffee franchise, and across the street is Starbucks. And she's got to work, work, work, work, work, so that she can compete with Starbucks. And her mother comes in and adds touches: cupcakes that she baked at home or things like that. So the pilot would wind up being the two of them in a somewhat uncomfortable, but for the daughter, a grudgingly beneficial partnership down at Ed's Coffee. And the homey touches that the mother brings, versus the marketing experience and the driven energy that the daughter brings, are, in combination, what can make the business work.

Since they work down at the business, and they work at home, they're never away from each other, which is another source of conflict: "Where are you going?" "Can I come?" "But you want me to meet a man." "Are you meeting a man?" "Well, can he come in?" The typical disruptions that a mother would make in a daughter's life are magnified here by the fact that the daughter can't get away from the mother, not only because she lives at home, but also because she works with her. So that would make it a story about both of them, so that—back to the business—your casting potential is that there's no real "second banana." So that if you were going, for example, to CBS, which skews a little older, and you could get Jean Smart, and you don't know who the younger girl is, you could get Jean Smart by saying, "It's not a secondary character. The mother's very primary. Or if you're going to Fox or NBC, and you could get Courtney Cox, you could say to her, "No, this is not a story about the mother and her transitioning her arc from the East Coast to the West Coast. It's a story about you and your mother." That's basically what I'd do—couple of funny neighbors. Some music. Some laughter. Some sweetening.

PD: How would you get a guy into this?

BM: First of all, it's easy to put a guy in at work. This is the guy who clearly has a crush on her, which Mom can see, but the daughter can't see the forest for the trees. So the sexual tension can come from him. He's not as driven. He's much more the mother's taste; he's much more what the mother would look for in a son-in-law. And the daughter has never even considered this guy. In the meantime, she's dating other guys, all of whom, in her mother's view, are wrong.

Let's go!!! [Bob pounds the table] Let's go pitch to some fourteen-year-old executive.

BM: My greatest nightmare is that I'm an aging writer—even "age-ier" than I am now—and I go into the network to pitch something, and I'm sitting before one of these baby executives, and I pitch my heart out and I'm waiting. The executive looks at me and says, "You know, Dad . . ."

JD (JEFFREY DAVIS): What would you do with this premise that would put your stamp on it if you weren't constrained by selling it in today's marketplace?

BM: How do you turn it into a higher concept, the kind of thing that they won't look at right now and say, "Well, it's been done; it feels ordinary; it feels yesterday"? I would probably look for that. Not only to satisfy my own sense of challenge, but also to satisfy what is right now—the network's need for something that is radically different, even though most of those are doomed to failure because on a week-to-week basis, you can't be radically different. You have to come back to character relationships and things like that. So how would I make it something that I would love? How big is my paycheck? That's the first question I ask.

Steven Spielberg said, "I like ideas, especially movie ideas, that you can hold in your hand. If a person can tell me the idea in twenty-five words or less, it's going to make a pretty good movie." This is another way of saying *high concept*. A writer has to walk a balance beam. The more "high concept" a project is, the more unique it seems to be, but the more difficult it is to sustain from week to week on a comedy series. And, of course, it's what the networks want—a perfect blend of stable relationships with high concept that is almost impossible to deliver.

Well, I would probably add a character to it who really created the imbalance in what is pretty much a very balanced concept. You asked before how would I get a male character into this. I would probably add a character. I've written a pilot on spec where the character's ex-husband is just coming out of jail. And I would probably throw in a variable like that, where somebody's coming in who is a brother, or an "ex," of the younger woman, of the daughter. This character is coming in from left field, just to crank the story up a little bit, just to get in her life. So maybe instead of the guy down at Starbucks, I'd bring this guy out of nowhere. He was a philanderer or he was in jail or he was an addict or something like that. A guy who has had a struggle and is trying to turn his life around, who her mother always loved. And Sarah can't stand him. So that we can get him into a relationship with both of the women that will skew the women's relationship to each other. And I think this guy might be coming out of a psych ward—something really a little bit out there; something you don't see on mainstream TV.

PD: He's not just chicanerous—he's a loose cannon?

BM: Yes, he is. He's not just a funny neighbor; he's somebody who has a life of his own that impacts your life, as opposed to, he is leeching off your life.

PD: He's very unpredictable.

BM: He could be very unpredictable, if you really wanted to go in a direction that I think many network executives could relate to, but I don't know how the heartland would respond. You know, this is a guy who's switching from one antipsychotic, or antidepressant to another. Or he can just be a guy who had a really bad past. And he's got a parole officer; he's got friends who are a little questionable. And so all these things, I think, get dragged into her life. And if you separate the two women, so that they have opposite feelings about him, that for some reason the mother sees through the veneer—the daughter does, too. She loves him—obviously, it's sexual tension; obviously, the series is heading toward somehow or other testing that relationship, getting them back together in some way. But the mother has always liked him, which gives the daughter an attitude: "But he stole cars, he killed somebody . . ." "We all make mistakes." Molly still likes him.

Molly says, "Who else is asking you out? Who else is so great out there for you?" And then the actual sensible comment: "You loved him once; there's got to be a little of that left." And, of course, the guy's got to have some redeeming qualities. He's struggling.

He's coming out of rehab or he's coming out of a psych ward or he's coming out of jail, which I particularly love. But whatever that test was, it converted him in enough of a way that he is trying to establish a normal life, a better life than he was leading before. Sarah just isn't buying it. [At this moment, Bob's face lights up.]

If you took Sarah, and had her coming out of jail, or Molly, and have her coming out of rehab, or something like that, week in and week out, you'd have to remind the audience that this isn't the nature of their relationship; it doesn't impact upon them anymore. It's something that she's already moved past. After a while, you don't want to have to answer that question; you just want it to be a study of the characters and their interplay. But if you take the third character, and it's because of his being a wild card that it impacts them, it's much easier to describe: "I see you're here without your car-stripping friends today," Sarah says. It's much easier to describe how he gets in there. He's a two-and-a-half-dimensional character, so it's a lot to get him in. And I forgot to tell you, he wears his pants up to here [Bob points to the middle of his chest].

PD: How would you go about making it darker?

"If it were darker, and an hour show, I would make it a ghost of her own past ... something she is trying to overcome."

BM: What I would do is make the profession darker, so she would be surrounded by darker characters. Not prostitution—we're talking about the marketplace again. If you're doing it for Showtime you could go there. That's actually a good idea.

I don't love this, but she could be on the crime beat of a newspaper. You know they do this on USA Network a lot. They take a crime show and put a funny character on it to lighten it up. They did it with *Monk*. They made Monk OCD. They put a lighter person in a darker arena. I'd try to find an uglier arena. Something where there's a darker side to the arena. Or I would try to find the ghosts of the past. If it were darker, and an hour show, I would make it a ghost of her own past. I'd make it something she is trying to overcome. What if she was still fighting a drug habit. If she actually had one and was trying to fight through it. That would darken it up considerably. I like that actually. I don't know how the mother fits in, but you take a thirty-year-old woman, who's had a roughish past and is trying to become a professional writer, for example. She works on the newspaper and her deep, dark secret is her habit, which she just can't kick. That darkens it up a little.

PD: That's like what they had in *Cheers* with Sam being an alcoholic.

BM: Yeah, and *Murphy Brown*, too, but they never explored it. That's what happens to high concepts. "Wouldn't it be interesting . . ." Only, ultimately, it's not. Because people like that ultimately grow. Like I said, the husband is a better person when he comes out of jail, not her, because she's trying to grow and if you hold her back, you hold up the drive of the series. It's the same thing with *Murphy Brown*. My thought about *Murphy Brown* is what would you do with Candace Bergen? Here's a woman who is beautiful, and seems very upper crust, and is coming out of the movies. and how do I sympathize with her? She's kind of cold, how do I sympathize with her? So they gave her, right out of rehab, coming back to her old job and finding that there is a younger, prettier girl competing with her. And so they gave her a real struggle. This struggle lasted two episodes and then the show was just about this curmudgeonly woman reporter, a woman anchor in this arena with a bunch of crazies.

So if you're on Showtime, Sarah could be a private detective, good at her work, a minor Sherlock Holmes. Holmes was a drug addict, so you actually give her the cocaine or heroin habit that she's trying to fight. Take it to a place where she goes through withdrawal and relapses. That's how you darken it up. She'd have to be funny out of her darkness, out of her self-loathing would be comedy. You know, when you hate yourself, you hate the world. So she would just hate everyone around her. Anger is funny. The negative emotions are the funny emotions.

PD: So once you develop a character like this, how would you flesh it out?

BM: In the pilot episode, I would probably start with a first act where you had no idea of her addiction. You just saw her at work and saw how good she was. And at the end of a quarter of an hour or half an hour, you'd see her make up all the chemicals she would shoot up. And you would go, "Whoaaaa!"

Then you'd go to her psychiatrist and see her lie to her psychiatrist, saying that she's over the habit: "I haven't done it in days." You know she did it the night before and she probably did it on her way over there. So you see her lie. And only the audience knows the whole truth. That way she becomes as dark as you want her to be, especially if she hates the world. She has no respect for the world. She'll lie her way through anything, and that could be very funny. Trying to get into the evidence room, for example, and she's just a private detective. And how does she lie her way into that because she just doesn't care? Here's a woman who, because of her drug habit, her life is sh-t, and she doesn't care if she dies tomorrow. But the one thing that keeps her moving is this—what she's good at. And this is something that she can't suppress.

PD: How do you make her likable?

BM: I think her dependency makes her likable and she's funny. And we like funny people. Second of all, she's pretty. You like pretty people. But she's also got a struggle and you're rooting for her. You want her to survive, you want her to pull out of this. And she's good enough at what she does and entertaining enough in how she does it that she can keep her friends strung along. Her friends haven't given up on her yet, and you don't, either. You still feel like there's something of value there. You probably need a Jiminy Cricket in the show. You probably need a sister who knows enough about her, who's constantly sitting on her shoulder. And someone she lies to, but somebody who probably knows about the lies.

JD: Do you take the mother and transform her into someone else?

BM: I would take the mother and make her into a contemporary, because the mother not taking really fast action makes her very weak. And that's not a character you would really love, but take a character who was a very dear friend, a sister, someone who knows her well, and there would obviously be an intervention show—right in the middle of an investigation. So she walks into her home, she's got the reports of the latent prints, the DNA evidence. She's coming home to pick up her hat or whatever it is she needs, but it's obviously her cocaine. She's got an interview with the guy she got to meet, and he's the deep throat. And she walks in and . . . INTERVENTION! There's comedy in that. I'm thinking of pitching it now!

PD: It looks like you develop a character by creating a property list. OK, I need this trait to make her quirky, I need this trait to make her dangerous, I need a trait to make her likable, and I need a trait to make her unpredictable. The functions derive from the character.

JD: How much of what Peter just described is conscious for you? How much of it are you aware of?

BM: Well, a lot of it was prompted by Peter's questions. Like, how do you make this person likable? And a lot of it comes from years of having it ground in by the networks: Unlikable leads just don't work. You just have to find a way to make a lead likable. The classic example is *Buffalo Bill* with Dabney Coleman. Now if you could find a more entertaining rogue than Dabney Coleman at that time, I don't know who it was. But *Buffalo Bill* was one of the best-written shows on television at the time. I, and most of the comedy writers of that time, were rooting for it because it would have broken the mold, but it didn't. You can make Louie de Palma, Danny DeVito, totally unlikable, but he's not the central character. You can laugh at him because you just know that he's never going to stop being grouchy and mean. And it's great for your secondary character. Later when the show matured and they needed to go other places for stories, they made him sort of likable. There was a studio executive named Glenn Padnick [cofounder, with Rob Reiner, of Castle Rock], who said, "Don't ever make Louie likable. The minute you make Louie likable, you've lost your character." But a lead—it's kind of a knee-jerk reaction—has got to be likable in some way.

This takes us back to Candace Bergen. There's nothing innate in Candace Bergen's character that suggests vulnerability. She was very strong, with her voice, in her appearance. She was beautiful, carried a lot of authority. How are you going to feel for her? You've got to give her a struggle.

Roseanne created her own struggle. She was a struggling mother trying to hold a family together in spite of her microcosmic economic disaster. Their situation was constantly never having two nickels to rub together. And that allowed her to be unattractive.

Which I never felt she was. I always thought she was adorable.

PD: You're so skilled at the craft of setting up a joke. Like solving the crime and walking into the intervention. Where did you learn that set of skills?

BM: I don't know. When they staff you, they try to put you into some type of category. Are you a story guy or a line guy? And I am only a competent line guy. If I had to make my living just writing jokes, I wouldn't be in the business. My mind works in juxtapositions and ironies. It just works that way. I can see situations better than I can see lines. And I can punch up lines and I can rephrase lines, and occasionally I will make myself very proud and come up with a line that the audience occasionally laughs at. But it's not the thing I do best.

PD: How do you know when something's funny? People who have done stand-up have developed a survival instinct because the situation is so immediate.

BM: People who play in front of an audience should always be funny. People will argue that because of that wonderful little laugh box, anything can be funny in an audience situation comedy. That's not true. As a stand-up, you know that it's funny immediately. But that's only with that audience. We had an act once where the act got stale. We took two months off and rewrote the entire act. We go onstage, and for one weekend our new act actually destroyed the audience. It was absolutely amazing. It was beyond anything we could have hoped for. We were so happy. From then on it died. Doing it in that same venue, on the same night of the week, but it died. Why? I don't know. And why does a piece of material that has worked for years for you suddenly stop working for you . . . that has worked for years for you? That also happened to us. It just stopped working for us—you don't know why. One audience differs from another. People who are writing without the illusion of a live audience, or for a laugh track, don't have to be that funny.

PD: How do you know when something's funny when you write it?

BM: Well, when you're writing them, the first thing you rely on is whether or not anybody else laughed. There can be lots of reasons why somebody laughs, or not. They could be sucking up—depends on who you are. If you're running the room and they laugh, they could be sucking up. If you're the omega dog in the room and everybody laughs, you're pretty sure it's funny; everybody in the room is pretty sure it's funny if they all laughed at the omega in the room. But there are other times, it's just a matter of why you're laughing, and were you laughing because it's a funny room joke. Does it really work for the show? And then you take a chance. You go down for a run-through, and you put that line in, and that's the one advantage that situation comedy has—you hear it right at the table on Monday, and Tuesday you'll see a run-through, and Wednesday, you'll see a run-through, and in each case, you'll have a crack at that joke; you'll be able to try it out in front of yourself as an audience in the context of what it's going to look like in a show; but even by your rewrite on Wednesday, you're still guessing.

PD: How about your instincts?

BM: Well, there are some things that you just feel have got to be funny.

PD: The intervention—you knew that was going to get a laugh,

BM: Well, I think that if I had pitched that in the room, that would have been the reaction to that—at least the moment that she opens that door and sees, in her urgency, that they've chosen that moment to intervene on her. That's got to get a laugh. Whether it continues to get laughs through the scene, who knows?

"Comedy is timing . . . the juxtaposition of moments or events, when they're slammed up against each other."

PD: I remember one of the writers in another interview said, "The telephone is always going to get a laugh. You make the guy busy enough when the phone rings, you've got a cheap laugh if you need it.

BM: Yeah. Comedy is timing. And it's true; it's just the juxtaposition of moments or events, when they're slammed up against each other. How do those moments interact with each other? The moment of her coming in, in haste and urgency, against something that everybody else is urgent about, something that is going to take hours, and they're not going to let her go. Immediately you know that those two things slamming up against each other—that's not going to work.

PD: Do you think those years of stand-up helped sharpen that instinct for you?

BM: I don't think it hurt. We weren't an ad-libbing act, so we didn't actually exist in the moment onstage. Everything we did was very, very set and it was a good act. It was very media-oriented, with commercial parodies with music and stuff like that. It was very set. And I think that we grew out of a sketch school.

PD: A writer we interviewed wrote jokes for Bob Hope. He said that Hope had incredible instincts for detecting what was funny. He said, "If gave him ten jokes, he would point out which six were funny, and which two would work for his character." He had that instinct that was so finely honed because he had stood in front of so many audiences.

BM: Well, all his life, even before he got into show business, he was making people laugh, and he knew what he could pull off. My partner and I are very different in appearance. I'm the short, Jewish guy, and he's a tall, thin, Waspy-looking guy from Tennessee, with a perfect American accent—the newsman accent. And we were doing an act for a while where all the lines were split up, and it was okay, because the act was clever. We were good together and the act was clever. And all my life I've been a mugger—short with the comic face and everything—and I had been a mugger all through my college years. I was in a performing organization, which is where he and I met, and I was the kind of guy who got laughs off my face. One night we're performing, or we were going in to perform, and I had laryngitis and I couldn't talk. So I said to him, "I've got to save my voice." There are parts of the act where I must talk, but there are parts of the act where we just split up the lines. "You know all the lines, so you just talk and I'll just mouth." It was an epiphany night for us. That night the act literally kicked up a level and became what our act legendarily became in later years, which was I just sat there and I was sort of the puppet, or the animated character, and he was the announcer. And we each got laughs off our individual skills. I returned to something that I knew I could make funny. I wasn't getting the laughs when I was reading the joke. The joke would get the laugh, but I wasn't. Bob got laughs because he's an announcer.

And going back to the Bob Hope reference: Roseanne had an idea. We were doing a show about a Lamaze class, and the situation that we set up that we thought was funny is somebody in the Lamaze class asking her about what her birth experiences were like. And we felt that since the audience really knew her feeling about her kids, this would be kind of a novel take. Did she go through Lamaze? Did she go through natural childbirth? Were there drugs? And stuff like that. It was pretty funny, but the moment that she wanted to do was, "When I had my third child, I hadn't lost the weight from my second child, and they said, 'If we give you drugs, enough drugs to sedate you, it could kill the baby.'"

This is her exactly, "It could kill the baby. So I thought to myself . . ." and that's the Jack Benny "Your money or your life" moment. "So I thought to myself," she says, and we're watching a run-through . . . because she invented it on the spot—we watch it in a run-through and I'm like, "Oh my God, oh my God, she's not going to do this. She's not going to say in front of an audience, "I considered killing my baby," so we wrote it out. We wrote around it, which is what we would do; we wrote kind of around it where a sense of those words were kind of in it, but ultimately it was a different joke, and we got a call from the stage saying, "She wants to do this joke; she feels she can make it funny."

And I said, "Who am I to argue with a woman who is one of the biggest stars in comedy right now? If she doesn't know how to make this funny . . ." Biggest laugh in the show. Biggest laugh in the show. When it was over she just looked at me—biggest laugh in the show. The audience just went bananas. They just went crazy . . . because it's Roseanne . . . and our thought was, "She would have a take like that, but I never thought it would be that one."

EXIT SARAH . . . ENTER BERNIE

 An Interview with Hank Nelken

A partial list of Hank Nelken's credits as a screenwriter include *Saving Silverman, Are We Done Yet?,* and *Mama's Boy.*

Hank Nelken is just another Jewish comedy writer from the Lower East Side—of Dallas. He went to school in the Lower East Side of Los Angeles—the USC School of Cinema. When he was just a kid, he saw *E.T.* and knew he wanted to be a filmmaker. By eleventh grade, supported by his theater arts teachers, he and a group of friends began writing and acting in comedy sketches broadcast live to his entire high school. Peter met him when he used his office to shoot a short video, *HOSTAGE: A Love Story* for Will Ferrell's Funny or Die website. His direction shows his comedy skills and when we heard his writing credits . . .

❌ ❌ ❌

HN (HANK NELKEN): Well, first of all, great job guys. I really love it. I think it's great—I love the character. I love the setup of it. The world of it. I've got a few notes, just a few thoughts and some questions. Overall, I feel like it's very situational, so it feels like a TV show. The big idea is that they were very well off, like the Madoffs, and he really didn't have what she thought he did, so now the mom is kind of screwed. It's such a strong situation.

"See it's my natural instinct, I'm trying to please you guys, like you're executives."

HN: I like the idea that it's these two women who live together, mom and daughter. And I like the idea that the mom is the one who is this sex-crazed, fun-loving, man-loving woman and the daughter is sort of the stick-in-the-mud. To me that's a fun dynamic. See, it's my natural instinct, I'm trying to please you guys, like you're executives.

JD (JEFFREY DAVIS): Let's say you didn't have to please us.

HN: I like this process. I feel very empowered by this. Truly, what I would do is I would make it two guys. I don't write women as well as I do guys. I would make it that the dad moves back in with the son. Same exact characters, stick-in-the-mud son, and this really wild, fun, bachelor dad. And I would give the son a new wife. Basically, the parents get divorced or the mom dies, and the dad has lived this conservative life and he's always sort of provided, but when the mom dies he doesn't know what to do. He's lost and he needs a place to crash.

He moves in with the son, who is this buttoned-down guy, and his new wife, and he never leaves. It's got the *Odd Couple* dynamic, but with trying to fit in a new wife and at some point a baby. And Dad will always be there in the way. I've always loved Rodney Dangerfield's *Back to School* and I love that dynamic between the two of them. It's a classic pairing of characters and I just loved that he was the wild and crazy dad and the kid was the stick-in-the-mud. It makes this kid the butt of the jokes and then it's sort of a Ben Stiller type of character, who plays the kid, and then you can have any fun, great, older comedic actor, maybe Nicholson, playing the dad.

There is another way to go, where he's a younger guy and he's not married. He's got a girlfriend. In some ways, maybe for a sitcom, that's better. The son has just finally gotten out of a roommate situation, he's moved into his own place, he's ready to face the world, and he's got a good job. He's getting his stuff together, and here comes Dad needing a place to crash. And so they become roommates. In some ways, maybe that's better because then they can fight over the same girl at some point. Dad can cockblock him. Just when he's decided he's growing up, here comes Dad. I think this is a rich situation. You can launch it from here and really mine that material for years and years. You would watch the son fall in love and the real question is, "When is Dad going to move out?"

JD: In your heart of hearts, movies are what you love most?

HN: Yes, although I just wrote a TV pilot. And I'm going to go pitch another one. I've sold one pilot in my career. Features are where I've been for my whole life. I want to branch out and be directing TV and film. I think for this premise, to make it into a feature, it needs an engine.

An engine is a drive. A thing that happens that is going to spin this character in a direction where he's got a mission he's got to accomplish. It's going to be difficult and full of obstacles. These two characters are going to go on the road together, like in *Rain Man*. It's a classic two-hander. Maybe it's as simple as, "All I've got to do is get from A to B and then I get my money." They need a goal and it would probably relate to the death of the other parent. Maybe it's getting the funeral together. And you're also looking for a high concept. There is something in here that really feels like the Madoff thing, which is so current.

PD (PETER DESBERG): How would you take it in that direction?

HN: I actually have some friends who thought they had all this money their dad left them. They had been spending all the money they made working and then they found out the dad was tied in to Bernie Madoff and all that money was fake. That changed their lives. But for a movie version of that, maybe their mission is actually to get the money back, or take down the Bernie Madoff character. If you can include the Madoff character, it might give them a goal, a drive.

Wait, let me go back to the female version for a minute. What if the husband died and Molly expects to get all this money, but then realizes there is nothing there when she goes to collect it? This could be the inciting incident or the page 10 event that gets the ball rolling. I think it works better from the female perspective because you feel like the men are dealing with the money. She could team up with her daughter to bring down Madoff. I definitely feel that gives it the high concept and gives it the drive of the movie. So now this unlikely pair, who don't have a great relationship, have this need to bring down this guy to get their money back.

And then there also needs to be some kind of ticking clock working. Maybe once they find out the guy is packing up shop and wants to go to the Caymans, they've got a week to infiltrate his company, figure out what's going on, and bring him down. There is something kind of fun there and, in some ways, that is actually more fun for the two women. You get that great *Working Girl* or *Legally Blonde* feeling of female empowerment while bringing down this Madoff-type guy.

PD: Now the two of them have a mutual dependency. How do they get along?

HN: This relationship is the heart of the movie. They are forced to work together. I guess you could keep it a mother and daughter. But in this version, I don't know what Sarah's personal stakes are. Why did she have to get in on this journey? I'm not sure yet. But it definitely feels like the two of them are similar. I love the idea that the mom is still the fun-loving one and the daughter is the stick-in-the-mud. So when Molly says, "Honey, we have to go do this thing. We have to get this money back," Sarah says. "No way!" The second act of the movie becomes all about their relationship. Neither of them wants to work together.

They've written each other off in some way. Maybe Molly says, "Look, we are going to do this. I know you don't like me. I don't like you. But let's do this. Get the money we deserve so we can keep financing our separate lives. And get justice and then go our separate ways." And they end up coming together. To me, that's the one that always ends up working the best when you have this push-pull, like *Midnight Run*, a classic two-hander. One of them is trying to take the other one in, and the other one is trying to convince him that he's morally innocent. So they're at odds the entire time, but they come to develop this great friendship and come to love and trust each other. All great two-hander movies have that "I don't like you, I don't want to be here" element in them. That's the engine that drives them together.

PD: How would you develop these two characters?

HN: It depends where you start. I either start with a character I've got in mind and then a story comes out of that character, or with a concept and then work backwards to fit the characters into the concept. Sometimes it's a back-and-forth process, like a crossword puzzle. You're filling in different parts until you figure it out.

PD: Do you have actual people you know in mind and start using their traits? Or do you start making trait lists?

HN: It's a combination of both. I use real people because that's a great place to start. You get those real traits. One thing I've been thinking about lately is that in reality people are very complicated, but in a movie, to have a great character, you have to strip away some of that complication. You want to depend on them being a certain way all the time. So I always take traits from real people, but then the process is also about heightening them, because great characters tend to be extremes. They are either incredibly cowardly, because you never write a character like, "Eh, he's kind of a coward." "He's a little nervous, he's scared, but he's kind of brave at the same time." You can't do that. It's either the bravest guy in the world or it's the most cowardly guy you've ever met. You have to take those extremes. Another way I come up with ideas is by taking that extreme character and figuring out what's the worst situation that character could be in. A great example is the cowardly lion in *Oz*. That's where you get the fireworks.

PD: So if you have a buttoned-down, stick-in-the-mud character like Sarah, what is she going to be like?

HN: You would want to put that character into a situation where she's got to be a free spirit. She's got use her heart. She has to use her imagination and really be uncomfortable. She's sort of an anal organizer, but somehow she's got to go into a world where she can't use her computer. It's just all kind of gut, and she's really bad at using her gut. If she doesn't have the protractor and the computer and the cell phone, then she's not good. So I'm not quite sure about her yet in this movie. Because she's trying to take down Bernie Madoff, she'd probably be pretty good at that. It would probably be a good thing for her.

JD: What about the mother?

HN: Molly is really fun for this story because she's been this woman who was a wife for her whole adult life. Maybe she was free-spirited in some ways, but she never had the responsibility and she was never taken seriously. She is the great character in the movie. She's had a life of leisure, and the big moment is when the husband dies on page 10. Molly is reeling from that and doesn't know her place in the world. She has no money. And when she finds out it's Madoff, she decides she's going to get her money back. On page 30 she puts on her business suit and goes into his office to infiltrate and bring down this guy.

So this woman, who has never worked a day in her life, is now going to bring down the most powerful guy on Wall Street. That starts to feel kind of good. That wouldn't be Meryl Streep. You wouldn't do that these days; she's too old to be the lead. You'd bring the age down. Make it Reese Witherspoon or Jennifer Aniston and roll Molly and Sarah into one character. Now you've got the same movie, but the lead is thirty-five. So let's say it's Reese Witherspoon. She's been a mom, she's been this total little housewife, and she's got this husband. He takes care of everything and he's got lots of money. It's great. Then he dies. She doesn't know what to do with herself. Then suddenly she finds out all the money he had was with this guy who scammed him. There's no money. The lawyers and everybody say, "Honey, there is nothing you can do. It's over." And she says, "No way. It's not over. I'm taking this guy down." She takes the kids to their grandma, and she puts on a business suit. Actually, this is a great idea because it's zeitgeisty.

Right now everyone is reeling from this feeling of being scammed. And then you have this great female character at the heart of the movie who thought she knew her place in the world. But she's never really had anyone's respect. Now she has a week to get her money back. Say, on page 30, she is working at the Madoff character's firm. She's in a low-level position. She has used her smarts to fake everybody out and get enough of a résumé together to fake an entry-level job. She thinks she's got plenty of time and that she's going to work her way up. But on page 45 she hears that Madoff is shutting down the whole shop in one week, or one month, and it's all over. He's going to the Cayman Islands and there will be no way to retrieve the money. Then suddenly she has to do what any normal person would take twenty years to do. But she's got to do it in one month. She's got to rise up through the ranks and win his confidence. And the only way to win his confidence is to be really savvy. Somehow she's actually going to help him close up shop and get him safely to the Caymans, but in fact she's double-crossing him.

JD: Would you have Molly's husband die in a funny way, as in *Private Benjamin?*

HN: It's a comedy. In this pitch we are going with now, maybe it's a divorce that sends her off into the movie. The husband dumps her. But then again, he can't just leave her because then he'll still be in the movie. So I guess it could be a comedic death. Death by blowfish. He's been on this exotic trip and she's told him not to go. He's an adrenaline junkie and something goes wrong in a bungee-jumping activity. Molly says, "Of course he died. He shouldn't have been jumping out of helicopters to ski." So, after some comedic death like that, she's left out in the cold. It really is like Private Benjamin. That is a great model.

This movie is not a two-hander. It's a vehicle for one of those great women. And then you populate it with fun ensemble actors. The other great role is the Bernie Madoff role. Then you pair up Reese Witherspoon with a great older actor. Nicholson or DeNiro. Or go younger and make the Madoff character Hugh Jackman. If you play it a little younger, you could potentially develop a love story between them that could be really interesting. She could be falling for him, despite herself. Or he's falling for her. But he's still the guy she's trying to bring down.

PD: Those guys are very charismatic, or they couldn't do what they do.

HN: Oh, of course. It's a great part.

PD: And that's an interesting conflict. On the one hand, she knows how this guy swindled everybody, but he is kind of cute, in his own way.

HN: Right. You talk about starting from complete opposites. Not only does she despise him, and not only did he personally screw her out of all this money, but she is on a mission to bring him down. But she can't help that she's falling for this guy. And he sees something in her, but he thinks she's very green and he's exploiting her.

PD: Do you also use this as misdirection? The audience thinks, "Uh-oh, now she's falling in love with him. Is she going to cave in?"

HN: Yes, I think you tease it all the way. I guess what you're getting to in the end of the second act is that she's become conflicted, and in the key moment in which she could squeeze him, she lets him off. Somehow, that's the kiss. That's the moment where she's fallen for him. And in the next moment, he has completely screwed her. He was playing her. The business is shut down. He's off to the Cayman Islands. She's completely humiliated and horrified. Now in the third act, she has to become determined to bring him down. She has the goods on him. She kept the incriminating data.

PD: Everybody's expectations of her are so low that there's a lot of room to surprise them.

HN: Right. That's the thing. Her husband's lawyer buddy, who is taking care of the estate, keeps telling her, "Look, there is nothing you can do." She's a housewife who is now thrust into this alien world, and she has this specific mission she has to accomplish. I actually really like it.

JD: You mentioned there would be some subordinate characters that would be fun?

HN: I think those characters are in the world she goes into in New York. Maybe Molly and her husband are from St. Louis or Milwaukee. People invested with Bernie Madoff from all over. It wasn't like they had to live in New York. So Molly's husband could have been investing with him for years and years. She's this very suburban housewife and she packs up and moves to New York City. She's a fish out of water in Manhattan. A fish out of water in this Madoff-like guy's firm. She doesn't know what she's doing, and the people she befriends—the fun characters—are all in their twenties. That's who she ends up connecting with because everybody else is so beyond her skill set. The female intern and the mailroom guy. She could potentially end up living with them.

"The lesson I took from USC was when you go shoot on location, always leave it cleaner than when you found it."

PD: All the USC film graduates we've interviewed have had a strong sense of story construction. Did you get your sense of story from there?

HN: No! The lesson I took from USC was when you go shoot on location, always leave it cleaner than when you found it. The other thing I learned from USC was networking. I had this meeting with a legendary producer. I was going to bring my résumé and he was going to take me by the hand and lead me. He was supposed to be my mentor. I sat down across from him. In my memory it's a giant office with a long table where you do the "pass the salt" joke. I've clutching my résumé. He said, "One word, kid—networking." And the next thing I remember, the doors shut and I walked out and I didn't know what the hell I was going to do. Life was beginning.

So I have to say, I learned story construction and everything after film school. My experience there was very lean on writing and much heavier on production. It was about directing. For every writing class, there were five directing classes. There was editing and cinematography. Actually, when I came out of school, I felt like I really didn't understand writing at all. I still had not written a feature screenplay and that is one of the things I feel like they should do. You should have a feature script. I guess you do if you're in the writing program. I was in production. But I think even production students should have a feature script coming out of there. You need to have written a feature and know what that feels like. I had only written shorts, so I didn't have the experience. A short film is just not enough.

My sense of story construction came from doing it over and over and over again. I hooked up with a writing partner who had come to LA from New York. He'd gone to graduate school in playwriting, and he really had the story construction side of it down. I had all the other stuff—all the gold, all the comedy. No, I'm kidding. He was really funny and I learned a lot from him. After we split up, about eight years ago, that was when I had to do it on my own. That was when I really internalized this feeling for structure, which has become an internal part of me.

"When people aren't laughing, it's like, 'Oh, I've written drama. How nice.'"

PD: Have you done dramatic writing as well as comedy?

HN: Sometimes my comedy feels dramatic. When people aren't laughing, it's like, "Oh, I've written drama. How nice." The closest I've come is writing a dramedy. Like a Cameron Crowe movie.

PD: Did you grow up a funny kid? Were you a class clown kind of guy?

HN: When I look back at videos and things, I was very serious. I remember I always loved directing. I loved film and I especially loved Steven Spielberg. When I went to USC film school, I thought my Spielberg story was really unique. I saw *E.T.* when I was nine or ten and it just changed everything. Even in that moment I knew I'd make movies. I got to USC and found out everybody had the same story. Earlier I was into filmmaking and made a very serious movie about drinking and driving and it won a big national award. I was very serious about the film and its message and that next year I just somehow dropped all that and got into comedy.

PD: When did you realize you could do it?

HN: Junior and senior year of high school I got into a great group. I went to this amazing high school in Dallas under the auspices of two theater teachers, Lynn Zednick and Craig Wurgo. It was under their tutelage that this great group of kids, who were creative, acted and did videos. We did school announcements in the morning, and instead of blaring over the loudspeaker they would have a TV in every classroom and broadcast the announcements. They were just straight news broadcasts. But then we decided, "Let's make them funny." On Fridays we would do the announcements and it was basically our *Saturday Night Live*. Once a week, we did an *SNL* kind of a show for the entire school. It was such a great experience. It would be ten or twelve minutes of material that we would create and everyone would see it. That was where I really started having fun with comedy.

PD: Just before we started the interview, you said that what we are doing with these interviews is what development executives hear all the time when writers are pitching to them.

HN: Yes. I wish I could be one of those development executives, just to hear what they hear. I've gone out for so many projects and basically you hear just a one-liner idea they want you to develop. There was one book I really loved, called *The Retired Kid*. It was about a little boy who decides to retire and moves into a retirement home. It's a great idea. But how do you know where that goes? You could do that in a number of different ways. I know they heard a lot of different takes and I wanted to hear what people came up with. So you're giving people a really cool way to experience that. I'm dying to read what other writers came up with here, using the same premise.

A NOBLY SEDUCTIVE STORY

  **An Interview with Tracy Newman
and Jonathan Stark**

Tracy Newman and Jonathan Stark's credits as creators,
show runners, and writers include *According to Jim, Ellen,
The Drew Carey Show, The Nanny,* and *Cheers.*

Tracy and Jon try to make each other laugh as they work.
They depend on it. If it works for them, they say, 50 percent
of the audience is guaranteed to go along. They met doing
improv. We're not talking about some obscure club in Duluth. It was
at the Groundlings, LA's premiere improv theater group. The key to
improv is the ability to take any idea that is fed to you and go with it,
rather than stopping the flow and questioning it. No hesitation, just
pure acceptance and then take it further. This background shows up
in how they work together to this day. When either of them throws
out an idea, the other grabs it and runs. Ironically, while improv
is all about fluidity and dealing with surprise, Tracy embraces
structure. Her songwriting background gives her a strong sense of
story structure. She wants to figure out where a story is going before
writing a word of script. Then Jon steps in and develops character
and dialogue. This combination has a lot to do with the success of
this Peabody and Emmy Award–winning team's amazing success.

�֎ ✖ ✖

TN (TRACY NEWMAN): Well, right away I want to go dark with this premise. So I'm thinking, what if Molly is the kind of mother who comes on to her daughter's boyfriends?

JS (JONATHAN STARK): I think that's a great idea.

TN: I'm playing with the idea that Sarah understands that's what her mother is trying to do. It's usually done where it comes as a surprise to the daughter.

JS: Well, you can turn that whole thing into a competition.

TN: Yeah, and she could be an attractive, young fifty.

JS: You can do an episode where she does that, and the boyfriend likes her. Is she too old for that?

TN: Fifty? Come on! Fifty's nothing. I mean to us, it's nothing. I know of a real situation where it went this far. Listen to this. The mother wrote a letter to the guy her daughter was going with, offering to take him to Europe. It was devastating for the daughter, but the thing that was great was, the young woman, the daughter, was so resilient and strong. And she knew her mother was like this. It wasn't so much that she forgave her mother, but they had a playful relationship, even as this was happening. Now I wonder how that can happen. I wonder if we can use that?

JS: What if we go to the fact that they become roommates— roommates in the sense that they are both in the same boat. Molly is nuts about guys. Sarah isn't nuts about guys. It drives her crazy that her mother has now become her roommate and girlfriend. Molly gets her all her dates and her mother is living a wild lifestyle.

Maybe even make Sarah a little more conservative than she is in the premise. Develop that a little.

TN: Sarah's attitude is probably, "Well, I know in my early twenties I was with a lot of guys." At Sarah's age, my career was the main thing that troubled me. Not so much guys. So what if Sarah's in a situation where she thinks, "Oh my God, I have to make it." I'd make another change. What do you think of this? Molly isn't broke. Molly has some money, and she's ready to live the carefree life. Maybe her husband was quite a bit older.

JS: Forget all that stuff about losing the money that's in the premise they gave us. Let's go back and say that Molly never actually did live the life she wanted to live.

TN: . . . she got married young and had kids . . .

JS: . . . and that stopped her.

TN: Sarah doesn't want to do that. She wants to have a career and is concentrating on that. They've done this sort of thing before but I'm not sure they've done the whole story. The whole story is that the mother wants to be the girlfriend.

JS: We should go even a little darker. You set it up where Molly never really loved Sarah's father. She always wanted to cheat on him. She tells her daughter this. And this is news to Sarah. She is floored.

TN: Did Molly cheat on him?

JS: I don't think she did.

TN: She tried to cheat.

JS: If she's actually not done that, then that's what she now wants to do. She wants to do all the stuff she didn't do when she was married to this older guy. And maybe Molly never really gave Sarah the time she needed, and now Sarah wants mothering. But she's getting exactly the opposite. The daughter has to be the mother and this is really pissing her off. "I wanted you to mother me. Now that dad has died, I want you to be my mother. You have time now."

TN: Sarah says, "You can cook. You can scrub."

JS: "I don't want to do that," Molly says. Now you have your conflict. I can even see the end of the first episode. They go through this argument and they finally come to some kind of understanding about their relationship and this new arrangement. Sarah says, "Fine. We'll just take it slow." Cut to the next morning. Sarah wakes up, and there's a guy coming out of her mother's bedroom. "Okay, I meant a little slower than that."

TN: I think that's good. Wait, though. Back up a minute. Is there any way we can do it that Molly really did cheat on Sarah's father? Is this too hateful? Because I think it's funny. Molly says, "Honey, your father wouldn't leave me. I even cheated on him with his best friend, and he found out about it, and he still wouldn't leave me."

JS: "I was cheating on him with his best friend the night he died. You have no idea how bad I feel."

TN: I think there are more people cheating now. Television has treated it like it's just a hateful thing. You just don't do that. Maybe Sarah is going out with somebody. She wants to break up with him and Molly says, "Here's what you do. You sleep with his best friend. He'll never get over it."

JS: That's a great first episode. Sarah says, "I've been going out with this guy, Tom, for two years and I really can't stand him." Maybe the mother takes it upon herself to break up the relationship by seducing him. You can take it further if you're doing it on cable. For network, she's too hateful.

TN: But really it's not hateful if what Molly is doing is showing her daughter that he's not a good guy for her. "You see, he slept with me!"

JS: "See honey, I helped you." "You banged my boyfriend!" I think what you want to do is have them be opposites. The daughter is the mother; the mother is the daughter. That's what the basic premise is. If I were going in to pitch it, I'd say they've switched roles.

TN: Once you're the person who takes care of other people, that's what you do. Nobody is ever going to take care of you. As long as you are a caregiver, the people around you will let you take care of them. That's who Sarah is. And we can add this element: When Sarah was really little and Molly was a young mother, the daughter took care of her. Molly would say things like, "Look how much she likes to clean. She loves to clean the bathroom. Look at her! Just give her a rag." That would be a good quality for the daughter because she's always been a caregiver and the mother has never been a caregiver.

JS: And Sarah is expecting that when her mother moves in, things will be different. "Now I'm going to have the relationship I never had."

TN: "Now I'll be able to go look for jobs, and come home and have a hot meal waiting for me," Sarah says. "And you'll read to me." "I'm not going to read to you," Molly says. "Tickle my feet before bed?" And then you cut to Sarah tickling her mother's feet.

JS: That is a great conflict right there.

TN: I don't think I've seen that. Where the caregiver continues to be the caregiver. Sarah took care of her mom when she was little, and now she's doing it again as an adult.

JS: Molly wants to live now. This is it. This is the way it is. But Sarah is pissed off about it.

TN: I think in isolated incidents the daughter is all for it. "You should be out there doing what you want." But as each little thing happens, Sarah disapproves more and more of her mother. She becomes the mother. A mother tries to subtly guide, and the daughter becomes that.

PD (PETER DESBERG): At the beginning, you said Molly seduces Sarah's boyfriend. That's a funny conflict, but what does that do to their relationship?

TN: Well, I think it wouldn't quite work.

JS: What we came up with later works better. Sarah wasn't happy to be with the boyfriend. It wasn't working out.

TN: Yeah, the noble seduction is how it works. If Sarah is saying, "Maybe I do want to date this guy now," that worries Molly, so she seduces him.

JS: Maybe seducing is the wrong way to go. Maybe Molly brings him to the point where she knows she could seduce him, and tells her daughter to get out of the relationship. She proves to Sarah that this guy isn't faithful to her. So she doesn't actually sleep with him.

TN: But I think that's your job, as a writer. You have to come up with something where it seems like, "My God, how can these people do this to each other?" And then, when you hear their reasons, you bring a lot of the audience with you. There are still going to be a certain number of people who say, "No, that's wrong. Just wrong." But there's going to be enough people being affected by it and think, "Yeah, I might do that myself."

JS: When we work, we'll come up with an idea and we'll say, "Well, this is crazy," but then you just try and go down different roads. You're trying to find a reality in it. You're not just doing something ridiculous. You'll go down a road sometimes, and you'll go down it for two days, and then you say, "Nope, got to go down another road. This one is taking us nowhere." So you just keep going down all these roads, and still there's no guarantee you're going to come out with anything.

TN: The interesting thing about the core of this mother/daughter premise, as it's developing, is the idea of a caregiver. Once a caregiver, always a caregiver. That's the premise of it.

If Sarah is a caregiver, her mother is a narcissist. When you're the caregiver, you infantilize the other person. Enable her. It also makes it easier to come up with stories. We know Sarah is always going to end up the caregiver and Molly is always going to behave like a narcissist. And yet, they are both lovable.

JS: I can see episodes. Molly wants to go skydiving. And Sarah says, "No, we could die!" "We're not going to die. We'll be fine." So Molly takes life by the horns and Sarah is right behind her, going, "I don't know about this. I don't know about this." And then maybe actually we do an episode where the daughter decides to do something a little bit risky. You see the "Molly" in her come out. You can do episodes where they're not always the same. Sometimes you see sitcoms where the characters are always like this, and you say, "But nobody is always the same."

TN: We knew someone on *The Drew Carey Show* who told us about her skydiving experience. Her chute didn't open. And you know, you're supposed to wait ten seconds and then pull another cord for the second chute. So during those ten seconds, of course, your whole life apparently really does flash before you. She was positive she was going to die, but she said to herself, "I'm going to do exactly what I was taught to do, but I'm sure I'm dying." I was talking to her about it, and she said, "That has totally changed my life." Her whole direction changed. She left the show shortly after that. She ended up getting married to an artist. She has a lot of kids. She has pets. Her life just drastically changed from that one incident. That's an interesting thing to have happen to somebody, and especially in the case of this premise of Molly and Sarah. Somebody goes through that—Sarah maybe—and she thinks her life is going to change. That's an interesting episode for Sarah. Because skydiving is just something she'd never have thought of doing on her own.

JS: What about Sarah's work?

TN: Are you thinking of a bank job? Or do you want her to be potentially creative, like a painter? Somebody who actually has the ability and is afraid to go for it.

JS: It could be anything. It could be a bank, an ad agency. The point is that she wants to move ahead. She'll do anything to move ahead. She's the one who does all the work at the agency.

TN: She's a caregiver. So whatever she does, she is so overworked because everyone knows she is the go-to girl.

JS: Right. So in the first episodes her attitude is, "I take care of everybody at work. How can I do this with you, Mom? I will not do it!" "Can you get me a soda?" "Sure." But the idea is that her whole life is taking care of people. That even makes it stronger.

TN: Oh, my God. What if Sarah became the director of a nursery school? She's been teaching at this nursery school and she's in line to become the director.

JS: And she tells her mother, "If they find out about how you go out with all these guys, I'll never get the job." There's that thing hanging over her. Her attitude is, "The lid has to be kept on this."

TN: Molly comes to the school and says, "And you think I'm going to ruin your chances of running this? You actually want to run this? What a horrible job."

JS: "And Mom, next time don't wear hot pants."

TN: We've got a lot of rules for this fifty-year-old woman. She's got to have great legs.

JS: Oh, yeah, I think she's got to look great. She's got to look really good. I'd even make her fifty-five. I'd go just a hair older.

TN: The mom could be forty. We could even do that if we wanted. Forty-five and twenty-five. That could be interesting. Because as a forty-five-year-old woman, having been there myself, you think your life's over. And then when you realize it isn't, you just want to dress up, look great, and go out.

JS: I just thought of a funny episode. The one we always wanted to write. Molly uses hormone cream.

TN: Oh my God! You know that testosterone cream for women? I'm not going to go into detail about what you do with the cream, but you become like the Terminator. You start scanning the horizon, and you realize, "I'm actually looking for a man for sex." I just think it's funny that . . .

JS: . . . Sarah literally has to lock Molly in a room until the stuff wears off. "I'm taking it away from you. That's it."

TN: Physically, it's like the woman's opportunity so see what it's like to be a man.

JS: Sarah can't go to work. She's babysitting.

TN: They're in line at the bank and the mother is perking up her chest.

JS: The thing that's so great about working with Tracy is that we just laugh all the time. We certainly had our fights. We had an assistant. Tracy's room was on one side, my room was on the other side, and the assistant's room was in the middle. And we'd have these screaming fights and she'd just sit there quietly. One time, I went out to her and said, "Just because Mommy and Daddy fight, doesn't mean we don't love you."

TN: People always asked, "Well, how do you and Jon work?" When we were in development, we would meet at eight o'clock in the morning at Disney. Nobody was there, and we would work until noon. We would work four straight hours. It was really laughter for four hours. But then we would go to lunch, and then we'd see other guys in development out there on Mickey or Goofy Avenue. They were sitting on the benches smoking cigars. They'd get there when we were leaving. But we wrote a lot of pilots.

JS: At Disney they'd always try and screw us with money. We were eating quite well, and all of a sudden one day we got the menus and all this stuff was blacked out. You couldn't have this and you couldn't have that. I went nuts. I threw a hissy fit and I said, "You get them on the phone and you tell them I'm not doing a show until they stop this petty, ridiculous nickel and diming."

TN: And they did. They stopped.

JS: So, let's continue with this. I would just like to figure out who the other characters are. We certainly want to write something for Tim Bagley [noted character actor, *Monk* and *Will & Grace*].

TN: Yes, Tim could be officious, but I'm thinking back to the caregiver and the person who gets taken care of. If Sarah's boss, let's say the principal of her school, is someone who needs to be taken care of, that's sort of funny, too.

JS: These are the satellites that go around Sarah and Molly. So I wouldn't put as much into them at this point. But how does a supporting character affect Sarah's life? That's what you want to know. Other than having to take care of him, how does he make her life more complicated? He could be another teacher who has a crush on her.

TN: He could also be an assistant who she has to give orders to. And she has trouble giving orders.

JS: But how do you get into the place where that character is in the show? How is he there every week? Because of work? Or do you go back and forth from work to the house?

TN: Maybe he's her assistant and he lives next door.

JS: Or he's Sarah's brother, who lives with her, and he is just so messed up that maybe he lives across the hall and he's over all the time. Is he the brother who is not a caregiver and isn't particularly well taken care of? He's just kind of floating out there. Now he's trying to bond with the family that he got left out of.

TN: Or maybe he's just someone who sees exactly what's going on between Sarah and Molly.

JS: Maybe he's the moral compass. Maybe he's the voice of the audience.

TN: Maybe he just turns to the audience and says, "What would you do?"

JS: That old fourth wall break. It always works, doesn't it? That's an interesting idea to have somebody like that because neither Molly nor Sarah are the eyes of the audience. If he's the brother, at the end of an episode he makes a speech to Molly. "And you, you never took care of either of us." Then he turns to Sarah. "And look at you, you're taking care of everyone." They both look at him and say, "Shut up!"

TN: He's the one who keeps saying the truth, and then they go right back to their lies.

JS: And he's the one who always gets sucked into the mother's schemes.

TN: He's got to do something for each of them all the time.

JS: Well maybe the daughter has a suspicion that the guy she is going out with might be gay. So they ask the brother to try to seduce him first, and that doesn't work.

TN: Or it does!

JS: Or maybe the mother tries to seduce the boyfriend and he doesn't go for it. And Molly says, "Wow, he really is a good man. He didn't even go for me. There's no man who doesn't go for me."

TN: And then Tim says, "Let me try."

JS: You talk about the main characters for a day or two and then something always pops up, and you go, "That's what we can do with an older man, or a younger man." Four characters are plenty.

PD: Did you two meet in the Groundlings?

TN: Yes, in the Groundlings.

PD: And were each of you actors first?

TN: Jon was definitely an actor. He's a really funny performer. He still performs. He still does shows every Saturday night. I was always singing and playing guitar. I was in the Groundlings for fifteen years, but before that I was singing and playing guitar and writing songs. I'm just back to that now.

PD: Do you come from show business families?

TN: In a sense. My real father—my mom divorced when I was five—was an actor. My mother was a singing, dancing kind of person in her late teens in New York. But when they moved out here, it was hard times. He started drinking. So I never really saw show business back then.

JS: So you were more from a drinking family then?

TN: That's the part that I remember.

JS: I knew her whole family. I liked your stepdad. One time her stepdad said, "Hey, we're going to get barbecue. Bring Jon."

TN: Remember, it's a Jewish family and he couldn't be more gentile.

JS: So we go to this place downtown, and I get the barbecued turkey sandwich.

TN: He gets a barbecued turkey sandwich on white bread. And there's ribs and these other things, and not only did he get one of them, he got two of them. And my stepdad couldn't get over it. He kept saying, "You're ordering a turkey sandwich here?" He thought it was so funny.

JD: What about your family, Jon?

JS: I'm from Erie, Pennsylvania. My parents were in local theater. They used to do shows and sometimes I'd go, too. They did *The Rose Tattoo*. There was a scene onstage where the little kids have to start the show off, where they're running offstage. I did little things like that.

PD: You were both early starters? You knew you had the calling?

TN: Yeah, I was doing comedy but I really was more of a folk singer. When I say I was doing comedy, I mean patter and stuff like that, between songs. It got funnier and funnier, just because it does.

JS: She has an excellent sense of story, and sometimes I don't quite have that sense. So it's always good to have that.

TN: But you developed it, made it better and better. It's amazing. I think improv training, that thing of not denying, of going with anything you're given, is probably the main thing in television right now.

JS: Keeping the story going.

TN: Just saying, "Okay, well if we do that, then what about if we do this, too?" Rather than saying, "No, I don't want to do that."

JS: We would also write twenty-page outlines when we did a script because we didn't want anything to be left to chance. Because when you're writing a fifty-page script you don't want to have to throw it away. We were very specific.

TN: Sometimes our biggest fights were over the fact that I can't even move forward if I don't know how it begins. If they walk in the room, what are they doing? And sometimes he would say, "Let's get past that and go to the second scene." I really need to know where each scene starts, but especially the whole thing because things fall into place. It's really true with a song. If you understand what you want to say, how you begin it is a major thing. We spent a lot of time on that.

JS: We spent a lot of time on the "Coming Out" episode of *Ellen* because we wrote the first half of it. So we had to come up with the characters and what they did.

TN: It was a one-hour special event. The first half-hour ends with her saying she's gay. So we had the responsibility of doing that part.

JS: So we had to set up everything. And we were lucky because we were only working two days a week on the show, so we didn't have to be there all the time. But you have to really figure out how these characters are going to be honest and real to ground this huge thing Ellen is going to do. And so we had to come up with pretty much what they did. That took us a long time to do, to get it right.

TN: We had the whole season practically. I mean, we worked on every show that season, but I remember you were reluctant because you thought that it would be under a microscope.

JS: I thought they'd kill us. Everyone talked about what a great show *Ellen* was, but when it was on, people just nailed it all the time.

TN: But I said to him, "Jon, we have the whole season to write the first half-hour. You think we can't get it so that we think it's great? Yeah, it will probably be smashed by some critics and they'll think it's terrible, but there will be people who will feel the way we do."

JS: Rewriting is really the most important part of the writing process.

TN: And the thing is, you really don't want to turn anything in that you don't think is the way to go. And so the only way to know that is to keep rehashing and keep really, really, really getting the details right. That's why our outlines made it pretty easy to go to script.

PD: Having been grounded in improv, you get feedback all the time. Your instincts must be incredibly honed.

TN: I figure that if I'm laughing at him maybe at least 50 percent of the people are going to be laughing at him. And every time he would do something, if he read it or said it, it would make me laugh. This is standing the test of time really. And if I said something funny and he laughed, we knew that was funny because that was really rare.

JS: I think you have to develop this attitude—it's a survival attitude—where you go, "This is what I find funny and interesting." And if somebody says, "Well, I didn't," then you go, "Well, then, you're wrong!" If you don't trust your gut, you're going to be all over the place. And these people behind the desks, they don't know. They don't know what's funny.

TN: I don't think it's that they don't know what's funny. I think they laugh when things are funny like anybody else does. The thing is, their job, in their mind, really is something else.

JS: Their job is analyzing. Our job is just putting it out there. You have to ask, "Is this funny for me? Because as soon as you start trying to please everyone, you're just going to be rewriting all the time, and then it just isn't going to be funny anymore. It's especially easy to write just what you like after you've had a successful series on TV for eight years. It's a little easier to say, "Well, I don't want to write that. I want to write this." The characters and a story are always what are going to sell a show, and are going to keep it working.

LOSING THE BUBBLE

 An Interview with Cinco Paul and Ken Daurio

A partial list of Cinco Paul and Ken Daurio's credits
as screenwriters include *Bubble Boy, The Santa Clause 2,
College Road Trip, Dinner for Schmucks,*
and *Horton Hears a Who!*

One of them works on visual humor, the other on verbal. Throw in a bathtub and you have the writing team of Cinco Paul and Ken Daurio. They feed off each other's ideas and often become animated as they develop characters, conflicts, and stories. Their process goes from brainstorming together, to writing apart, coming back together to try to make each other laugh, to improvising dialogue, to getting stuck until Cinco takes a bath to figure out the solution to a problem. Thankfully, they didn't demonstrate this part of their process during our interview.

❖ ❖ ❖

CP (CINCO PAUL): I would make it father-son, that's what I would do.

KD (KEN DAURIO): Right . . . Who knows what women are thinking?

CP: So almost everything we've done—we just do "guy" stuff. It's easier to be funny with guys, I think, so that would be my first suggestion.

KD: We're both sons.

CP: And we both have complicated relationships with our fathers. I think of the dad whose wife took care of him his whole life. He never had to do anything and now she's gone.

I think he hated this woman he was married to, and now it's his chance to be free and freewheeling, right? He wants to be a single guy again.

KD: Yeah, that whole dating thing with the son, I see that. To me, that's easier to see with the two guys.

CP: Especially if you're thinking of a movie. What's the hook? It seems like it would need some sort of bigger hook than this.

KD: Right, this is like the setting. And that's what sitcom is.

CP: For a movie, you're going to want something that pushes it—like the second bump—and it would be trying to find that. Obviously, the son is Ben Stiller. And then the dad is . . .

KD: Jerry Stiller.

CP: Yes, yes. And the opening scene is Anne Meara's dead and they're burying her, and then it's like the thorn-in-the-side movie. We love that sort of movie, which is *Planes, Trains, and Automobiles*, and it's *The In-Laws*. And Stiller was made to live in those movies. The dad is a thorn in the side. He cannot get rid of his dad. His dad has now moved in with him and wants to be part of his life.

JD (JEFFREY DAVIS): Is that the second bump [plot point] you were talking about?

CP: I don't know if that's the second bump yet. The second bump might be trying to fix up his dad with somebody. What is the hero's goal? And which obstacles are going to come into the story?

It's similar to *Dinner for Schmucks*, a project we worked on which is a French movie, and we did the American version. A guy who's very much like Stiller has a boss who has a group of friends who get together and each one tries to invite the schmuckiest guy to dinner. It's sort of a competition. By the end of the night, who has invited the biggest schmuck to dinner? And so, the boss' schmuck drops out, so he gets Stiller, his VP guy, and says, "You've got to find me a new schmuck by tomorrow night." And so Stiller finds this schmuck, but then ends up not being able to get rid of this schmuck for twenty-four hours. So the schmuck is with him for twenty-four hours, and ends up totally destroying his life in the process. And then it leads to a nice moment where he also sort of becomes friends with the schmuck, and so at the end he's got to choose: Do I . . . ?

Whatever Ben ends up doing, in this premise he's like a VP somewhere. But it's got to be like the biggest week of his life, and unfortunately, his dad is there with him. It could be a business trip. Maybe his dad wants to come with him.

KD: Wanting to help out.

CP: Right. What if Stiller is in advertising, and his dad was like an old jingle guy, back in the days when they still wrote jingles. Ben's got this big presentation he's going to make. But his dad is like, "I'm going to help."

KD: But, where's the jingle?

CP: Right, there's no jingle.

KD: You can't sell pharmaceuticals without a catchy song. Write one of the old songs. Like "Plop, plop, fizz, fizz." How easy is that?

CP: It'd be great if his dad has written at least three or four classic jingles that we all know.

KD: Like, "I'm a Pepper, you're a Pepper . . ."

CP: Right, he wrote, "I'm a Pepper . . ." or "Look for the union label . . ." And so if you put his dad in a room with people and a piano, he's like the life of the party. I think that's what the key is to these movies. Everybody else loves his dad.

KD: And the dad doesn't understand why Ben hates him.

CP: Right. "Your dad is the greatest guy. He wrote 'Plop, plop, fizz, fizz.' How could you not love this guy?"

KD: Ben says, "Yeah, I know. He wrote 'Plop, plop, fizz, fizz.' I get it!"

It's the big business dinner and Dad's there to sit in with everybody, and Ben says, "Dad, just go wait in the bar."

CP: A key scene would be this: We're at the bar, and there's a piano, and his dad sits down and starts to play. "Here's another one I wrote," he says, and everyone's gathered around the piano, and they're like, "Plop, plop, fizz, fizz." They're all at the piano [clicking fingers and singing], "You! You're the one!"

KD: His dad's going to help him work on the presentation— whatever he's there for—and Ben is going to reject it. So it's going to be the breakup scene.

CP: What this creates is a conversation between the new methods of advertising and the old school. And what's great is advertising right now—they don't know what they're doing, right? They're freaked out because everybody is TIVO-ing past their commercials.

There's the Internet. Maybe what Ben needs to learn is the sort of spirit his dad has. I guess his dad would say, "It was all about people and connections." It wasn't about paying people to tattoo the corporation's logo on their faces.

KD: It is going to be about the jingle. And Jerry Stiller is going to have to save the day.

CP: They check into the hotel room and his dad has ordered the keyboard and the whole setup and says, "All right, let's get to work." And whatever client it is, a jingle is completely inappropriate.

KD: It's Vagisil . . .

PD (PETER DESBERG): Singing the side effects . . .

KD: [Singing] "May cause nausea . . ."

CP: "Dad, please!"

KD: We've got to tweak it . . .

CP: It would work in the classic way, where it's just like every time he thinks he's gotten his dad out of the picture, his dad keeps popping back up. Wherever he is, he thinks, "Oh, I'm rid of Dad," and Dad just keeps on showing up. You want to set up as many things for his dad to ruin as possible. I think the son has got to have some sort of office romance and she's with him there, and Dad's going to screw that up as well. It could be something along the lines of . . . years ago, in his dad's opinion, Ben should have asked this girl to marry him. Right? Because his dad is more traditional, so his dad is sort of pushing him in this direction. Maybe trying to orchestrate a proposal against his son's will.

KD: "Here's how we proposed in my day!"

CP: "It's been three years now with this girl and you haven't asked her to marry you?" And Ben says, "We've discussed it. We don't want to get married. We don't need that. That was your world. That's not ours." But his dad would be pushing him, and ultimately, it's going to be good. Stiller needs to ask her and probably she's secretly wishing he would. But at the end of Act II, it's got to be that his dad has completely destroyed everything, right? The girl has left him. He's lost the account. He's fired.

KD: I'm thinking about the end—the scene where dad overhears his son ridiculing him in front of everybody. "That old coot. He doesn't know what he's talking about." It's that moment when Dad's heart just breaks, and he walks away.

CP: It's not the funniest moment, but it's the one that kills you. You see his dad overhear. Yeah, I like that.

KD: And then, in the end, I think it's Ben's choice to use his dad's method, even though his dad isn't even in the room.

CP: Right, so that he's not doing it at all to make his dad happy.

KD: Yeah, I think he does it because he's still guilty about what he'd said about this great old guy, and maybe they do sort of think he's a joke now. And I think it's just Ben realizing, "You know what, my dad is right and this is all wrong." You know, there's the big presentation and he's got to do what we don't expect him to do, which is to use his dad's approach.

And in the end, Ben does the jingle and he's fired. And they hate it. He's fired. But the relationship with his father is much better and he's marrying the girl. And everything is fine. Maybe.

"You want some sort of rival there. Someone his dad can help him take down at the end. Because otherwise, there's no bad guy in this."

CP: I'm trying to think of what else is going on. We would want a rival for Ben at the agency, who's there trying to sabotage him.

KD: Or, he's the guy who's nine steps ahead of everybody, like in Japan, how they have those bus stop ads . . . there's all these advertising techniques, where it's like on the buses, as you pass certain points, there's computer sensors that trigger screens to come on in the bus for the stores that are outside. He's way ahead of the game.

CP: You want some sort of rival there. Someone his dad can help him take down at the end. Because otherwise, there's no bad guy in this.

He thinks his dad's the bad guy, but then his dad can help uncover this smarmy guy.

KD: Or it's the other agency that's up for . . .

CP: . . . Yeah, it would be . . . the other agency—not someone within his agency. There's another agency. It's highly competitive. "Can we get this huge account?" And that guy is really trying to screw over Ben Stiller and make him look bad and nail him. His dad maybe comes to the rescue. Somehow. I don't have the exact details of how he does it.

Maybe there's a moment where his dad does need to realize . . .

KD: "I need to let it go."

CP: He needs to let it go. But it is that classic John Candy moment when he tells Steve Martin, "I like me. My wife likes me. I talk too much. Well, I also listen, too."

KD: Well, going where you were saying, maybe if Ben does the jingle at the end, and it flops, it's like Dad can swoop in and fix Ben's technique. That's more of your feel-good, happy ending.

CP: That's what everybody wants.

KD: Okay, but what about the backstory? Stiller's dad is going to suddenly show up? Maybe he's lonely. Maybe he's gone through the other kids and now it's . . .

CP: . . . no, no. What if Stiller brings his father on himself? That's the smarter way to do it. Instead of his dad just showing up. It's like, "Dad, this is sad. Mom died a year ago. You need to get out, you need to do something." But he means, "Far away from me."

KD: "You miss your dad, don't you?" I got the message. You don't have to say it.

CP: It's like, "Oh, no, I was thinking more of you going on a cruise." "No, but this is so much better." And what we would usually create is the incident in the past, a moment when his dad completely humiliated him as a child. It's great to go to a flashback of that. I don't know exactly what it would be. Did he make his son sing in front of people?

KD: You know how they used to do the live commercial in between the show. An in-studio commercial. What if he was supposed to sing the jingle?

CP: He was going to have his kid do it and Ben froze. It was humiliating. How far back would that be? It's like, *The Texaco Hour.* Too far back.

KD: Well, maybe Ben wanted to do a commercial. Like he was the original Oscar Mayer Wiener Kid. But he couldn't pull it off. He choked.

CP: He blew his chance to be on cereal boxes. And it's great. The advertising world—and his dad was part of this, because everybody knows these ads and these songs. And it's good to meet the king— the jingle king.

PD: Has the Oscar Meyer event haunted Ben?

CP: It's something he always resented his dad for. Maybe he went into the same business to prove he's better than his dad, right? "I'm going to be more successful than him. I'm going to do the same exact thing he did. I'm going to end up more successful."

KD: Although it's nice if he was supposed to sing a song, so that at the end, when he has to sing the song in the meeting, it's sort of like he gets a second shot. And his dad's in the back of the room just crying. That used to be the lullaby he would sing him to sleep with it.

CP: But he wanted Stiller to sing the song in a commercial when he was a kid, and Stiller wouldn't sing the song. "I hate that. I'm never going to sing that song." And then at the end, he sings the song in the middle of the presentation.

KD: Yeah, and then in the middle a bunch of funny stuff happens.

CP: They'd be set pieces.

KD: Those take months to create. We do an outline, and then we'll . . .

CP: . . . do a scene list. We look at the first act: "Here are all the scenes. You do this one and I'll do this one." And then we go off and write our scenes. The goal is to try to make the other guy laugh at what you wrote.

KD: If it doesn't make us laugh, we try again. That's when we'll get together and look at a scene. After a first pass, if something's not working we go at it together.

CP: Ken is more visual. He gets the visual stuff. I get the more verbal stuff. I will go off on my own a little, and figure out structural problems. And then I'll say, "I got it!" And then I'll pitch it to him and he'll make it better.

"You want it to lead to a moment of truth. This guy is a schmuck, this guy has destroyed his life, but he only did it because he wanted a friend. It's like, Do I deliver him up to the lions?"

KD: And generally, that's done in the bathtub. I'm not part of that process. He goes and takes his bath, comes out—"I got it!"

CP: Well, since he brought it up, a lot of times I'll say, "I need to take a bath to figure things out." Because really it's not worth starting until you know where those big beats are, especially at the end. Like *Dinner for Schmucks* led to a really nice ending where it's a moment of truth. You want it to lead to a moment of truth. This guy is a schmuck, this guy has destroyed his life, but he only did it because he wanted a friend. It's like, Do I deliver him up to the lions? Or what do I do? And you want it to lead to that moment, and I don't think in discussing this premise we've found those moments yet.

KD: Do you have a bathtub? Twenty minutes and he'll be out, wet, and writing things down.

CP: Then you just populate it with the characters. This is basically a two-hander, which is a two-star movie like *Planes, Trains, and Automobiles*.

PD: Before you go in and pitch something, do you have a pretty good idea of what's funny?

CP: We know where the big laughs are going to be. We've gotten a feel for them. I think the main reason we do it this way is it's faster. I once tried writing something else in collaboration, where we were writing the scene at the computer together, and it was like pulling teeth. It was just a nightmare. This is much better. We just go off, write, and then we'll come back and combine it. Yeah, we try to make each other laugh.

PD: How did each of you get a grounding in comedy?

CP: The reason I'm in movies right now is because when I was in the fourth grade I saw a Marx Brothers movie on TV. That was it for me. I'm a huge Marx Brothers fan now. I became really obsessed with that. I'd go to the library. They had Super Eight Chaplin and Keaton. We had this little Super 8 camera and I just started making movies. There's the Marx Brothers, Woody Allen, Monty Python, there was the old revival house. I'd go all the time to watch them. I was schooled by that sort of stuff. But you have to be born funny. I was always able to make people laugh.

KD: Well, to some degree, we both have that same, sad experience in that we weren't the cool kids. For me, a lot of it was a defense mechanism. I could always make people laugh. Maybe I wasn't as good at sports, but that was my thing. So that was sort of what I had, and I used it a lot when I was a kid. Movies were always my escape, when I wanted to get away from realizing I wasn't the cool kid.

CP: I don't think, for either of us, that it came out of suffering or pain. A lot of comedians are very depressed. That's not us. We're both very optimistic, easygoing guys.

PD: Did you pick up the craft or were you mentored?

CP: I didn't know anything about structure until USC. Three-act structure. Eight sequences.

KD: Right out of high school I started making music videos with a friend of mine. We figured out a way to connect with a band. Once we got one, we got another one. I did that for ten years. I made over a hundred music videos. So that was great experience, just holding the camera and editing. But making music videos isn't really storytelling. You try to get a little story in there, but the goal was ultimately to go on to features. So during that time, I'd written a couple of little things. And I've always wanted to make movies, and be in movies. I just loved everything about it. Cinco and I met at the end of my ten-year music video run. We started talking about things. It was our mutual sense of humor that clicked immediately. Cinco said, "We should write something together."

JD: Were you the original writers on *The Santa Clause 2?* Or, were you brought in to rewrite?

CP: We were brought in to rewrite, but here's the story on *The Santa Clause 2.* Every scene in the script was our scene, but they rewrote almost all the dialogue. Then they brought in guys after us who changed almost all the dialogue except for a couple of scenes.

KD: It's exactly what we wrote, but nobody says the words we wrote.

JD: You started from character on this father/son premise. Is that how you typically work?

CP: This premise is character-driven, although I've never been accused of being a character guy. Usually, we get a little criticized for that. We're more story-driven. I know that's how my brain works. You saw us trying to work out what the story is.

KD: What are the moments? We need those moments.

CP: I cling to the emotional beats, the moments, because it makes everything else easier. You kind of riff on that character, yeah. It's kind of like improv. The more real you make it, the funnier it gets. We try to resist stuff that's too crazy and broad. *Bubble Boy* is broad but it has a layer of reality to it.

JD: Do executives ever ask you to funny it up?

CP: We do hear that. The sad thing is we'll get a lot of scripts to rewrite because we do comedy and they want us just to make it funnier. But they don't realize that the reason it's not funny is because it's broken in a lot of other ways, and usually they're not willing to fix that other stuff. They just want icing jokes.

JD: What's the dumbest note you've ever gotten?

CP: On *Bubble Boy*. It was from the senior VP who bought the project. He said, "We've got to get him out of that bubble as soon as possible." He wanted him out of the bubble at the end of Act I. We told him, "The movie's called *Bubble Boy*. He cannot spend only the first act in the bubble. The whole idea is that in Act II he's in the bubble suit, and that's what makes him the "Bubble Boy." He says, "By the midpoint he has to be out of the bubble." We didn't have any choice. We did a draft with him getting out of the bubble halfway, and it was . . .

CP: . . . it was a horrible, horrible. That was the craziest note. You should've seen our faces. "Well what does he do?" we asked. "He's all germ-a-phobic."

KD: Like, are we changing the name of the movie to *Boy*?

IN NO MOOD FOR NICE MOMENTS

A partial list of Heide Perlman's credits as a creator,
show runner, and writer include *Frasier*, *Cheers*,
The Tracey Ullman Show, *Stacked*, and *Sibs*.

A warm and open person, Heide Perlman nevertheless embodies what we describe as a sweet cynicism about television. It's a love/hate relationship. Too often, Heide believes, situation comedies try to cram "happy" stories into half-hour, neatly wrapped packages. For the most part, network television is afraid of the meaner side of life. She suggests that not every character has to be likable. She points out that by broadening a situation, by using parody and satire, skills developed as a writer on *The Tracey Ullman Show*, life's absurdities are revealed.

Heide Perlman trusts that great comedy can stem from deep-rooted scars left by unresolved relationships between people who are related but may not necessarily love each other. It's interesting to compare Heide's interview with Leonard Stern's. They are opposite sides of the same coin. Leonard creates conflict that springs from love.

❇ ❇ ❇

HP (HEIDE PERLMAN): Okay, I would make it that the daughter and the mom's relationship was never good and Sarah is extremely jealous of her mother. What I would do I'm sure would never sell.

All the sympathetic relationships are so sickening, so I would have it that Sarah, to spite her mother, has made something of herself, and she's focused. And Molly has always undermined her in backhanded ways. So now the dad's dead. The dad was really the only constant connection in the family because Sarah and her mom, from Sarah's perspective, never got along, although Molly may not be aware of this. Molly sees herself as a good mother. She's an extremely self-centered person who took the gravy train by marrying the wealthy guy and never had to work, and was like a lot of other women, kind of the hostess.

Okay, so now Molly finds out she doesn't have any money. Her parents aren't going to give her any because she somehow burned her bridges with them, so she needs her daughter. Her daughter is only compelled by guilt to take her mother in and she can't actually refuse her. But she takes her in even though it's at great emotional expense. Molly is totally unaware of this. Molly thinks she's to the manor born. Her attitude is, "Of course this is going to be great."

So the arc of the series would be to have their relationship be more of a real, honest relationship than it has been. I'd like it to be more torturous than anything else. In a mother/daughter relationship, it's really hard for a mother to change her role. Maybe if Sarah's grandparents are starting to go mentally, it could actually be good for Molly. If Molly's parents were always really uptight and always disapproved of her, maybe now they've mellowed toward her. So there's something perverse about Molly celebrating that her mom, Sarah's grandmother, is losing her mind. That could be fun.

I saw a documentary about this daughter and her mother, who had Alzheimer's. The mother had always been the kind of character who was very contained. The Alzheimer's, in a way, made her go back to her youth. The daughter saw parts of her she never saw before. She would sing, for example; she never did that before. So in a way, the Alzheimer's enabled her to have fun, like the kind of fun that she repressed and contained her whole life. For the daughter it was a revelation. But that would be the nice side of it.

What if instead of the grandparents, it was Sarah discovering it in Molly? What if Sarah sees things in her she never saw before. You could have that moment. I'm just not in the mood for nice moments.

I guess you could have situations, going along with this idea of the senility or Alzheimer's, that bring out this part of Molly that was repressed. What if she finds some guy to hook up with and is obviously going to exploit him? She should really still have all her hot stuff. Rather than having the typical attitude of, "Oh I've been protected by this man my whole life and now he's gone. I don't know how to survive in the world." Instead, Molly has all those qualities that can make her survive, because she's so self-centered.

Sarah's kind of torn between getting rid of her, putting her in a facility, because she went off with this rich guy, and she's going to take him for a ride . . . torn between that and letting her have the fun Molly's never allowed herself to have. That's if she has the characteristics of the stodgy grandparents. Molly's really out of control. And the guy could be someone Sarah works with, just to make it more complicated and sitcom-y. I'm interested in a mother who's totally frustrating for her daughter. I think you need the younger character of Sarah. Sarah's an autonomous person. But when her mom is there, her mom pinches her butt to such an extent that Sarah reverts to all of her childhood behavior. I think that could be funny.

JD: Can you think of something that makes you revert?

HP: My mother has a habit of saying, "Right?" after a statement, forcing you to agree with her, even if you don't. "Oh, you love tuna fish, right?" "No, I don't." "Yeah, you love it, right?" And then even if you try to move on, she keeps forcing the issue. "Right? Right?" and you're thinking, "What does it matter if I say 'Right'?" I know I don't like tuna fish, but it's the fact of being forced into agreement that's frustrating. And if someone has Alzheimer's, how do argue with her? That's even more frustrating . . .

JD: What do you see as the arc of the series?

HP: Well, obviously, if the Molly has Alzheimer's, it's not going to be tough. I have a family member with Alzheimer's. When we talk on the phone, she sounds fine. You can talk about stuff in the past. Then it's like, "So did your sister have Thanksgiving at her house?" "Yeah, everyone was there." Then she says, "So, where was Thanksgiving?" It's hard to make that funny.

PD: But you made the Molly character unsympathetic. She's opportunistic and calculating.

HP: And I think that might work if this part of her nature has come out or she's always been this kind of person. As a writer, I've written so many of these shows and been in so many rooms where someone asks, "Well, what's the takeaway from this?" You still have to learn a lesson from a sitcom that's twenty-one minutes and four acts. and the credits over the last moments of the show? How can you feel that this is any sort of reality?

PD: Does Molly have any sort of maternal instincts?

HP: I think Molly would feel like, How can Sarah be so inept? Like anything she teaches her she would teach her the hard way. "Oh, my darling daughter, let me help you. This is how you get a man. Here, dear, put on this wig." As long as it was something that hurt her daughter's feelings. And you can make her daughter overly sensitive to that kind of stuff, because she's traumatized. Molly would say, "You're going to wear that?" Molly would dress Sarah and she'd look horrible. She wouldn't be Sarah anymore. And Molly would kind of be forcing her to go out like that, and it wouldn't work for her. And then she would have to change outside. Like whatever she does makes it even worse. Molly, in helping her, screws things up worse for her.

PD: So Molly would actually be frustrated by the fact that her daughter was inept.

HP: Yeah! "You had the best teacher in the world growing up and you didn't even take notes." The daughter comes home complaining about her work and how hard it is. "You don't have to have a job. You can use your resources—get way more money than you're making now." Maybe Molly doesn't understand that kind of self-worth. Again, this might work whether this is the new Molly brought out by Alzheimer's or if she's always been this self-centered.

PD: When Sarah says, "That's not the way I'm living my life. I've got plans and ambitions," how does Molly react to her?

HP: She would think that's ridiculous. "Fine, live your stupid way!" I think every daughter wants to throttle her mom, even the ones with the good relationships. There's something very special about that relationship in terms of frustration.

JD: On *Frasier*, there were always dark and light moments. Just the whole fact of the father living with the son was done differently. This guy who never understood his son.

HP: When you conceive something, it changes completely once an actor gets hold of it. I wonder if the actress playing the part of Molly would want to be quite this unsympathetic. A writer is a puppet master. You can get out all your hate and all your bad thoughts and your manipulations. This is how I would get back at my mother! I'm going to put every bad trait of every person I've ever met and had to deal with into this character, but you know, that actress won't do this unless she's British.

I think of *Ab Fab*, because that's the basic self-centered mom with the frustrated daughter. But yeah, just that she was such a buffoon, that she was so pathetic. And that's another example of the writer playing the unsympathetic part. So maybe that's what you need. You need a bunch of Larry Davids being willing to be the unsympathetic character people relate to. Relate to, and like to laugh at and enjoy.

This show I did was about three sisters who were going to see their dead stepmother, a woman they feared and hated. So I wanted it to be the scene from the *Wizard of Oz*, where they were walking down the hall to see the wizard and they were really scared. At the end of the scene the cowardly lion runs out and jumps through the window. I wanted to do that scene, only they're walking down a hallway in an apartment building and they knock on the door. The stepmother opens it, and one of the sisters runs down the hall and dives through a window. But the actress didn't want to do it because she couldn't find the motivation for that cartoonish of an action. She did it but not without a big fight and of course it didn't come out exactly how I wanted it. Tracey Ullman was playing the stepmother in makeup and I wanted the sister to go like this [Heide screams], run, and jump through the window.

"...I tend to pitch the most cartoonish ideas just because it's hard for me, at this point, to think of these shows as reality..."

JD: Would you add some of that cartoonish element to this premise?

HP: In rooms I tend to pitch the most cartoonish ideas just because it's hard for me, at this point, to think of these shows as reality because once you've done a lot of them you have to play with it to stay interested. I still like the small story. It's the daily hell of everybody's lives that I find interesting. Basically like being stuck in *No Exit*. It's just that things don't really change that much. Especially in familial relationships.

PD: Network sitcoms have a lot of rules and structure. Is it easier writing for cable?

HP: You'd be surprised. First of all, the cable outlets are very, very specific as to what they want, and they all say, "If it can be done on network, we don't want it." But then, that's not necessarily true, because every character has to be sympathetic down to their core, really, and they have to really love each other, after all. I guess people get upset if they feel like people really don't like each other. *Seinfeld* was none of that. Okay, a show like *The Office*, I don't think it would've been made without the British version. I think there's British versions of shows that give permission for the American version to be made.

If the network has deemed that it worked somewhere else, then it's okay. But if someone comes in and pitches that, it's like, "No, no, no, that's way too dark." Or, "We'll never like that character." And then it turned out, like on *Seinfeld*, the audience didn't care whether they liked each other or not.

JD: *The Tracey Ullman Show*, which you were an important part of, had a cartoonish element.

HP: But it took risks.

PD: A number of writers started by saying, "These days, if I can't produce or direct, I don't want to be part of it."

HD: Oh my God, can I just tell you one experience? I did this pilot years ago. It was a mother/daughter, but like a mother and a four-year-old. And it had a scene where the mother is trying to go out, and the four-year-old says, "Mommy don't go, don't go," as four-year-olds do. "Don't leave me." And she throws a fit, and then as soon as she goes, she's fine! The babysitter says, "You can have ice cream—whatever you want." And then as soon as her mom walks out the door, she says, "So, can I have the ice cream?" So we got the kid to cry and even though that was the scene where you know the kid's fine, and it's on film, the executives said, "You have to take this scene out. It's too sad. We won't show the pilot unless you take this out." And I took it out and that was really a knife in my heart. I was just trying to do something that was real, that happens to people every day, and that I think every mother can relate to. Every little kid uses emotional blackmail.

It just kills you. I shouldn't have done it. The changes you make that hurt you usually turn out to hurt the whole project. You might as well say, "No, this is how I want it." The executives will say, "Okay, f--k you, go away anyway," and then at least you have your dignity.

JD: Jerry Belson was your mentor.

HP: My first job was *Cheers* and he did one day a week. And I saw immediately that this guy is different. You know he was always a curmudgeon, but he had the most original mind—just funny, funny, funny. And the things that he would say, that everyone would laugh at, would go in the script, but usually only worked if he said it. And sometimes they were just so outside. He pitched this joke where Coach goes into Sam's office, saying, "There's a small, black man asking for you," and then he says, "Oh wait, it's the phone." Talk about bizarre.

PD: How did you get into comedy writing?

HP: Nepotism!

PD: Did you always write?

HP: I always wanted to be a writer. When I dropped out of college, I went off to be a writer, but of course that didn't work out.

PD: What kind of writer were you trying to be?

HP: Oh, something very deep, like Beckett. By that time, my sister [Rhea Perlman] was married. Her husband Danny [DeVito] was out here doing *Taxi*. They also were trying to do their own projects, and I would just write little things to send them. That was one of the things I did to entertain myself and my friends. They said, "You could write as well as these guys out here." So I just came out here for a while and I read all the *Taxi* scripts because Rhea had them. And I also hung around *Taxi*, but mostly it was from reading the scripts. I learned, "Okay, here's the dumb guy, here's the selfish guy." I basically learned sitcom from reading *Taxi*.

They had their own structure. They used the same basic structure on both *Taxi* and *Cheers*. After I read all the *Taxi*'s and I hung around there, I read that pilot the Charles Brothers wrote for *Cheers*. It wasn't on the air yet, but I thought, "Oh, well, I'll try this." So I wrote a *Cheers* spec script and because I had my way in, I knew them. I had met the Charles Brothers and my sister was on the show. I gave them the spec script and they didn't have a staff, as they did later. There was only Isaacs and Levine on staff, and then they had Jerry Belson one day a week.

They thought I got the characters, so they gave me an assignment, which was bizarre. I had no idea of what it was at all. I wasn't a production assistant. I didn't work in the mailroom. I just was there all of a sudden. I think it was extremely helpful to me because I probably would've sunk myself somehow if I thought, "People write spec after spec before they get a job." So I wrote one spec and they gave me an assignment on *Cheers*. I wrote the outline and they hired me on staff from the outline because they needed stories. It was really right place, right time.

They gave me a bunch of outlines, and so I thought, "Okay." They were substantial outlines, where each scene and jokes in the outline were laid out. Although they changed a lot, you put a lot in those outlines. I wrote a joke where Diane's cat dies and Sam takes advantage of her emotional distress and tries to hook up with her. The joke I wrote in my outline, which they loved, was that Carla comes up to Diane and says, "Oh, I'm so sorry about your cat. I've been through it all with the kids—the turtle, the fish . . ." Diane says, "Yeah, but cats are different." And Carla says, "Yeah, you can't flush a cat." I think that was the joke that got me the job.

IT SUCKS TO BE IN A MOVIE

 An Interview with Charlie Peters

A partial list of Charlie Peters's credits as a screenwriter, director, and television creator include *Three Men and a Little Lady, Blame it on Rio, Her Alibi, Paternity, Hot to Trot, My One and Only, Music from Another Room, Passed Away, Krippendorf's Tribe,* and *CBS Summer Playhouse: Tickets, Please.*

By the time you finish reading this interview, you will feel like you have earned the equivalent of three credits in a university writing class. Charlie Peters is the college professor you would have loved to have a beer with after class. His interview blends premise development, comedy theory, and story construction with personal industry stories woven in. Charlie's working style is a blend of technical virtuosity and creativity. He makes the point that, in a good script, the characters want the story to end, but as you're reading this interview, you'll hope it never does.

❊ ❊ ❊

CP (CHARLIE PETERS): My inclination would be to develop this premise as a movie. The difference between television and movies is that a television premise is more situational. It has to promise much more story. You pitch a pilot and you have to come in with fifteen plots. A movie can be about a single day or a single hour. So a movie is much more event-driven in terms of the comedic. If I refer to movies, I refer to classic movies that most people have seen. Like *Tootsie*. The situation is a man pretending to be a woman, but the event is essentially romantic.

Unfortunately, some writers create a whole movie, and I will read it and very often I will find very little conflict in it. Because with the amateur, no conflict actually exists in the movie. The thing about writing movies is that it's a very unnatural thing to do. Because the whole point of everyone's life is to make life easier. And what you're asking a writer to do is to figure out how to make someone's life harder. And you know, in the morning, you get up, you take a leak, you go downstairs, you get the coffee, you get dressed, you get the keys, you get in the car, and you go to work. In a movie everything has to go wrong. You go downstairs and the coffeepot doesn't work. You can't find the car keys . . .

Look at Woody Allen's really good films. There are no scenes in which people are *not* arguing. And it's what we all by nature try to avoid. So we're being asked to be incredibly *un-human*, because drama is all about conflict. You have to know the motivation. The motivation for every character in a movie should be to stop the movie right now. It should be to get out of the movie. Once a character is enjoying the movie, the movie is over. If they had their choice, they would get the guns of Navarone on page 2. No one should want to be in a movie for exactly the reasons I told you. It sucks to be in a movie. You want to watch the movie—not be in it.

You start to fall in love with your characters and you don't want them to have problems. But you get to page 120 and you have this whole problem-less life for them and it's a really boring movie. If this were a feature premise, it would read like an ensemble movie with a young woman looking for love.

The first thing they would do is cast it. The story now is not really important to a movie. The story is only important as bait to an element. An element is an actor. In movies, actors are now the only elements that matter. The studios would say, "Who would be in this?"

The other thing they think about now when you tell them a story is the opening weekend. They mention one word. *Poster.* They want to see the poster. I worked with a man who was the head of Paramount Pictures, and I was told he was a genius. I pitched him an idea he really liked. And maybe he had too much to drink or maybe he didn't have enough to drink because he looks at me very seriously and he says, "What do you think the opening weekend will be?" I said, "How do I know? Probably be cloudy, maybe like sixty, sixty-five degrees." That was ten years ago and it's gotten worse since.

So here you have a story that could be trigenerational. Sarah is a youngish woman, living with her mother; there's the influence of her grandparents who are Molly's mother and father. The feature people responding to this would be looking for an event. So what if we kill the grandparents off. There's an event. The death of the grandparents. The funeral. Funerals are always good. Big laughs. Funerals and weddings. Weddings are in movies a lot because they are a much more highly used device. I don't think you find it that much in Europe or South America, but because it is really the only place where we are, in this culture, allowed to openly show our emotions. The event is orchestrated to allow us to show emotion. It opens a wound. People behave at weddings like they behave nowhere else. As opposed to cultures where people run up to each other, kiss, and stand really close. We have to be invited to weddings, but we're expected to go to funerals. We're very cheap with our emotional joy, but we're very generous with our grief. But I'm only going to invite people to my funeral. This is how I'm going to be different. If you're not invited, don't come. And come with a gift.

So Sarah and her boyfriend, who she brings to the funeral, decide to move in with Molly and within a month they're looking for assisted-living housing for themselves. Molly is a charming socialite. What she does is she hijacks the role of the younger woman, which can be funny as long as her mother is cleverly cast to be two years older than Sarah. In fact, if the mother were younger than her it would probably appeal to the studios.

It never occurred to Sarah why her mother is younger than she is. If Sarah is twenty, the mother could be forty-five. We can make them both attractive. One is essentially Lolita and the other is a slightly older Lolita. So I would look for episodes in which Sarah is attracted to some guy who's attracted to Molly, although I'm sure he doesn't want to bed the mother, although there's another episode.

There's a sophistication and grace to older women that younger men find comfortable. There's an ease that's there, so you have that element between Molly and Sarah. You could also have the dead grandmother come back to life and there would be the guys that she would be attracted to.

Probably being a TV series, they would want one who's attracted to the grandmother, that she's not attracted to. A romance is about two people who don't get together. The classic thing is that if they're going to be together at the end, they have to be as far apart as possible at the end of Act II. And if they're not together at the end, they have to make love at the end of Act II. In most romances, the couple is together at the end, but it's finding the obstacles. Today in romance, the obstacles are essentially neurotic, which makes for good psychiatric visits but not very good films. When I say neurotic, I mean the guy who's saying, "Well, I really want to marry her, but I still want to f--k a lot people, too." And then the woman saying, "Well, he's really cute and everything, but maybe he still wants to f--k other people and maybe he doesn't make enough money." I mean it's all about your interior problem, which means there are really not that many obstacles.

Conflict and obstacle. Obstacle is sort of like a physical obstacle. Conflict is what you feel emotionally. Again, you have to have that obstacle. You have to have that conflict.

PD (PETER DESBERG): How would you find the obstacles?

CP: In the story of Molly and Sarah, I suppose illness, you know, classic things . . . falling in love with someone you find out is married. Falling in love with someone you find out is a Republican. I want to see people in a romantic comedy sit down and say, "Yeah, I want to have sex with you, but what do you think about the death penalty?" "How do you want to bring the children up?" Clearly, it's a fantasy, as is most love anyway. And then you put it in a movie and then it becomes fantasy to the nth degree.

JD (JEFFREY DAVIS): What would make this premise more interesting to you?

CP: By putting Sarah and Molly in a situation they can't get out of emotionally or physically and then have them find their way out of it. Right now the obstacle in the premise—the mother moving in with Sarah—is annoying, but it's not really an obstacle. It's not the German Army arriving just when you're about to blow up the guns of Navarone. A lot of times I'm given things that are high concept. In a high-concept story, the attraction of it is that you're able to present it in a short period of time, get executives to see it. But it's an easy sell for the studio executive to go to his or her boss, because the person you pitch it to is never the person who says, "Yes," unless you're a major filmmaker. So what you have to do is wrap the idea in a way that they can take it to their person and make it seem palatable. And very often, by human nature, we do know what makes a good story. You have to give them an event, an obstacle.

But it's a dangerous thing because the concept sometimes overwhelms the story. You look at the really good stories. Again, I'll mention *Tootsie*. It's a perfect balance of high concept and story because of the brilliance of the writing and the acting and the direction. But the high concept is the sort of booster rocket, the conduit that exists all the way through the story, until the second-to-last scene. But the writing of the obstacles of the romance is so good that it's always seen as a means. Once the high concept becomes the most basic, the most interesting part of the movie, you're really dead. Which is true for a lot of these movies. They're about people in their thirties, because most of the executives are in their thirties, looking to have sex or love or sometimes both.

Now that's a high concept, that sex life. But it doesn't work because it's just the notion of wanting to find sex or love, but it's not enough to carry something unless it's well written.

PD: If you were talking about it with a producer, and he said, "Give me some examples of conflict that you would put in here," how would you go about choosing?

CP: Well, we see the conflict between characters. If you have conflict, you can separate it. Mother versus daughter. Daughter versus father. Parents versus daughter. But the father's dead, isn't he? I think he should be dead. He and the grandmother run off together, *dead*. There's a high concept.

So you can have the father as a ghost. But the story could also be about jobs. Sarah's job. What does she do? She could be let go and Molly tries to find her a new job. She goes in with Sarah and maybe meets someone. And the person wants to hire Molly and not Sarah. And then there's the conflict of jealousy. I think much more so with mother and daughter jealousy than there is between fathers and sons. Or a son and his mother. That's a whole different kind of jealousy. Like who's wearing that red lamé dress tonight. Now that my mother's dead, I don't have those problems anymore. I've got all her clothes. Or this: Molly and Sarah could be evicted from their apartment.

PD: When I asked you for those examples, you said, "Okay. I can take conflict A to B, B to A, A to C, C to A." It was really logical, and then you started going out from there. Is that the way you work?

CP: I guess so. Sometimes it's good, in a scene or a sequence, to do a writing exercise. I'll rewrite the scene, saying, "Okay, what if the person were a dog?" I mean something just totally outrageous. Just to stretch it and to see it in a new way. It's very difficult to rewrite your own stuff because you've been through the process of doing it.

JD: If you could do one thing to this story that would reflect your sensibility, what would it be?

CP: My instinct now, after twenty-five years of writing romantic comedies, after *Three Men and a Little Lady* and all the rest, is to do very dark stuff. And I'm having fun doing it. I'm trying to think of the things I'm doing now and how they would relate to Molly and Sarah. They're very personal. I think it would be wrapped around a mystery. All parent/child relationships are about what's unspoken. What if it were the father's funeral, not the grandmother's? It's about the mystery you find when one parent, Sarah's father, is gone and maybe Sarah is discovering mysteries.

My parents got a sixteen-millimeter camera when my brother was born and so, of course, they took home movies. And my brother put together a little video of those home movies and the most fascinating thing is this: Home movies are, in a sense, the opposite of life. They're the simple moments of these short reels at a party. Or Fourth of July. Or Christmas. And when there was blackness, when there was a piece of black between the shots, that's when my life really happened.

So this blackness between the home movie idea would be when Sarah's father died. This is when their house burned down. This is when they all got sick. They didn't have home movies of these moments. Home movies are such a small part of what the relationship might be between Molly and Sarah. And finding goals for each of them that not only don't match, but goals that collide. You could make the story about a mother and the daughter who are criminals. They're con artists. They work together as con artists and then of course something happens where one of them falls in love with somebody. And they can't do it anymore. That could work.

You can, if you have two characters like this, Molly and Sarah, bring in what I call the third object. If you can't find a clash between the two characters in a scene, there is the third element, or the third character. The best example is in Cocteau's *Beauty and the Beast*. I remember seeing this as a kid. It's their first dinner together and they're at this long table. He's at one end and she's at the other end. She's kind of like, "Well, he's not such a bad guy. He's a beast, but he's very gracious and actually quite wonderful." And at the end of the meal they go for a walk on his property. And suddenly they're walking and they're talking and he points and there's this beautiful fawn grazing in the field. And they do this two-shot of the two people. And they don't see each other. Only you see them. And she looks and she goes, "Oh." And he looks and he gnarls his teeth and the drool comes down. That's the third object, the deer. That tells you exactly why this marriage is not going to be great.

Without the third object, there is no movie. Often, in a seemingly emotional or a comic thing, the third object is very clear. I call it the third object because if there is only one character and an object, you need someone to bounce off one's feelings to another during the movie. It saves you from writing voice-over. But the challenge is finding a third object in a situation like this. The mother and daughter could be quite happy together. To make it a little edgy, in walks a guy they both find attractive, like *Lolita*, which is my favorite book.

Back to the notion of the high concept. I could see people pitching *Lolita* today. But it's actually quite tragic. Obviously, it's about the middle-aged guy and the young girl. But I mean she dies in childbirth and it's very, very sad. But that's an example of a mother and a daughter. The mother doesn't kill the daughter, but in certain ways she sort of drives her to the madness of this car crash. So you can find that third element. I guess, taking what we said earlier, the third element should be the least comfortable thing to deal with. It's the thing that causes the most conflict.

It could be this attractive person coming between Molly and Sarah. Whatever creates jealousy. Movies are about people being less than good. There aren't many movies about Mother Teresa.

"... I said, 'What's the difference between a device and a trick?' He said, 'A device is a trick that works.'"

PD: Do you think, "I've got this sort of dial. How dark do I want this conflict to be?"

CP: Generally, I do that within scenes. What ratchets up the tension? I had a scene last night in which a guy is dealing with the woman who was his son's teacher. It was kind of okay, but I needed somebody outside the scene to call the guy and tell him really bad news. To get into a conflict with him. I mean, there are devices or tricks that are pretty obvious to the audience. I went to school in England as a kid, and I spent some time in Ireland. Brian Friel [a famous Irish playwright] once told me, "Make sure it is a device and not a trick." "Well," I said, "what's the difference between a device and a trick?" He said, "A device is a trick that works."

JD: Do you always know where your ending is?

CP: Most of the time I know the ending before I know much of anything else. People talk about characters driving their stuff. I think that's true, but I think characters are essentially plot anyway. What are you but what you do? I think it was Graham Greene who said, "Plot is character and character is plot." Cause you've only got so many pages before you've got to get there.

JD: What do your second, third, and fourth drafts look like?

CP: I just go through and say, "This is terrible." I'm very, very easily bored. I'm sorry, what's your name? When I directed my own movies, it was depressing. Writer/directors are notorious. They love everything. My director's cut would be eleven minutes. I go, "Oh my God, I'm dying here. Cut this. Cut this. Cut this." Literally, if it was more than ninety-two minutes. I hired famous actors to do specific scenes because I had to call them up and say I cut it out of the movie. I've met a lot of them and I've worked with amazing directors.

JD: After you've written a couple of drafts, are you able to tell if it's funny or do you have to go to someone else?

CP: The problem with writing a screenplay that's funny is that it has to be funny to the executives. For the first ten years, I used the same twenty-five jokes in the first thirty pages of the screenplay to get them to know it was a comedy. Those jokes never made it into a movie. If they made it into a movie, well, then I couldn't use them again. But you have to tell the guys it is funny because very often what's funny in the screenplay is not funny in the movie. The difference between a screenplay and a movie is such a huge difference. And the ability of those in the business to make that jump is virtually nonexistent anymore.

PD: What if an executive says to you, "Punch it up"?

CP: I did it for *Snowdogs*, that Disney movie. There were a lot of TV writers in the room. They were fun. They were cool guys. But I stopped because I said this was the film moment. Because they were just going on about the gags and I said, "No." They built up this one moment and the producer said that was what they paid me for, just to show some sort of sense of what the story was about. And they cut it out of the movie anyway.

JD: How did you end up in the arts?

CP: My mother was sort of a journalist and I used to ghostwrite for her sometimes. She had several jobs after my father died. So I would help her and we were paid three cents a word. So it's odd that I was introduced to writing as a job and only later, when I became a boring, self-absorbed adolescent, that it occurred to me that it was artistic. It is usually the other way around. It is usually, "Well, this is my love. Poetry. Poetry is what I want to write." And then finally, stepdad says, "Who's going to pay the rent?" But it literally was three cents a word. My mother would write a story and send it in to the editor and it would come back with red pencil marks through words. This meant there was three cents less for everything we needed. So we had to learn to write. She wrote some whacky stuff. She wrote an advice column for teenagers, which I ghosted for her sometimes. I was twelve years old and I was writing advice for young women. Now there's a story. Molly could be a famous columnist and she's starting to get early senility and Sarah has to take over.

But the other thing is, I went to school in England when I was a kid and I just got involved with the theater over there. The way they teach it, it's more like a subject. It's not like an after-school club to sort of keep kids from doing crime or jerking off. In fact, theater is probably a way to make them jerk off even more. But it was really funny. It was just one of those things where you had just one teacher who was a catalyst and several of my roommates and classmates became really famous. I mean world-famous. Charles Sturridge, who directed *Brideshead Revisited*. Edward Duke, an actor who did the P. G. Wodehouse shows. There were about ten of us and we're all sort of in theater and film. And I just always liked to tell stories. I was always a liar.

My stuff is situational in the sense that it's sort of like an uncomfortable comedy. Sometimes in movies, comedies really don't get that much laughter. I remember going to see *Working Girl*, which was directed by Mike Nichols. It was quite a brilliant comedy, but the audience laughed only once during that movie. They laughed when one of the executives says, "Let's have some coffee." And the main character is a secretary pretending to be an executive and she says, "I'll get it." It wasn't even a particularly funny moment, but the audience was given a *cookie line*. In a cookie line, you keep all the tension going, and then at the end of the scene, or somewhere in the scene, you have to burst it. You ask people coming out of the movie, Was that funny? "Oh God, that was the damn funniest movie." But there wasn't a lot of laughter in it.

JD: You've probably written yourself into corners. What do you do when that happens?

CP: I usually just keep going. I just finish it. I have, you know, dozens and dozens of scripts on the bookshelf and in the bottom drawer.

JD: How many scripts do you work on simultaneously?

CP: I've worked on as many as two or three at the same time. Right now, I'm just doing one, but I've got two or three in my mind. I've realized that I have really good plots. A lot of my friends who write books say they're jealous of me because I have so many plots.

I have a very bad attention span. I work for very short periods of time. I mean no more than twenty minutes at a time. That's where the dog comes in handy. Most people say they don't walk their dog enough. I walk mine fifteen, twenty times a day. I have a very short attention span. I write in short periods of time. I write no more than a couple of hours a day, but it gets done.

PD: Does your attention span differ when you're editing?

CP: When I'm editing, it's actually a lot easier to stay with it because it's all there. I can sit in front of the screen and spend a half an hour editing and I look up and it's three and a half hours later. But it's a little indulgent. People spend hours and months and years changing things and it's irrelevant to the reader unless you change something in a movie that is dramatic. *He dies. She kills him.* To change a line here, a location there? It's all indulgence. To really change something is to change the event.

"Having been brought up on three cents a word, you can't exactly sit around and wait for inspiration."

JD: What do you do when you aren't feeling inspired?

CP: Having been brought up on three cents a word, you can't exactly sit around and wait for inspiration. As Samuel Johnson said, "Anyone who writes for any reason other than money is insane."

JD: Who mentored you?

CP: I had some really great teachers. They weren't writers, they just let me do what I wanted to do. I am a voracious reader and seer of movies. I'm always going to movies. It's actually depressing to read so much because there's just so much better out there than the nonsense that I do, which is fine. I make so much more money than they do. No, I could buy and sell those schmucks.

PD: When you go to the movies are you analytic?

CP: No. When I go to movies, I am the best audience. I see everything. When I see a movie, I really want to be seduced. So you have to see it a couple of times to really study it.

PD: It sounds like some of your mentors were flesh and blood and some were celluloid and paper.

CP: You look at something and say, "Wow, I like how he did that. I can use that."

What I usually say is, "I can steal it." I think I learn somewhat subconsciously from watching what I like. I like a certain kind of British humor. I think that's because I came into my adulthood in Britain.

PD: Did you enjoy teaching?

CP: I did enjoy teaching. I think the hardest thing about teaching is being just as good with the students who you aren't impressed by as you are with students you are impressed by. As with my stuff, I get bored very easily. I did a graduate screenwriting course at USC. They actually came to my house and had dinner. Five or six people. Once a week. And the first year I did it, I had this hugely successful movie come out of my class, which was the second biggest movie of the following year, *The Hand That Rocks the Cradle*.

I do find that I'm steering people toward television more. Because I think cable television is the most interesting medium that there is now. Feature films? I just don't see the chance of most people getting in there. That's why I would love to do something on TV. But something that takes a little bit more time, like HBO or Showtime or the countless cable outlets. USA, FX, and American Movie Classics.

That's why I tell these kids, "Think TV." All of them go, initially, "Oh, television. I don't want to do television." But they all come back to it. Because their friends who graduated a few years ago, none of them are selling anything. There's a large industry of developing movies for studios. I get a lot of those jobs, but I am quite aware that they will never make them. Because the producer has to develop a certain number of projects to justify her discretionary fund and her salary.

WRITE YIDDISH, CAST BRITISH

☞ An Interview with Phil Rosenthal

A partial list of Phil Rosenthal's credits as creator/show runner and writer include *Everybody Loves Raymond*, *Coach*, *Down the Shore*, *Baby Talk*, and *The Man in the Family*.

Only two things in this interview did not surprise us. One, that we were interviewing another comedy writer who was Jewish and, two, that Phil Rosenthal turned out to be as nice as many of the other writers in this book told us he was. Co-creator of *Everybody Loves Raymond*, Phil could be called a professional nice guy. Along with all those Emmys, he has earned an industrywide reputation for being as old-school gracious as he is creative and shrewd. It shows in the way he chose writers and managed the writers' room on *Raymond*. Almost everyone on the staff stayed with him throughout the nine years it was the number one comedy on television. Even when they had lucrative offers to go to other series, they stayed. In all that time, Phil had one rule: If something didn't ring true, it didn't make it into a script.

Watching him develop this premise, you notice his deep understanding of human idiosyncrasies. Phil values believability and humanity over jokes. He does this without devices or tricks. He's as universal as he can be by being as personal as he can be.

❎ ❎ ❎

PR (PHIL ROSENTHAL): If I was in charge, if suddenly you proved incompetent and brought me in . . . I'm not going to help. The first rule for everybody is you can never win that way. But if I was given this rough premise, the first thing I would do is to make Sarah a guy. That is how I approached my show. I don't know if I would have written *Everybody Loves Deborah* as well as *Raymond*. I can identify with *Raymond* because I feel I am Raymond. I know what it's like to be that guy. I don't think it hurts your premise. It may even be more commercial. Everyone always tells me that shows with a male center sell better. It would be foolish not to address the business side, yes?

I've seen the mother/daughter show before. *The Gilmore Girls.* That's another reason it's more interesting to change Sarah to Sam. We haven't seen the mother/son show. What if I was suddenly in this situation? What if I had to live with my mom, when maybe I'm closer with my dad and he's dead? Now what Mom wants is to be my buddy and I don't want to be buddies with my mom. I want a mom. I think it's even better making Sarah into Sam. Maybe he has a boss who's a woman and he's trying to do the typical male thing and advance. And while Sam's trying to advance, this woman is keeping him down. I think that's a better dynamic. Ideally, I think you want a Tom Hanks/Shirley MacLaine dynamic between Sam and Molly. Of course, it could be even more different.

JD (JEFFREY DAVIS): What would you do to make it different?

PR: I would make it as Jewish as possible, but call it Italian. That seems to have worked before. Write Yiddish, cast British. I would make a pilot that served this premise. Where you go from here is the question.

This is a perfectly valid premise. You see him at work. He's going for vice president, but he has a female boss who's not going to allow it. He's not going to get the promotion, and to make his day even worse, his father dies. You always want to raise the stakes. You guys have done that. I made a big change here in making Sarah into Sam.

So now I think you put a funeral at the beginning, where you are seeing and introducing your characters, and maybe it's a one-camera show, which seems to be in favor these days. And maybe during the father's funeral, we are doing flashbacks of Sam's relationships with his dad. And maybe forget what I said earlier about how Sam was close to him. Maybe he was an absent father so that Sam's not devastated by the loss. To do that right away in the pilot, it's such a downer. Of course, I'm just spitballing.

Here's the thing: You don't want something that you can't recover from. "Oh my God, he lost his beloved father. Now he's depressed for the rest of the show." I think it's better if he didn't really know his father. Sam says, "I haven't seen my father in fifteen years. Never mind loved him." Maybe the dad skipped out on Sam and Molly. Now it's the funeral and Sam's obligated to go. Everyone else is going. Maybe there's money, but he gets there and the bad news is, maybe there is no money. But Sam gets his mother instead. So maybe that's the act break.

Now his mom is moving in and suddenly this is not the upwardly mobile track he thought he was on. Women are ruining it. Bubbe and Zayde, the grandparents, have always been close by, and their daughter Molly is not as close with them. In fact, maybe that's the comfy, distant relationship, instead of the way you had it here, where the mother and daughter had a comfortable, but distant relationship. What if it's Molly who has one with her parents? And maybe it's Sam who enjoys having the grandparents nearby and likes to check on them once in a while. So maybe he moves them closer. Now he's at the center of a fight between his own mother and her parents.

What often happens is you become the parent of your parent. Maybe that's the relationship between Sam and Molly. If you flesh that out a little bit, you see that he's between his mother and his grandparents. He identifies more with his grandparents than his own mother. Maybe she's kind of a hippie. But, absolutely, she must be a pain in his ass.

That's kind of where I would head in the pilot, and it's what you always want to do. You head down the road until you see it doesn't work. You start writing with this in mind until somebody throws you a question. "What about this?" "Oh, I didn't think about that. You're right. That's terrible." I find in writing, you have these decisions and you make the decision and you run as if that's the best decision. You run toward it until you fall. Now you say, "Maybe that's not the best decision." That's what happens in the room. That's what's so great about the writers' room. You get to have these different, hopefully brilliant heads, challenging your ideas and coming up with their ideas of what's good and what's not, and then debating it, discussing it. Many people hate the writing-by-committee approach. I only loved it because if you had bright, funny people in the room they only made you better. Of course, you should also have a strong sense of what you think the show is.

If this was my premise, I would be protective of it. I would have a feeling of ownership of it, but that's not to say I would be closed to other opinions. A good idea can come from anywhere, even from the network or the studio. At the end of the day, they're actually people, too. You want your show to come across to them, too—the people you are writing it for. They may ask a question that someone in the audience may very well ask, but if they are only coming from a purely commercial standpoint and you smell that, you say, "I will take a look at that." And then you do what you want.

"Do the show you want to do because in the end they are going to cancel you anyway."

You say, "That's very interesting. I'll take a look at that." But you must do what you want. The best advice I ever got from anybody was from Ed Weinberger (writer/producer *The Mary Tyler Moore Show, Cosby, Taxi*). He said, "Do the show you want to do because in the end they are going to cancel you anyway." You can't go to them when they are canceling your show and say, "But I took all your notes." They don't care.

PD (PETER DESBERG): You started with a great conflict with the boss.

PR: In the pilot, your last scene would probably be back at work, if that's where you started. However, once we got into developing episodes, we might find the strength of this show is at home. We'd see very little at the office. Or we might discover that the strength is at the office. You don't know until you get going. I always like to use the example of *The Mary Tyler Moore Show*. The strength of the show is at the office. As the show went on, that TV station is where the series lived. It could very easily have gone the other way, where we are only concerned with Mary in her apartment and her dating and all about how her friends at the office were going to take it and interfere.

I do believe it always tips to one side. Raymond was a sportswriter. Who cares what he did? The money was in the living room when the parents came over and bothered him. What he did for a living didn't matter. We picked sportswriter in 1996 because the job of comedian was already taken by Jerry Seinfeld. That's what Ray would have been most comfortable doing, since that's who he is, but we made it sportswriter because that's a male-obsessed thing. We wanted him to be the typical male, obsessed with sports. Ray certainly wasn't the first sportswriter on TV. Oscar Madison is my favorite.

JD: You rarely saw Jack Klugman and Tony Randall at work. In *The Odd Couple*, you saw the relationship of those two characters.

PR: I think that is, to this day, the most successful adaptation of a play, to a movie, to a situation comedy in the history of the business.

JD: I remember my father [Jerry Davis, producer of the *The Odd Couple*] saying the network was worried about two guys living together. The show lasted nine years.

PR: I'm ten years old watching the show. Gay never enters into it for me. Of course two guys live together. Why wouldn't they? They are friends. It's a perfectly reasonable premise. It was funny to me at ten. I remember thinking, "Look at that guy. He acts like the wife. Felix is bothering Oscar the way my mother bothers my father when he's late for dinner. That's funny because he's a man."

JD: If you could just throw the network out the door . . .

PR: . . . Okay, sounds good. Keep going.

JD: Is there something you've always wanted to try on TV?

PR: Honestly, I would love to unashamedly make them Jewish. That's what I know. Not because they need to be Jewish. Last year, I pitched a show where the characters were decidedly Jewish. The wife wants to have Friday nights at home. I wasn't stupid enough to say the word *Shabbos*. The wife wants Friday nights at home, and she wants to light the candles. I think that when you are true to what you know and who you are, that's when you reach other people. Take *My Big Fat Greek Wedding*. I'm not Greek, but I identified with the specifics in her life because they matched some of the specifics in my life.

PD: Where would you take this if you made the pilot?

PR: It's a tone. It's the specific things they do. Maybe Sam's not religious and Molly is. That's funny to me. Not only is she going to impose on him by being in his apartment, she's going to impose religious rituals he doesn't believe in. Or switch it. What if he's religious, not Molly? Sam identifies with his grandparents, who are observant. Maybe Orthodox. That may be interesting. Molly comes in and she's not at all a religious Jew. She's a hippy. She's still stuck in the 1960s. Sam is shocked and embarrassed that she's like this. The networks are deeply afraid of Jews on TV. I couldn't get a pilot shot of the show we were pitching because the characters were Jewish. I guess you could do a movie.

PD: If it was a movie, how extreme would you make it?

PR: As extreme as need be. If I found it was working that way, I would go as far as I could go with it, keeping it believable. That's the other thing. You want to keep it on planet Earth. I always find the moment you do something that is not believable, the audience won't buy it and you've broken that covenant with them. Now they are just waiting for the next hilarious joke. We only had one rule on our show: Could this happen? Not that it would happen that way in real life, but could we believe it was plausible—that it could happen?

JD: Like the Thanksgiving episode of *Everybody Loves Raymond*.

PR: With the tofu turkey. We were experimenting with healthy alternatives because we were all getting fat on the show. On sitcoms, the only sunshine coming in the room is the menu for lunch or dinner when you order whatever you want. You get fat. We were all talking. Tofu was discussed, so that's where that came from. So, yes, it could happen. A writer goes all the way with that and makes a tofu turkey.

Food is such an obsession with everybody. We do it three times a day. It's what we look forward to. Every culture. We identify. In this show about Sam and Molly we're developing, there might be an obsession with Jewish foods. Maybe Molly's parents or Sam are obsessed with it.

Maybe Sam's tie with his grandparents is that his grandmother's a wonderful cook. It was essential in *Everybody Loves Raymond*. It was essential that his wife was a terrible cook and his mother was a great cook. Why would Raymond put up with that mother? Why would he continue to live across the street from that mother? You had to give him a damn good reason. The reason there was that nobody cooks better than she does. You're willing to put up with a lot for that.

PD: Where are some other places in the Molly/Sam premise you would heighten conflict?

PR: It looks like four main characters. Sam, his mother, and his grandparents. To create tension, we could throw in a girlfriend for him. He could get involved with his boss. I'd like her to be the same woman who won't allow him to rise in the company. Maybe he decides that the way to defeat her is to date her. That gives you two areas of conflict to play with. The office. I might play it as a secret that they're together. And then home, where the grandparents and Molly are. Once he bridges the personal gap with his boss, now she can come over. They can't be seen together at the office, but now she can come into the house.

PD: Is she Jewish?

PR: Probably not. My gut reaction is you always want an outsider.

PD: How does she react to this family's Jewishness?

PR: She does what all gentiles do. She reports it to the authorities. She's a stranger in a strange land. Don't hold me to any of this because it's all spitballing. Why not? You go down the road until you can't. I try to jump right in. It's a better way to go than if you fret, worry, and think. Why not start running and see where that goes without pressure? Let's assume your first idea stinks, and let's get that over with. Then you have something on the wall you can address. It's not nothing. You want to start from a believable place. Hopefully, you do it with a sense of humor, thinking of comic possibilities.

"... I don't feel I am good enough yet to write what I don't know."

I get movie scripts to rewrite and I just don't believe them. I think it's a lack of self-confidence, if we are going to be honest. At this point, I don't feel I am good enough yet to write what I don't know. I feel to do my best work I have to be inside the characters' heads. That doesn't mean I can't do a lot of research and get inside. So far, I really haven't had the opportunity to do that. I think we need to bring ourselves into whatever we do to do our best work. That's why my immediate idea was to change it to Sam instead of Sarah, so I can have a way in. It's about making a strong, hard choice and following through and really committing to it. That may be a terrible choice, and may be destined to fail. Once you make your choice, you live with it and go with it.

JD: You come from the theater.

PR: That's all I ever wanted to do. When you're a kid and watch *The Honeymooners*, you don't think there is writing and directing and producing. In my case I saw Art Carney, and started imitating Ed Norton. I wanted to be Ed Norton. That's who I loved. You start seeing other shows and you try out for the school play because that's all you know. My parents were kind of funny. My dad was a tummler [entertainer/master of ceremonies] in the Catskills. He hosted in the evenings. I never saw it. I remember one time seeing him in the city. He got up for a relative and did some shtick. I was so proud of him. I remember thinking I wanted to be up there with him.

PD: Was humor prized in the house?

PR: My parents' laughter encouraged me. If they didn't laugh, I wouldn't be here. My little brother, if I didn't make him laugh, I wouldn't be here. These are the people first and foremost. Then you try out for the school play and other people are laughing. So you think, "Wow, I'm famous. Wow, this is what I'm supposed to do." Then you graduate from college and realize, "Oh, there are others."

PD: How did you get into writing?

PR: Failing as an actor.

PD: Was there a place you learned the structure?

PR: My real school was the years and years and thousands of hours of childhood, adolescence, and young adulthood I wasted in front of the television. It becomes a part of you. You understand it. It's in your makeup, how you think. I can't explain it better than that.

I would have liked to have gone out with girls more. Who's to say I would be in this nice house? I did get a nice girl.

PD: You have an excellent reputation for the room you ran on *Raymond*. How did you structure it to keep the dynamics working?

PR: Well, first you read a ton of scripts. Once your show gets picked up, your home becomes a fire hazard with all the paper that comes to the door. I was stupid enough to say to every agent who called, "Send me your top three people." Oh, my God. I should have said, one person. Scripts were piling up in my house. You read the first ten pages of everything and beyond that, you read all the way through the ones you like—maybe. Then you meet with people. You never know what they are going to be like until you work with them. I was going to call my book, *Everybody's Nice in the Meeting.* You don't really know until you work with them that they're ax murderers. "Oh, you were totally different when I met you. You never really wrote this spec script. I was stupid enough to believe you." That's maybe the number one reason television is lousy. People get through on false credits. It's a dirty secret of show business.

So you find your people. Usually, you're going to take people you worked with before because you know them and you like being in a room with them. You need to be in that room more than your own home. Welcome to your family for good or bad. I pick very, very well, I think. The proof is that 90 percent of the writers on *Raymond* stayed all nine years. We became sickeningly sweet, in that we are bound together forever. I'll never have that again. You hope and pray you get to work at what you love, and with people you love doing it with you.

PD: After you picked the people, you had to do more than that to manage them.

PR: I never ran a show before. I never ran a shoe store before I was a writer. You can be this nebbish who never comes out into the sunshine and never has to talk to people until your show is picked up. Now suddenly, you're the head of a giant corporation. That's literally what's it like. You have to make executive decisions. You suddenly have to understand budgets. You have to understand personalities and manage personalities. If you're not used to doing such a thing, you can stay up all night worrying.

PD: You were in rooms before *Raymond*. You knew a lot of the dynamics.

PR: You know the dynamics, but you're not in charge of the dynamics, and that's a very different thing. You can leave your worries there when you go home. If you're in charge, you can't. I learned from my experiences being on terrible shows what not to do.

Before *Raymond*, I was lucky enough to be in another hit show. One day we got this memo: "We noticed that some of you are putting milk on your cereal when you come in in the morning. The milk is for coffee. The cereal is for snacks. Please do not put milk on your cereal." I remember distinctly thinking, when I got this memo, "If I'm ever lucky enough to have a show, we are going to have milk on the cereal." That's how I ran my show. An army travels on its stomach. The food is the most important thing. If you are working hard, it could be the only nice break in your day. It should be nice. That's how you make a family.

JD: What are the different roles for writers in the room?

PR: It naturally comes to the surface for each individual. Lew Schneider [also interviewed in this book] is maybe the funniest person I know. Lew's role on *Raymond* was room monkey. He'll admit this. When you needed to jump-start something funny, a comic spirit in the room, he would pretend to have sex with the thermostat.

It's essential to have that monkey. I had been the monkey in the rooms I had been in before. You can't do that and pretend to be in charge and be the captain of the ship. Thank God for Lew. He was a better monkey than I ever was. He's absolutely hysterical to the point where you are working now and you have to say, "You must stop. Please put your pants back on and come back to the table because we need you."

DRIVING MISS MOLLY

 An Interview with Lew Schneider

A partial list of Lew Schneider's credits as a writer
include *Everybody Loves Raymond, Less Than Perfect,
The John Laroquette Show, Wish You Were Here,* the *HBO
Comedy Special, Men of a Certain Age,* and
The New Adventures of Old Christine.

Lew Schneider got his start in comedy because he was a good
Jewish boy and listened to his mother. Following in her
footsteps, he attended the University of Pennsylvania. She
suggested that he join Mask and Wig, the famous campus comedy
group. Once he began writing and performing with them, he knew
he was going to become a comedy writer. Along the way he did
some acting and a lot of stand-up comedy, which strengthened his
writing skills. Throughout this interview, his acting and stand-up
background are evident as he uses them to express his original ideas.

❉ ❉ ❉

LS (LEW SCHNEIDER): Everything's coming through the filter of what
I'm working on right now. I'm currently working on this show about
my mother, a sixty-eight-year-old licensed clinical social worker.
So, I feel like you've handed me something similar, in that it skews
older: "Hey, what great old lady characters." All right, but never

mind that. How funny is it? These characters are no better or worse than any other characters. It's how you fill them out.

I get freaked out by the high-concept show. So I would hate it if you'd given me a thing that said, "Now Sarah's an albino welder. She's the best welder in the world, but the proximity to sparks makes her skin glow abnormally." Then I'm like, "Oh, we can only do four shows." So this is okay. You've given me a generic sort of premise. In order for me to jump on this and write this properly, I would have to cast these people in my head.

So I always do it by name. So you have the name, Sarah. You need a couple of character traits, but nothing that you would go, "I know this voice right now." We'd really have to figure out how to get the grandmother and grandfather into the same location with Sarah and her mother, because I think you want to catch Sarah—I think she's your hero—in the middle. And I think if you put her in the middle, you've got plenty of stuff with the grandparents. If she's like these old people, first of all, it makes a young person crazy to find out that they're not like their parents, but like their *grandparents*. Oh my God, that's even worse. And it would highlight how immature her own mother is. So I think I would have Molly be flat broke.

Yeah, what I'm thinking is maybe they are all in California together. I know a guy who's going through this—he realizes that his dad never had anything. His dad gave his brother a car for his graduation, and he wondered why he didn't get one—because there was no money at that time. You know what I mean? There sometimes was money and then you got a car. And this guy's brother got lucky enough to graduate and get the car. His poor wife has her mother-in-law working for her. I would probably steal that idea. I think maybe I'll have the grandparents out here. I think Sarah's the dutiful grandchild. I could buy that she's so efficient and so composed and so steady at her job. Although I'm not seeing how any of these things are funny. All these are unfunny characteristics, unless Sarah is really obsessive.

She's living with her grandparents, or helping her grandparents because she thinks that's what the dutiful child should be doing, and that's what her mother *would* be doing if she lived here. Then when the father dies and Molly is flat broke and she moves here, Sarah realizes, "My mother wouldn't be doing any of this. She's a big screwup." That would be a funny thing, maybe, if what happens is that Molly doesn't move in with Sarah. Molly moves in with her own parents, and Sarah then has to raise her mother, manage that relationship—the mother and grandparent relationship. Sarah thinks now that Molly is here, she'll take care of her parents. "I don't have to baby-sit Nana and Papa." Sarah says, "I can start having as much sex as I want, even though it'll be responsible sex because that's the way I am."

> ### "If we're going to do this as a premise pilot, we're going to introduce our characters. We'll show how the situation came to be.... That's the premise pilot. Networks don't love those."

And then Molly comes out here and doesn't want to deal with her parents. That might be a funny episode. Molly tells Sarah, "I've got an idea about our living situation . . . I'm going to downsize Nana and Papa, and you and I—we're going to switch. You're going to go live in your apartment, that's perfect, and then you and I can live together." I wouldn't do that as a pilot necessarily. There's always that question of *premise pilots*.

JD (JEFFREY DAVIS): What's a premise pilot?

LS: If we're going to do this as a premise pilot, we're going to introduce our characters. We'll show how the situation came to be. In other words, Dad has just died, and we're moving Molly to the Coast. Molly's coming out here, she has no money, and she's going to live with Sarah. That's the premise pilot. Networks don't love those. Seventy percent of the time you don't write a premise pilot, you write a show where Molly is already living with her parents and Sarah has to come and take care of everybody. So the premise is in the backstory.

Here's a funny episode. Say you had Molly living with her ninety-nine-year-old parents. Sarah's grandfather calls, complaining about his daughter. "She's playing her music too loud. She's entertaining men here. She used all our Mrs. Dash. Do you have any Mrs. Dash? Ours is gone. My Stim-U-Dents are gone." "How do you know?" Sarah asks. "I count them." "Why do you count them?" "What else am I doing today?" These are old people. I used to look for a place to put "Stim-U-Dents" in. In an age when many of us are caught in the generation where we have to take care of our parents, the only thing worse than that is taking care of a parent who's supposed to be taking care of her parents. So that might be the show. Sarah, this poor woman who has everything to take care of at work, is then taking care of her mother, who she thought had been taking care of her own father and mother, and never really was. This may be a workable show.

Her parents never had to be parents because she was always so good raising herself, and Molly can say, "You practically raised yourself." I think I could wrap my head around that a little bit. Of course, the grandfather character has to be a virulent racist. Of course, I think that all old people are Jewish. I guess there are some old people who aren't Jewish—some of them are Italian—but Jews are the funniest old people. No one ever says, "I saw the funniest old gentile."

It's a young person whose life was taking care of her grandparents. Her life gets worse when she finds out that she has to take care of her mother, who she thought was going to take care of her own parents—finally. Sarah has a moment when she realizes, "Oh my God, my mother was never a suitable mother, and now she's not a suitable daughter." And the grandparents say, "We could've told you that. We did everything we could with her. But she married well, that's all—and he made a beautiful dollar." "No, he didn't," Molly sets her straight. "You were so smart—went to college on a scholarship. It's a good thing, too. We didn't have any money." "You didn't? I never would've gotten the scholarship if I'd known the pressure was on." Now *that* I think I can write. It's a funny Episode 1. But I don't see this as a series yet. What if there's a lot of planning for funerals? There should be a constant mention of the grandparents' funerals.

Old people are always worried about when they go. They want to make sure all their affairs are in order. So they have their daughter, Molly, help organize their stuff. Good luck! She puts all the money they have into a boat or into a restaurant—a floating restaurant. Sarah sees this and says, "No, no, no. We're not buying a time-share in Darfur." Maybe Molly's redecorating the house. Somebody should break a hip. Got to figure someone breaks a hip. You know what I also like? The old people. I know we've seen this a lot, but there's this funny relationship. Very, very old people don't get along. I had grandparents whose marriage was "iffy" for like sixty-five years. Who knows if they'll even be together? Everybody knew! In a world where soup can't possibly be hot enough, I'm trying to think of other stories.

I guess when Sarah does date men, they can't believe how great Molly is. They just think she's great. "Everyone thinks my mom is great. I want to kill her." "Your mother's so great!" "I know. On paper she's great." I think it's funny that Molly would confide in Sarah like an adolescent. "Look at your grandfather. You know, my parents are impossible." "You're fifty. Your parents can't be impossible." "Do you find me impossible?" "Yes, because you are impossible."

All these are bits. The question is, What are stories? I'm having trouble coming up with stories in this. I guess it would be nice to make Sarah beholden to Molly in some way. Maybe Sarah's boss has a soft spot for her when he sees her dealing with Molly. So he decides that because she's so fantastic at managing *that* situation with Molly and her parents that she *will* get her position as vice president, which only adds more work for Sarah. Maybe the whole reason the boss was unwilling to move Sarah up was that her boss believed, "No one can do this as well as I can." Now Sarah has proven that she really is Superwoman and can do all this. It should always go bad for Sarah. The key for any sitcom is it has to go bad for your hero, and you have to be able to root for your hero. I don't think Sarah can be particularly gorgeous. She should be cute.

I think that the grandparents were very competent in something—they should come from competence, so they would blanch at every attempt Molly makes to fix things. For example, Sarah says, "You should take care of them. They're your parents. You're here now." So maybe Molly tries to do things and the grandparents know better. They were doing just fine. But they have a sense of obligation, and they want to do what's right, so they have Molly move in with them.

Wait, as part of this sense of obligation Sarah's trying to instill in her mother, maybe Molly would have to drive her parents around. She'd have to show up. Oh, wait. That's funny. If these grandparents still drive—they're eighty, and they still drive.

Molly thinks that she's trying to do the responsible thing, and she takes her parents to the motor vehicle place to get them retested. Or there can be a big fight. She thinks they should stop driving, but they say, "*We* drive great. *You* drive poorly." She tries to get them surreptitiously tested, or she tries to videotape their bad driving. So she thinks they're bad drivers. The funny thing is if Molly's a really bad driver. And then you have an eighty-year-old person saying, "Let me drive."

Yeah, Molly's from New York. That's funny. She has to get her license. Molly has to move to California and get a license because, in that eventuality, she's saying, "Someday you won't be able to drive," and the grandfather says, "I'm going to drive my car 'til the day I die."

PD (PETER DESBERG): Who teaches Molly to drive?

LS: Molly's father, of course. That's a much funnier scene. It's always funny to watch a father teach a daughter to drive. It's funny when the father's forty and the daughter's sixteen. It's got to be funnier when the father's eighty and neither one of them can see! Molly's nearsighted. Neither one of them is seeing very well. And the grandmother, she's along for a ride in the back. She's backseat-driving on two people. That's a funny show. We got another story.

Molly's the fly in the ointment. Say she decides she's going to start her new life, and her new life may be, "I'm going to get a master's." Sarah says, "Don't you need a bachelor's?" She's in school and needs a work-study job. Molly appeals to Sarah to give her a work-study job. The more complicated you can make Sarah's life, the better. She's overwhelmed at work, now add her mom being there. She's always refereeing the fights between Molly and the grandparents. Sarah's a woman caught between her mother and her grandparents. She would have to be very upset with these people, and that would be the fun part to watch. Watching her lose her temper—that was the fun part of watching Ralph Kramden—

watching him explode. So watching Sarah's anger would have to be funny, or her sadness would have to be really funny. You have to find a Mary Tyler Moore out there to play this. We can talk about this all day long, but you have to find the right funny people to do this, and then if they're super funny, characters that people love. Some of this writing doesn't have to be so great.

"The [writers'] room's a great break from the writing and the writing's a great break from the room. The two sides serve each other."

PD: What is it like working in a room versus writing a script?

LS: I love the room so much. That was the most fun for me. Let me get my hands on somebody else's crap, and get a few jokes in, and screw around, and that was always great. Then, I found myself dancing down the hallway, after getting notes, going, "I can start writing the script. I don't have to go in that stupid room!" So the answer is, I like both. The room's a great break from the writing and the writing's a great break from the room. The two sides serve each other.

It can also be bad; there can be some comic intimidators. There can be one sort of guy who sits there looking for reasons to hate your stuff. I'll pitch a million things and somebody goes, "How can you have both?" I go, "You can't have both. I just thought they were both funny. Pick the one you like. I don't care. Just pick the one you like." Sometimes I'll pitch a bunch of stuff, and someone will say, "That was great, why didn't you pitch that first?" "I don't know. I just like to talk."

JD: Now that you have all these ideas for Sarah and Molly and the grandparents, what would you do next?

LS: I would get a decent spine for the story, and then I would start writing dialogue and bits of action. And I would write scenes, and then I would realize I would be rewriting that stuff too many times. You have to know the story so well first, and know what each character needs in that scene first, and then the funny stuff will naturally fall on top. You'll be able to layer it. It's like putting icing on the cake. That comedy stuff is all icing. You don't start with the comedy. You certainly don't start with the dialogue. Funny dialogue, that's really the last part of the icing, and before that it's funny behavior that might get comic. And before that it's all the story.

PD: Do you have a good sense of what's funny?

LS: I really try to give other people the benefit of the doubt. "Wait a minute. I'm being judgmental here. Let's listen to this writer and hear what he has to say." I try to see it from his angle. And I find myself not doing it as well in comedy. I sound so cocky, but I'm more sure about me thinking I know the comedy answer and I would get called on it. A friend of mine would say, "Oh, it's funny. Why? Because you say it is?" "Yes." "Why?" "Because I'm the arbiter! Because I know what funny is and everybody else should line up behind me." And then he would yell at me, and you know what? He's right. You hate to analyze. As soon as you start analyzing comedy, it becomes very dry and unfunny.

PD: You've done stand-up. Do you think that makes a difference?

LS: I used to think that stand-up guys were going to be the funniest. But that's wrong, because most stand-ups stink. But then I found that the stand-up guys were just as funny on the page, so it was, "Oh, you know what, there's no right or wrong answer." Anybody can be funny. Often, you pick up a script, and you go, "Holy smokes, this is hilarious. Who wrote that?" And it's the guy who's not talking—the quietest person. Everybody has a different process.

One of my favorite things in the comedy room is sitting next to the quiet people. First of all, I'm proud of myself when I don't interrupt and can keep myself quiet for a few minutes. I'm thrilled and I can hear somebody else, and there's a good joke—I love it. I also love it when someone pitches something, almost under his breath. I just think it's hilarious, but the room didn't hear it. So I'll say, "Pitch that again." And he'll ask me to pitch it for him. And I would pitch it and they would laugh, and I'd say, "That's great. It was his." Then they would tell me to shut up. What's so gratifying about that experience is, first of all, that means someone thinks enough of your skills to have you pitch something of his that he considers dear to him. If the idea tanks, he knows you'll fight for it, because you already were a champion of the idea. You'll go, "I thought it was funny. Okay, you guys don't want to use it. That's fine."

The idea of spending eight hours a day in a room with these people—it's the most gratifying experience. You're screwing around so much. Everyone's looking to laugh, whether it's about the script, or somebody else, because you're just trying to break the monotony until lunch comes. *Raymond* was the greatest group of writers I've ever come in contact with. I always compare it to summer camp. That room—that felt like camp. We kept our group together for nine years.

PD: What did you study at U of Penn?

LS: I was a history major. But I really majored in a group called Mask and Wig. My mother went to Penn, and she said these guys are the funniest guys on campus. I joined my junior year and got heavily involved. It was a great experience. In college, it's rare to do a show every weekend because it feels like a professional job. You have exams. That's too bad. You have to do this show. My grades went up during that time because, the more you're doing, the more you get done. So after college, I knew I was not going to become a lawyer. I was going to do comedy.

In Mask and Wig, you had to write two different shows a year, and one of them was done thirty or forty times; the other one was done twelve times. But you had to write the material and that was like a room, too. You wrote it with other guys in the show. It was mostly scenes, and there was a lot of editing. You could've learned a little more about writing for character and about writing, about not doing all the jokes. We never cut a joke. We did all the jokes every time.

Then I went to Chicago. I had a director who said, "You should go with Second City." So I went out there to take classes and I never auditioned for the group because it was in 1985, and they needed stand-up comedians. It was like the Army. They needed you as long as you didn't have flat feet and could do five minutes. You got to go on a mission. So I worked with some great guys in Chicago, and they took me out on the road as their opening act pretty quickly after I started doing stand-up. And then I was an actor and I got a couple of shows. I went to New York first and did a lot of stand-up there, and then came out here. And when the acting dried up, my writing staff buddies—guys who'd been on shows that I was an actor on—said, "You should write. If I get a show, I'll hire you." I didn't realize what a magnanimous thing that was.

A PLOT, A PLOT, B PLOT

An Interview with Sherwood and Lloyd Schwartz

A partial list of Sherwood and Lloyd Schwartz's credits
as creators and writers include *Gilligan's Island*,
The Brady Bunch, The Adventures of Ozzie & Harriet,
Love American Style, Alice, and *The Munsters.*

Sherwood and Lloyd Schwartz are one of the rare father-and-son comedy writing teams. Watching them work together, and seeing their mutual respect, was very uplifting for us as the parents of teenagers ourselves. Then you realize that this is where *The Brady Bunch* and *Gilligan's Island* came from. Most teenagers have no idea, or interest, in what their parents do and are totally clueless about their grandparents. What made the interview even more interesting to us is that Lloyd's sixteen-year-old son sat through the entire interview in the background, clearly impressed by what his father and grandfather were able to create within a very short time. Lloyd and Sherwood have evolved a successful system of working together in a way that enhances both their personal and professional lives.

�֍ ✖ ✖

LS (LLOYD SCHWARTZ): When we were doing our shows, people would come in with a premise. We'd listen to it, and then we'd say, "You know, we saw something like that on *My Three Sons*," and we'd say no to it. Now, when somebody comes in with an idea, the network says, "Yes, that's perfect because we saw that on another show."

SS (SHERWOOD SCHWARTZ): If I have any fame or glory, it's that the two shows I did [*The Brady Bunch* and *Gilligan's Island*] had nothing to do with anything that had ever been on before.

LS: If you look in *Variety* or the *Hollywood Reporter*, it always says, "This is a *Brady Bunch*–type show." Or "This is *Gilligan's Island* set on the moon."

SS: I didn't write two shows. I wrote two type shows that now everybody compares. If you want disassociated people brought together, that's *Gilligan's Island*.

LS: Somebody actually told me about a thing called, "A Sherwood." They teach this in a New York film school. It's an outline format using the way that he developed an episode. It's the plot, the subplot, and the act break. They hand this out as a form that you fill in. It was named after him, and he didn't even know about it.

SS: It was the form I used to give to writers to discuss their story, and tell them to fit it into that plot line.

LS: So it's A Plot, A Plot, B Plot, and they come together; and you see that to the extreme in a *Seinfeld* episode, where things are so outlandish and then they always come together somehow. But we always managed to do that. It always ends up with everybody at a square dance.

This premise lends itself to a verbal show. That would be three-camera. One-camera shows are much more physical. The thing that's missing is the specificity of what Sarah does for a living because we're going to travel with her. And then you have a mother who's going to get involved in messing up her business life as well as her personal life. We would see her meddling. You'd have subplots of the mother somehow getting involved in the business Sarah's involved in.

What I would probably want to do is figure out an ethnic thing here, either in terms of whether she's Jewish, or not Jewish, or black, or not black.

SS: I think that's good.

LS: You want the mother black, and the daughter . . .

SS: No, I don't want it to be that good! No, I think they should be whatever they are, which is mostly whites and blacks separately, for the moment.

What about the grandparents? What if one of them were dead?

LS: Ghosts? You want ghosts of the grandmother and grandfather in this?

SS: We could do that. Don't pass it up.

LS: But ghosts don't have strong work ethics.

SS: They go through walls. They're terrific people.

LS: You know that work ethic thing can sometimes skip a generation. It's like talent. Sometimes we skip a generation [Lloyd turns to Sherwood, smiling]. I don't mean that personally. So here's what we've got. Molly's parents had a strong work ethic, and Molly's husband who died, had a lot of money and spent it, right? So now you have Sarah, who's also got a strong work ethic.

SS: And Molly, apparently, didn't have such a strong work ethic.

Probably she was a big spendthrift. Meanwhile, the husband was out trying to make good money.

LS: So they're both responsible for the financial situation. They were obsessed with appearances. He made it, they spent it.

SS: Yeah, now we should figure out what business Sarah's in.

LS: I think one of the neat things is that so many people who are parents of young people starting off today have no concept of some of the kinds of businesses their children are in. Sarah might get involved in some kind of high-tech business that Molly would not understand. It's like you and the computer. You know how you can't even scroll up or down.

SS: Look, I still work with a pencil. I need to graduate to a fountain pen.

LS: So Sarah is doing very well. I see a scene where Molly says, "I'm not going to be any problem," and the doorbell rings and the moving men move all her things in. So you have some physical humor right at the top.

SS: I think that's a great idea for an opening scene because she arrives unexpectedly with a change in the dates and the daughter isn't even expecting her that day. And all her stuff starts to arrive with the moving man.

LS: That's right, and Molly's directing everything. When kids go to college, they gain independence, and then when college is over, if they move back, it's not like what they want it to be. They move back and the parents now resume telling them what to do. But they've already tasted independence. Sarah's at the stage where she's done with her parents. She's got her own life; she's got her own boyfriend.

The boyfriend stays over sometimes. Well, my God, he has to stay over when the mother is there. So in the first episode, it would probably deal with all that stuff coming back, and then hiding the fact that the boyfriend sometimes stays over.

SS: Well, if her mother's furniture arrives, that's one element of the story. The other element is her boyfriend arriving. So you've got these two clashes.

An "A" story and a "B" story.

LS: This is like your Uncle Bob. This happened seventy years ago. His uncle married a non-Jewish girl. They kept it from the family. Then, finally, their kid was about to be Bar Mitzvahed.

SS: They had to invite their families. And they didn't even know he was married. Oh, that was so funny. One of the sisters was very Jewish. The other brothers and sisters, and the mother and father had to keep the news from her. And I happened to be in New Jersey, on a visit, when they had to break the news to this woman. They knew she was going to either collapse or grab a knife and commit suicide. And I was there when they said, "Look, a lot of things happened here and I'm just going to tell you everything right now. Bob is married to a non-Jewish girl and their son is about to have a Bar Mitzvah."

And she said, "Oh, is that right?" and went on with her conversation. For thirteen years they'd been hiding that fact from her.

LS: So how this story could apply here is that after the furniture's in there and Molly's telling everyone what to do, Sarah goes to her grandparents and says, "What do I do about my mother?" They say, "That's not your biggest problem. Your biggest problem is that your boyfriend stays over." At the end we find out that Molly did the exact same thing with her boyfriend. She was a little bit ahead of her time. So I think that's kind of the overall shape.

ss: Yeah, the only thing missing so far is what Sarah does for a living. Let's go back to that.

LS: Whatever it is, it ought to be something Molly is not used to. So I'm saying it's a more of a high-tech area.

ss: The ad agency business is a foreign business to most people.

LS: I don't think it's a mother-daughter relationship show. I think it's Sarah's show. Television is based on the idea that you don't change brands over the age of thirty-five or forty-five. So all television has to be skewed to the people that are under that age. The truth of the matter is that people over forty-five are the baby boom generation, who change brands in a second. That's the age that has all the money and that watches television. So just looking at selling this premise to network television, I would have it all focus on Sarah, with the influence of the Molly character. At Sarah's job, there is a guy running the business who could develop some kind of relationship with Molly. He could be some kind of a possible suitor who she finds attractive.

ss: So he's an older gentleman.

LS: Maybe he founded the ad agency, and there's a similarity between him and Molly. We have Sarah's boyfriend, maybe as a continuing bit, where Molly never knows that he's there. Sarah sneaks him in and out. I think that's very today. So the people she would explain that to are her grandparents, who are simpatico. It's that skip-generation thing with Sarah. They're the people she can confide that in.

SS: Yeah, I think it's good so far. I'm just searching, as I always do, for stories. The magic of the *Brady Bunch*, which made it different from all other shows and made the writing easier, is you not only had sibling rivalry, which other shows had, since it's two different families, and there are children from each family, you had cross-sibling rivalry. And the two youngest kids are rivals, so there were sixty ways to go for stories, instead of the traditional twenty. So that kept it alive and made it an icon for new shows that came along with different family relationships that weren't traditional.

JD (JEFFREY DAVIS): So you were always looking down the road to see how many stories you could get?

SS: Yes, absolutely.

JD: What would you do to "Sherwood and Lloyd-ize" this premise?

LS: One of the things networks don't like are dream sequences. I would love to have a parallel universe using skipping generations, showing the grandparents at a younger age. We could go into sepia tones for that in the grandparents' story. This is something that people are always advised not to do, and I always try to do it.

In the sepia sequences, Molly would be the same age as Sarah is in the present.

SS: I love the idea—sepia tone—with Molly and Sarah as a little girl, shown in a previous generation.

LS: Yeah, I'd do that. Also, that makes Sarah's father alive for those sequences.

SS: So it wouldn't be a ghost. This would make him a real person, but only in sepia.

LS: Does he get less? Do we have to pay him less?

SS: Let me just say a very important word—*impact*. Why is this show different from all other shows? That's impact. If you tune in to a show, you should know instantly what that show's about, even if you don't like it. When you see seven castaways on an island, you immediately know that's *Gilligan's Island*. Now like it or hate it, you know what that show is, and most people liked it—fortunately.

LS: *Gilligan's Island* was just raked over the coals when it first came out. Now we read articles that talk about the "acclaimed *Gilligan's Island*." This has to do with the identity he's talking about, where just—boom—you know what it is. If you see most of the shows that we're talking about, with the heavyset father and the beautiful wife, you don't know what show that is.

SS: Let me tell you what the impact was on *The Brady Bunch*. That staircase! Impact! When you see *that* staircase, you know that that's *The Brady Bunch*. It doesn't look like any other room, no other staircase with a thundering herd. You know how often the kids came down that staircase? Very, very seldom, because you couldn't use kids like that all the time.

The recognition factor of this show will be the word *sepia*. It will be on no other show. The word *sepia* indicates two different generations. It will be the same as the kids running down the stairs.

LS: We have often been the first people to do something. We were the first people to do a movie on videotape. The first ones to have the kids sing the title song. None of those things, including this "sepia" device, is done for the purpose of being different. It is all done for the purpose of what's right for the show.

SS: Sepia, don't forget, will just be a small section out of twenty-two minutes—maybe a minute and twenty to thirty seconds. But that will be an identification factor.

JD: How involved were you in the two Shelley Long *Brady Bunch* films?

LS: I produced them. That was interesting. I wish there'd been some article somewhere that gave us a little bit of credit for being the first people to satirize our own work.

PD (PETER DESBERG): How did you work on that?

"You couldn't just string a bunch of episodes together and call it a movie. That's stupid."

LS: It was a brutal experience. Paramount said they wanted to do a *Brady Bunch* movie. Dad and I discussed how there was no movie; there were six kids and a house. Unless we did it as a satire.

SS: You couldn't just string a bunch of episodes together and call it a movie. That's stupid.

LS: We went back to Paramount and we said we'll do the movie, but it has to be a satire. And Paramount said, "We don't care," because they just thought *The Brady Bunch* would be enough.

SS: They didn't understand that a name is not a show.

LS: So we wrote a movie and it got a green light. Brandon Tartikoff was running the studio, and gave us a green light. We were ready to make the movie and excited about it. And then he was deposed as president of the studio. The new president comes in, and refuses to read our script. I said, "Could they at least read the coverage? [Coverage is a summary report of the contents of a script or project with an evaluation of its viability.] It says how funny it is." All right, so they bring in two other writers, they rewrite it, and they do a brutal satire. We wrote an affectionate satire for people who loved *The Brady Bunch*. The fans would laugh at it, and for people who didn't like *The Brady Bunch*, they'd laugh at it, too. These writers had all the girls as prostitutes.

SS: Three girls, my three girls—all prostitutes.

LS: Then they green-light *that* script.

SS: And they're not living in that house; they're living in a slum in Hollywood.

LS: So we said, "Okay, we recognize you own the copyright, you could do this movie. However, we, as individuals . . .

SS: This is a direct threat from me to Paramount.

LS: However, we, as individuals, have the right to go on every talk show advising people not to see this movie, which we were going to do immediately. So then, all the notes we'd given to those people were accepted, switching it all back to what you saw, which was this affectionate satire. We don't do that very often. But the line was in the sand and we had to do it. We made a lot more money for Paramount than we got out of it. We're involved in the *Gilligan* feature. We have certain guidelines for that, and we've had to take stands against people who want to do it in a certain way.

SS: It's hard to take stands, because studios promise you things. "If you'll do it our way, we'll somehow inject your ideas into future episodes, you'll get what you want." And it's all bullshit. Because they're just trying to get their way, and if you let them do it their way, it's going to fail.

JD: How do the two of you work together?

SS: Lloyd writes first drafts quickly off the top of his head. I don't do that. I write much more slowly.

LS: More carefully, too.

SS: We adopted a technique as we were writing. He does a first draft.

LS: We spend a couple of days talking.

SS: . . . with a yellow sheet with the stripes.

LS: We do a broad-strokes outline. And then we agree on it. And then I go away and write my rough draft.

SS: I don't like to call it a *rough draft*. Until I'm into the seventh draft, I haven't even started to write the script. Anyway, he gives me what he's got.

LS: Then he does a draft.

SS: It's not too careful, but it's a lot more careful than his, because his is just the thought process. Mine is more a *considered* thought process. And then we just go back and forth several times.

LS: And then we usually take his, and then we sit down and agree, and then that would be our first draft. We started one time—I think it was when we were doing the movie called *Rough Draft*—and we started to write it together and I don't think we lasted a day. We stopped speaking. It was awful.

PD: How did you get into joke writing?

SS: I needed money. I was here taking a master's degree in biology. My master's thesis is here.

LS: It's not a big seller.

ss: Only two copies were made, and one of them didn't sell.

ls: The musical rights are available.

ss: I grew up loving a book called *Microbe Hunters*. That's really what influenced my life. It was about the great humanitarian doctors who were guys, like Dr. Banting, who discovered the islets of Langerhans. He was the one who discovered their relationship to diabetes and the effect it has on your body. I wanted to become an endocrinologist. And instead I wrote for Bob Hope.

ls: His brother Al was a Hope writer.

ss: I came out of school with a master's degree in biological sciences at USC. I stayed with my brother, Al, who had gotten a job writing the *Bob Hope Radio Show* in 1938. I was in the house hearing Al and the other writers and it didn't seem to me to be very hard to write jokes. So I said to my brother, "If I write some jokes and you give them to Bob, maybe I can get $5 or $10 a joke."

In those years, for $10 you could eat like a king for a whole week. So I wrote some jokes and he gave them to Bob, and they got big laughs. And after two or three weeks of that Bob said, "Why don't you come work on the show as a regular writer because you write very funny jokes." So I said, "Well, I'm supposed to be going to medical school." He was a really nice man, Bob. You hear a lot of stories about famous people, but to me he was really nice. He said, "Why don't we draw up a contract for seven years. If you don't get into medical school, you'll have a job as a writer." And that's what happened.

Yeah, now most of the time a comedian, if you leave him, he will hate you. If he fires you, he will hire you back any time. It's traditional. It was that way with Henny Youngman, or Ed Gardner, or any of the old comics. They love you and they will hire you back if you love them; but if you don't love them, which is indicated by the fact that you have left them in the lurch, then you are banned for life. When I left Bob, it was the most difficult meeting I ever had in my life. I was drafted from *The Bob Hope Show* and I spent four years in the Army writing *Command Performance* and *Mail Call*, a lot of comedy shows for the Army, during which time I used Bob on some of these shows. So we remained friends.

But after the war was over, I didn't want to go back to writing those same kinds of jokes again. I went to work for *The Adventures of Ozzie & Harriet* after the war because I wanted to do story shows. So I had to explain that to him, and not have him hate me. We were in his dressing room at NBC and I said, "I know you expect me to come back." He said, "Of course." I said, "Well, that's what makes this tough because I really don't want to go back to writing the same kind of material." In the Army, I had written story shows with important stars like Clark Gable, and other stars of that magnitude, and they were good; they were comedy, but they were stories. So I said, "I hope I can explain it so you understand it, Bob." He was very nice and remained my friend.

I think it was his 90th birthday—some big hotel, it was on Sunset. It was a combined event: It was Bob and George Burns. Burns was 96 and Bob was only 90. The two of them were up on the stage at the same time and they hugged each other. It was a moment I'll never forget. These two giants. They hugged each other, and one of them said, "Do you realize we have a 186 years of comedy between us?

PD: Was writing for Bob Hope like going to school?

SS: I wrote a script. Everybody wrote a script. And Bob was a master of knowing what he could do, and he would take these different scripts and put them together somehow. So he had a choice every week of six scripts. He worked just as hard as we did on the scripts in those years.

JD: Lloyd, how did you get into this with Sherwood?

SS: He started at the bottom. He was on the stage with *The Brady Bunch*. He read scripts with them.

LS: I had done a summer job on the show he did—*It's About Time*, with Imogene Coca as a dialogue coach. And then he created *The Brady Bunch*, and I was going to graduate school at UCLA and he said he wanted me to be a dialogue coach for the show with these six kids, and I said, "No, I don't think so." I was a comedian at the time; my partner was a Black Panther. I wrote for *Love American Style*. And I said, "You're just giving me that job because I'm your son and I don't want that." And he said, "Well, who should be a dialogue coach for this show? I've got these six kids on there." I said, "Well, you should get somebody who works with kids." And he said, "Well, you ran a summer camp," and I go, "Well, yeah, I did that, okay." And I said, "You should get somebody with an English degree." "Well, you've got a bachelor's in English."

SS: I was describing you.

JD: You let him think it was his idea!

SS: I always do that, I truly do.

LS: That's right, and then he gave me more and more, and we never talked about it really. Yeah, but I didn't know if he had to take anybody on to say, "Hey, no, he's doing it," we never discussed that. And then by the end of the third year I was directing episodes. And then I produced and then since that time we have been just about executive producer on everything together.

"Writer/directors fall in love with what they've written . . ."

JD: Did you direct episodes of *The Brady Bunch* and *Gilligan's Island?*

SS: I never directed anything. I think it's wonderful to write and produce. I don't think it's wonderful to write and direct. I think you need a different kind of guiding influence after the script, and it's not producing—it's directing. And that's a separate form. Writer/ directors fall in love with what they've written and find ways to direct it.

LS: We're talking television. In movies I think the writer/director is a valuable animal, but on TV I think it's better being a producer.

JD: How do you feel about staff writers?

SS: I never used them. The danger is that a show can go to hell because everybody wants to get his joke in, whether it fits or not, or else he'll be fired. So people expand the script with bad jokes just to stay alive.

LS: Dad says, "A show is really only good if you erase all the names of the characters and you can look at it and know who says what."

SS: That was my test of every joke. Erase the name of who delivered it. No one else could say that line. There was no line where you had to say the Professor or Gilligan or the Skipper said it. That's why the show has lived as long as it has.

JEWS DON'T SQUARE DANCE

👉 **An Interview with Marc Sheffler and Paul Chitlik**

A partial list of Marc Sheffler and Paul Chitlik's credits as writers include *Who's the Boss?*, *Perfect Strangers*, *The Happy Days Reunion Show*, *The Twilight Zone*, *Harry and the Hendersons*, *Charles in Charge*, and *Small Wonder*.

Our role changes from interview to interview. In this interview, our biggest challenge was to realize that we weren't necessary. The creativity that flowed between Marc and Paul made us want to jump in and contribute; we wanted to play along with them. They made it look so easy. This team proves that a mark of professionals is economy of motion. They are playful, innovative, and free, yet they always pay attention to structure. They jump freely from content to process issues without missing a beat. The results are original and funny. A few weeks after this interview, Paul called and said they were going to use some of the material they dreamed up here in their work.

❈ ❈ ❈

PC (PAUL CHITLIK): Sarah's parents live on the East Coast? Okay, we just moved them to Palm Springs.

MS (MARK SHEFFLER): Sarah's parents are swingers.

PC: Big swingers. They go to square dances. Square dancers are among the biggest swingers in the country. They square dance and after the square dance they pair off and they f--k their brains out. There is more venereal disease among square dancers than there is in punk rock. My ex-girlfriend's mother, when her husband dropped dead, started to square dance and she just became a nymphomaniac.

MS: Because we all know how erotic it is.

PC: Well, have you ever heard of it? No. So it might be interesting to do for this show.

MS: "Dance of the Seven Veils" and the "Three Barn Doors"?

PC: Well, they've got plenty of places to go, the barns, with all the animal smells.

MS: The animals would be like, "Look at these idiots."

PC: "What are they doing?" You don't see a lot of Latinos square dancing.

MS: No, it's a very white thing. You don't see a lot of Jews doing it, either.

PC: One thing I learned when I was a producer is that you always have to have an answer. It doesn't have to be good. So the protagonist is Sarah and she's got a workplace and a home.

MS: There don't seem to be enough complications for her. What if Sarah's at a point in her life when everything is settled and all hell breaks loose? Just when you think you have it figured out, the world throws you a curveball.

PC: She thought she was going to be the vice president of this company, but she doesn't get promoted. What kind of company is it? Let's figure that out, too. Let's not set it in Los Angeles. Let's set it in Phoenix. It's hot, they've got a lot of retirement . . .

MS: . . . a hundred thousand miles of kitty litter . . . I don't know Phoenix.

PC: My brother lives in Phoenix. That's where he goes to Harley-Davidson Mechanics School. Maybe she works for Harley-Davidson . . .

MS: . . . or a motorcycle repair shop.

PC: Why would Sarah work at a motorcycle repair shop?

MS: Not a repair shop. A manufacturing company.

PC: Okay, it's a manufacturing company. So she's dealing with a lot of macho types.

MS: She's the only woman.

PC: She's the only woman in the place. Okay, there's the conflict right there.

MS: Run by a former Hells Angel.

PC: Okay, that's good, we're on track here.

MS: Sarah's the only one in the room who never killed anyone.

PC: She's the only one who doesn't know a thing about engines.

MS: The only one who doesn't have to report to a parole officer.

PC: Molly lives with her. Does she ride a bike? Some of these older people buy Harleys and they ride them. But I don't think so. Molly's against her daughter working there. How did Sarah get this job?

MS: Ex-boyfriend. A bad boy.

PC: Right, every woman loves a bad boy. So, she got the bad boy and then the bad boy got arrested and then that was the end of him. But she likes the job because she likes the hum of the Harley.

MS: Right. She's the financial brains behind the company. She's turned it around . . .

PC: . . . because it was floundering . . .

MS: . . . It existed only to transport meth.

PC: It was a front for the drugs because outside of Phoenix is like outside of San Bernardino. You know what; let's set it outside San Bernardino because that's where they have the best meth labs in the country.

MS: And you know this how?

PC: I just told you, my brother is a Harley-Davidson motorcycle mechanic.

MS: And they have a class in meth-making?

PC: It's big, it's huge. It doesn't really matter. San Bernardino or Phoenix.

MS: It matters because you're close to Los Angeles, closer to things we're familiar with.

PC: So San Bernardino's good. It started off as meth running with a bunch of motorcycles. All those guys got arrested and they ended up with a bunch of motorcycles.

MS: There's a concept. Make motorcycles and sell them. Wait a second. What if she's a court-appointed receiver?

PC: That's interesting. All right, go on.

MS: So she shows up on orders from the court.

PC: With orders to sell everything. She goes through the books and realizes . . .

MS: . . . that this thing could turn a profit. This could actually be a business.

PC: Okay, so she talks the guy into it and he says, "Okay, you run it." So she's running this business with nothing but Hells Angels and former meth runners and mechanics.

MS: And these are all macho guys, you know, women are objects used to sitting in the back of the motorcycle, getting the second hit on the pipe.

PC: So how does she control these guys? How does she whip them into shape? Withholding drugs?

MS: No, they're all recovering. If they're all straightened out, they're not funny anymore. That's rule number one. If we do this normally, they're not funny.

PC: So they're not normal? So let's create some of the characters. So we've got one mechanic.

MS: Blind.

PC: He can tune it by the sound.

MS: A blind mechanic.

PC: He can feel when the piston is rough.

MS: Totally by feel.

PC: Totally by feel. Okay, that's funny. He can't see himself in the mirror.

MS: He needs other people to dress him.

PC: For sport, he's got a wife.

MS: Every morning she dresses him like an idiot and tells him how good he looks.

PC: "You look so handsome today, honey."

MS: In fact, it could be funny if somebody gets a phone call and all you hear are, "Uh-huh, khaki pants, blue shirt, brown shoes, uh-huh. Got it." The guy walks in and he's dressed like Bozo the Clown. And the wife cheats on him in front of him.

PC: She likes the danger of almost getting caught. Okay, but what challenges does he present to Sarah at work?

MS: Nothing, but I think there's an antagonist who opposes her.

PC: The owner?

MS: I don't think so. Let's take the legal side of it. She came up with the idea that it could actually make money and she petitioned the court. She said, "Give me a year to turn it around."

PC: "Just don't shut it down."

MS: "A lot of people work here. Closing it is not good for the community. There are some real reasons why it should stay open."

PC: Okay, it makes sense now. Who is against that?

MS: There would be somebody who wants the space.

PC: A landlord. The landlord doesn't get his full rent.

MS: Yeah, and it's somebody on the outside paying somebody on the inside to f--k things up.

PC: Well, let's do both. Let's make the landlord's son a mechanic there.

MS: I think this is a place that employs parolees. Let's get a little dark with it. Everybody's got a dark criminal background of some sort.

PC: I was just thinking the criminals sit around asking, "What are you in for?" "Murder." "What are you in for?" "I slit the throats of three guys I robbed." "What are you in for?" "Tax evasion." Something that's like, "I didn't pay the fine on my . . ."

MS: . . . you don't get paroled for spitting. You can pay a fine. I think these are hard-ass guys who are in for drugs and . . .

PC: . . . gang-banging. This is a dark comedy.

MS: Sarah has to walk into hell. It's got to be primal. And she's got to be the opposite.

PC: She wears the suit. She wears high heels. She goes into this place. Everybody's dressed like gangbangers.

MS: . . . they don't work, they just hang out. It's like a big warehouse . . .

PC: . . . with a bunch of parts and motorcycles all over the place. There's a frame over here. There's a couple of wheels. There's a tank. There's probably about thirty motorcycles there if you assembled them. How does she motivate these guys to work? And who's paying them?

MS: That's the thing. If there was money in the bank from the meth business . . .

PC: . . . which they can't use.

MS: Sarah talks the court into releasing the funds so she can disperse them, but only for the business. How does she motivate these guys? I don't think she knows.

PC: She has to find out. That's her challenge—to figure out how to get these guys to do stuff.

MS: I think that she's one of those people who goes along in life and kind of copes and doesn't ever do anything spectacular or ever do anything other than maintain. And without even realizing it, she's put herself into a situation where in a very short amount of time she has to succeed or fail. It's a new feeling for her.

PC: So why does Sarah take a chance for the first time in her life?

MS: Why does she take a chance? She has to. Bringing that personal thing in, that thing with her mother.

PC: On her salary, Sarah can't afford to keep Molly in her own place.

MS: On her salary, she's stuck with her mother.

PC: But if she makes more money, she can get away from her mother. Is that enough?

MS: No. Okay, let's go back to basics. Sarah's brother is successful. She has a successful sister. She's the one in her family who's never done anything. And her mother is all over her about that.

PC: Yeah, but her mother wouldn't be staying with her if that was the case.

MS: Yeah, but she's the only one her mother can control. The other ones are successful and don't give a sh-t.

PC: But her mother could go live with the siblings.

MS: No. They have the money and the money gives them the power and Sarah has no money and no power. They always go after the weakest one.

PC: Like in the wild.

MS: The mother is a predator.

PC: Another issue is that the father died suddenly and he had a false front and he left them with a lot of debt.

MS: . . . which Molly tries to put on Sarah because she's a predator. She's got three children and Sarah's the weakest of the three.

PC: It could also be that maybe the father owned the condo that the daughter lived in and had borrowed up to the hilt.

MS: Yeah, that could be. I'm just trying to come up with the reason why she takes the chance and has to succeed.

PC: She's a court-appointed . . .

MS: . . . yeah, she's an accountant . . . a numbers cruncher, a bean counter.

PC: She's only, what . . . twenty-eight?

MS: Twenty-eight, twenty-nine. Master's degree in business administration. Accountant.

PC: CPA.

MS: CPA. Boring. Has no life except simple math.

PC: So was there a fiancé, a boyfriend? What?

MS: Nothing. Zero.

PC: The first guy she ever falls in love with is one of the guys in the shop.

MS: Bad boy. She finds herself strangely attracted to a bad boy. Clearly a man who never had a Bar Mitzvah.

PC: He was one of the chief runners. And maybe he's on parole or maybe he's the only one not on parole. Maybe he never got caught. Maybe he was always smart enough to get out of whatever it was. I don't want to make him too bad. Maybe he's the opposite.

MS: She has to do this to prove to Molly and herself that she's more than a bean counter.

PC: And that she's also an individual, that she's separated from her mother.

MS: The thing is, we're searching for the emotional through-line of this story. One of the things you learn about good situation comedy—and I learned from the masters—it's got to be somebody's story. And that journey has got to be that person's journey. And she has to go from here to there.

PC: Sarah's father ran a motorcycle factory—that's what everybody thought. But as it turned out, her father was the meth-runner. And the motorcycle factory was nothing. And when her father dies, she goes to close down the factory and finds there's nothing to sell off.

MS: No, I don't like it and I'll tell you why. I like her. If her father ran a factory, there's some preexisting knowledge. It's too much of a blind for her *not* to know something.

I like her walking into a strange environment. I like that fish-out-of-water thing. She comes into something that she thinks is one thing and then—surprise! Let's look at the structure of a story. You got this factory and all these whack-jobs running around. A blind guy who dresses funny and whose wife cheats in front of him. So you do a couple of minutes of that, just to establish where we are. They're all sitting around doing nothing. Sarah comes in and they're dressed like Hells Angels and she's dressed like a bean counter, and she announces to everyone who she is. "I'm here from the court. I'm not going to be here long. I'm just here to liquidate."

PC: What if the guys go into the office and say, "You can't do this. I'll lose my job. I have a family to support. They'll put me back into prison if I don't have a job." And the next person comes in and says, "I have a family to support . . ." It's the exact same speech.

MS: Exactly. No, and he says, "I've got a family to support. I've got three . . ."

PC: ". . . four children."

MS: "And I will go back to doing hard drugs." Then a parole officer . . .

PC: The parole officer comes in and . . .

MS: . . . he's the romantic interest. He's the guy. So that's who becomes her love interest.

PC: So she's got to keep him happy. She wants to keep him coming back.

MS: You remember that episode of *Seinfeld* where George was collecting unemployment and the woman had a daughter. And in order to be friends with this woman, George went out with her daughter. Well, this girl should be a hidden beauty. This parole officer hits on her and she's so unused to guys hitting on her that she has no idea what it is, okay?

PC: Sarah knows she feels pretty good after he leaves. So who does she call to tell that to?

MS: She's got to have a friend.

PC: I don't want it to be the "gay" best friend. Let's have another best friend. Is she a single woman? Or is she married or does she have a boyfriend? I'm thinking she would like a parole officer.

MS: Maybe it's a girl who is the opposite of her. A party girl? A flight attendant?

PC: How would they get along?

MS: A flight attendant who's in and out of town.

PC: That might be how they get along. She's in town for just a little bit.

MS: A friend from college. An old college roommate, just somebody she hangs with. Somebody she talks to. We'll worry about that later because we know we're going to do that.

Okay, so the crisis is . . .

PC: . . . that's what makes us want to stay there. It's not about fixing the factory. It's the guy. Is that enough?

MS: It's enough for the beginning. So what happens is she's in this thing and she's got all these rough characters and he's the wrangler for these guys.

PC: And when do we see Molly? Only when Sarah goes home?

MS: The mom is . . .

PC: . . . Molly's gone. We don't need no stinking mom. Now we've got the basic emotional incident.

PD (PETER DESBERG): It was interesting watching you guys start. It was like watching musicians warming up by playing scales. You were fooling around making jokes.

MS: Oh yeah, that gets you warm.

PC: You just have to completely open it up to let it flow all in and around.

MS: We all knew kids when we were younger who were funny at parties. It's a whole different ball game when you have to do it on a button, do it on command, and you develop over the years a mechanism for beginning that process. When I first started writing on shows, I had to learn, "Okay, they're paying me a lot of money. They expect me to perform and I can't say I don't feel it right now. I have to find that place inside of me where it exists and develop a system to access it at will." There have been times in my life when I've overdeveloped it.

PC: But you develop as you work more and more in comedy. You develop a certain way of approaching things and you know what's important in a comedy. The number one thing is the conflict. And the number two thing is the emotional through-line.

MS: Every writing team has a different process because it's so out of the box just to do that thinking about what you do, but you have an ultimate goal. Sam Denoff [writer on *The Dick Van Dyke Show* and co-creator of *That Girl*] taught me this a long time ago. When any comedy writing team is doing it right, if somebody else reads the script it looks as if one person wrote it. It's not schizophrenic. You could put one name on it and it could be plausible that it was written by one person. When you have two strong personalities—two adults with a tremendous amount of experience—that's a lofty goal. So we worked out quickly how to do that. And if this were a project that

Paul and I were really doing, at this point I'd leave and Paul would get at the computer.

PC: I'd write up the first draft the roughest possible way. Just to get the tone of the story. And then I'd send it to Marc.

MS: E-mail it to me.

PC: And then he would rewrite it and we would go back and forth fifteen or twenty times until we got it to where we wanted it to be.

MS: We find a time in the daytime when I've completed my work and he's seen it. He prints it out. I have a copy of it. We meet. We go over the notes. And then I go to sleep and then he does his draft. He e-mails it to me. I get up. I pull it off the computer. I do mine and we continue that process back and forth and back and forth until there's nothing about what I send him he wants to correct and there's nothing about what he sent me I want to correct. And that's how we know we're finished.

PC: About how many times did we do that with *Whitley Grove?*

MS: Thirty times, maybe.

PC: This was just a pilot. For the pilot, we gave each draft a letter. We went through the whole alphabet twice up to Q. So it's *Whitley Grove*, Draft I, QQ. Sometimes that's just proofreading. I have thirty or forty drafts of *Whitley Grove* on my computer. And that's our process.

PD: How would you guys describe yourselves?

PC: I'm more of a structural guy, and I'm always looking for the emotional content. Marc is very quick with a joke and very good with character.

MS: I think that we're like two kids flying a balloon—a helium balloon. Paul is the kid holding the string and I'm the balloon. You know, we're both there to have fun, but we need each other to make the experience work. Paul provides grounding and a rooting for whatever it is we're doing and I provide the opposite.

PC: I'll just say to Marc sometimes, "You know we need a joke here. And he'll go, "Uh-huh," and then he'll deliver the joke.

MS: I see things in images and pictures, and Paul sees things in structures and words. I see things completely, especially now that I'm directing. I'll see everything in images and pictures. And then we kind of meld together and make it words.

PD: Paul came up with structural ideas in several places and Marc came up with jokes.

MS: Mostly that's my area. I have a background in stand-up comedy, so being funny instantly on my feet is just a reflex reaction for me.

PC: One that's gotten you into a bit of trouble from time to time.

MS: Oh, yeah. At the nadir of my first marriage, my wife decided she was a lesbian. She announced it one day in a marriage counseling session where she began to volcanically explain what she was feeling. So we get back home and our marriage is over and she couldn't even look at me. So I turned to her and I said, "Hey, I got a question for you. Now that you're out of the closet, could you still be in the hallway?" And she looked at me, and she said, "This is all a big joke for you, isn't it?" And I said, "Well, I'm a comedy writer and this is a horrible event. I mean, what do you expect?"

And then I went off and did like twenty lines. I said, "Hey, now that you're like this, when you go shopping in West Hollywood, do they give you a discount?" It was like line after line after line. Clearly, it was pain and anxiety that was producing this. And it was the pain and the anxiety that was being filtered through the prism of my personality. It was coming out as jokes. Where some men would have screamed at them, or worst-case scenario, smacked them around, I pummeled her with jokes. She didn't laugh much. She got upset that I wasn't respecting her. She said, "You'd better behave yourself because I've already been to the Gay and Lesbian Legal Defense Fund and I've got a lawyer." And I said, "Hold on, I'm just a regular guy heterosexual."

JD (JEFFREY DAVIS): You've both been in writers' rooms.

PC: Oh, God, I hate writers' rooms. The problem is there are two kinds of writers' rooms. There's the smart writers' room and the stupid writers' room. The smart writers' room is run by an executive producer who understands that he's not the smartest guy in the room and not necessarily the funniest guy in the room. He's open to listening to other ideas. Then there's the guy who thinks he's the king of the world and if he thinks he's the king of the world, the politics of the room are going to be terrible. You've heard the saying, The fish rots from the head down? It's awful when the king of the room is like that because you can't be funny in a room like that.

MS: The thing about running a room is that if you're running the room, you don't always have to be right; you just have to know what *right* is.

JD (JEFFREY DAVIS): What's the difference between writing drama and writing comedy?

PC: I was on *The Twilight Zone*. It was a lot less stress. It's a lot easier to write a dramatic program. First of all, there's no late-night rewriting. You have your dramatic ending and you move on. So you don't have to sit for fifteen minutes trying to think of that joke. I can write drama completely on my own. Comedy? I feel that I write much better if I have a partner because I need somebody to work off, to see if it's funny. Stuff that I think is funny might not necessarily be funny, as Marc will tell you.

PD: What were you doing before stand-up?

MS: I had no life. I came to Los Angeles, having sold a movie of the week to NBC. So I came here surfing on that wave. Suddenly I had a ton of cash and I was living in Los Angeles on credit. And then I got an agent and I did stand-up, not because I wanted to be a comedian, but to perfect my ability to pick up women.

So I hung out. The guys I started with are Jay Leno and David Letterman and Tom Dreesen, Robin Williams, Billy Crystal. These are all guys I hung with and still know. I had an agent who was working for me getting me writing jobs and I was doing stand-up and I never had any formal training in writing other than watching a zillion shows and understanding the structure on an unconscious level. I didn't know what anything was called, but I knew that I could bullshit my way through a story because I knew how the stories evolved. And I learned the names for everything. I just knew it belonged here or you had to do this here because this is how it worked. I kept my mouth shut long enough and pretended that I knew what I was talking about until I actually knew what I was talking about.

PD: Do you think people have a tendency to start writing too soon?

MS: Writing is a developmental process. You have an idea and it grows. It is a life form that gestates. And often the energy of a young, inexperienced writer makes him sit down and stare at the page and say, "I've got this great idea. Why can't I write it?" Well, because you're not ready to write it. You have to know your material and you have to know when it's ready to write. And I always know when it's ready to write when I've got so many nonlinear notes about what it is that I have to *now* write. I can't make any more notes. I have to see what it looks like. And I don't rush that process. It's very intimate. If you don't get intimate with your work, you end up writing very thin material.

PC: You really have to think about who your characters are, what the conflicts are. Well, we do that in the projects that we've written together. We talk about who the people are.

MS: What I do is, I carry a notebook with me wherever I go. The creative process is nonlinear and astructural. So what I do is this: I know movies are written in three acts. So let's say it's a movie I'm working on. I think of moments that I think are in this story. And it doesn't matter to me how I think of them or in what order. I fill up a seventy-page, spiral-bound notebook. And when that notebook is finished, I open my computer and I go, "This belongs in Act I. This belongs in Act II. This belongs in Act III." And then I put it into the computer. I put all the Act Is together, I put all the Act IIs, I put all the Act IIIs together. And then I say, "This comes before this. This goes here. I don't need this." And suddenly—without thinking about it, without forcing myself, without pressuring myself—I have an outline.

And once I have that outline, it's a chip shot. Then I just get a draft. I put myself in a movie seat, in a theater watching a screen, and challenge myself to entertain myself. How would I tell this story? What would make me really dig it?

PC: It's all about the story and the people. You just have to have a story to tell.

JD: Can you come up with stories like this on demand?

PC: In my early years, I wrote for Reuters. I had a 4:00 p.m. deadline. Not a 4:01 p.m. deadline. So if I didn't have my stuff ready by four o'clock, that was the end of my job. Every day I just started writing about the subject, whatever it was I had to write. I just had to write about it until I found out where I was going.

MS: It's like lifting weights. You develop muscles. I wasn't even awake. You have to give yourself permission to explore.

PC: To go outside the structure.

MS: To be nonlinear. Putting things in order is the easiest part of it. The hardest part is coming up with those moments of magic.

PC: And try to keep yourself structural and at the same time magical because they work at cross-purposes. Let yourself go. Be free.

"The goal of any writing team is to create something that looks like it was written by one person."

PD: You guys also have a real good sense of each other's strengths.

MS: That's why I'm directing now, because once it gets through the script stage, I'll take it from here.

PC: We have a movie we're doing together. He'll be directing and I'll be producing, and that's the way it's going to be. But as for the writing, which is where it all starts, yeah, that's mutual respect and that's also because it's the product that's important.

MS: The goal of any writing team is to create something that looks like it was written by one person. Because whatever we finish up with is the best of Paul and the best of me. And Paul's the judge of what's the best of me and I'm the judge of him. So I give up control of certain things to him and he gives up control of certain things to me. And at the end of the day, we always have something finished that we both like.

HOW MUCH DO YOU TIP A CAB DRIVER ON THE WAY TO YOUR SUICIDE?

 An Interview with Elliot Schoenman

A partial list of Elliot Schoenman's credits as a show runner and writer include *Home Improvement*, *Maude*, *The Cosby Show*, and *Cheers*.

Some young science types sit in a room and come out years later having proven math theorems or understanding the laws of thermodynamics. Young science guy Elliot Schoenman watched tons of sitcoms in his room and emerged understanding how to write them. Shortly after leaving his room, he had the good fortune to begin his writing career working with the legendary Norman Lear on *Maude*. He says working with the Lear writers was like going to graduate school in comedy writing. It was certainly a long way from trigonometry.

There is a structure in the brain called the corpus callosum that connects the left and right hemispheres. Elliot's must be burning on all eight cylinders. His work is a wonderful balance of left-brain logic and right-brain creativity. He develops the premise, bringing tremendous discipline to story structure while at the same time demonstrating an uncanny instinct for finding authentic humor in real life, often with dramatic situations, which makes his writing both moving and funny.

⊠ ⊠ ⊠

ES (ELLIOT SCHOENMAN): What I'm writing about now is the father/son relationship, because I have my book coming out about tracking down my father. So my own instinct would be immediately to change the premise to a father/son story.

I come out of the Norman Lear School. I'm interested in finding some kind of social significance in anything, even if it's minor. I would look for an undercurrent in this. Maybe make it into a play, although it might work as a series. It just seems like we've seen this "when a parent moves in" situation a million times. I'm not sure how you would do the frivolous spending of the money if it was a guy, although it would still work. He loses his wife—he's been frivolous—or a father/daughter thing, which I know less about.

The thing that interests me most is the father dying suddenly. My book is about my father's suicide when I was eighteen. There is some humor. More and more I'm learning about how to mix the two. My father was a stockbroker, and he left his office on Sixtieth Street, took a cab, went to the Hudson River, and jumped in. My sister and I duplicated the trip. We took the cab. And you know, I'm writing about it in my book and describing it, and you can't get a heavier moment. It suddenly occurs to me: My father's a German who was notoriously cheap. What did the guy tip a cab driver on the way to his suicide? I wrote that in the book, and thought, "Do I put that in? Does it break the moment?" But it's really what I thought about.

So what interests me, too, is finding out more about who Molly's husband was. I like the concept of the mother, and subsequently the daughter, finding out more about the father and this whole existence being disrupted. That's where I would take it, whether it was a mother and daughter, or father and son, or mixing the two.

If Sarah's father died suddenly, and you did it as a sitcom, there's no way in the world they're going to let Molly be the main character. It doesn't matter if it's a man or a woman—the parent is a fifty-year-old. So it's going to be about the daughter. So you're restricted right away. Do I want the mother's life to be turned upside down by finding out about the father's having an affair with one of her friends, or do I want Sarah to find out more about her father's affair herself?

One of the major things I learned from my days working with the *Maude* writers is to go for the character and go for the story and not worry about the comedy. It was very hard running shows, not so much on *Cosby*, but on *Home Improvement*, to get people comfortable with that concept. You've got to get the story right. A lot of writers fall in love with jokes, and they'll bend a story to keep them in. Sitcom people tend to hold onto the joke at all costs, and one of the things that was interesting is, we would have a reading of the script on a Monday, and a lot of times it would read really well, really funny, really interesting halfway through, and then it would take this tremendous dive.

I would ask young writers, if the comedy isn't that much worse in the second half, how is it possible that there are no laughs in the whole second half? It's because we lost the audience. So we fixed the story, and it took a lot to get used to it. Let's get the story right, and we're not going to go out of our way to make it funny, and during the week we'll find the humor.

Nowadays, with something like this premise you've given me, my instinct would be, forget the comedy. I can't write without comedy. You can go as far as going to your father's place where he committed suicide and without forcing it, there is humor.

My cousin Leona is a stunning blonde, who is older than I am. We all grew up in the Bronx near Yankee Stadium, and my father was a German immigrant. We were very embarrassed by this family who didn't know anything about baseball; the whole neighborhood was all Yankee fans. I was telling this to a cousin of mine I hadn't seen in years. She said, "You know about my affair with Mickey Mantle?" It turns out that my cousin had a three-year affair with Mickey Mantle, from the triple-crown years—'56 through '58. I said, "Do you want me to reveal this?" and she said, "Sure." Once she got involved with Mantle, she became friendly with all the players and she would invite them over on the off-days.

I said, "My father was schmoozing with the Yankees. And he knew about Mantle?" She said, "Absolutely. Everybody knew." And she said, "I wish you knew. I would've taken you to the clubhouse." And when I thought about my father, my reaction literally was, killing himself is one thing, but not telling me about Mantle?

That's my idea of good comedy because it's not a joke. That's your thought at the moment. So I would pursue something like this in our story, or almost anything from the standpoint of, What's an interesting story? What can we relate to as an audience?

JD (JEFFREY DAVIS): Would you talk a little bit about Sarah discovering the circumstances of her father's death? How would that play out?

ES: I think it would be interesting to start in the past and see the relationship. If you had complete freedom of amounts of people and sets, I would say it'd be interesting to see the dynamic when Sarah was a teenager with her mother and dad. We'd see how her family acted around the dinner table, and what job her father had. You say he was successful. I love color, so I would look for an unusual profession where somebody makes a lot of money, but I want to make the job unique. Another cousin of mine invented a new jar lid for mayonnaise that used a rubber top. There was the person who invented White Out. I'm tired of everyone using the same old professions. Every film you see is about a writer or about an advertising executive. I've had a butcher as one character, another guy who worked for the Sanitation Department. I think you're better off with just regular old people. So I would look for an interesting background. I would establish them kind of on the way up.

PD (PETER DESBERG): As you pick an occupation for him, would you link that to the character?

ES: Yeah, I would try to. Going by my instinct, when you read something like this you tend to think of the silver-haired, fancy executive. My own instincts take me more to a guy who made it in the garment center. I think a self-made guy is a more interesting character. It's my own background from observing New York characters. I would make it a guy who is self-made, and is proud of himself, and has his own characteristics. I always equate it to real people. This wife might live through her husband, but they have an understanding. She spends a lot of money.

And the other thing I would immediately go to is, Are there siblings? Does Sarah have brothers and sisters? How does that affect the dynamic of this? Is there an age difference in the siblings? I would look to more and more fill it out. I also think that in the premise Sarah doesn't really have anybody to talk to. I would make it a sibling and look for territory within that.

To me, it's the puzzle, and I'm constantly moving stuff around in this treatment. "This is too soon" or "I've already said this; the audience already knows this." The other thing I've learned through playwriting, which is different than television, is the audience knows a lot more than you give them credit for, and there's nothing like watching the audience, and saying, "All right, they get it. The boat's sailed, keep moving." What do you need and what don't you need? The most fun part of the process is the laying out of the pieces.

JD: Would you lay out a few of the pieces of the puzzle?

ES: First of all, I'm not that interested in Sarah's work situation. My eye is drawn to the piece of information in the premise you've given me about how Sarah has a great relationship with her parents. I would take "great" with a grain of salt. What would interest me is a starting point of some family dinner to establish the past and the family dynamic. Maybe here it all looks like the perfect family. Let's keep it a young woman for now. We'll start with Sarah at fifteen. Then I would flash-forward to another scene where Sarah's in a marriage. They're having some sort of problem, maybe about money. And it's here that she gets the call from her mother saying her father has died.

I think it would be interesting to break it to Sarah that there was more to the story of her parents' marriage than Sarah knows. The audience would find out at the same time as she does. My instinct is Molly and her husband were a terrific couple at the beginning. Sarah's talking to her husband about whatever issue they're dealing with, and she gets the call from her mother. "Dad died," and it's surprisingly unemotional, and she doesn't get it. It turns out there's more to the story and Molly's pissed at him. "Mother, the guy died. How could you be angry with him?" Molly says, "Because he died doesn't mean he didn't do this." I think that's an interesting scene.

What happened? He died two days ago. Molly got a call from a jewelry store. They called because he never came in to pick up a bracelet. Molly went in to pick it up and it's inscribed to another woman. Maybe this brings out Molly's eccentricity. Sarah asks,

"When did he die?" "Molly says, 'Three days ago." "You didn't call me?" "Well, there's been a lot going on." This gives Molly a new color. She didn't call her daughter.

Where Sarah's dad died, what the circumstances were could lead to a delay and another complication. When Sarah hangs up, the young husband says, "What happened?" "My father died." "You don't seem very shaken up." "I'm trying to process the whole thing." Now does her husband know the mother? Has he met the mother? Maybe it's kind of interesting if he hasn't met the mother and he's magnanimous about it; maybe they've been together four months, and they're on the upswing. "You don't know my mother." "Let her come," he says. It might be interesting that he talks her into it, not knowing what he's getting into and then Sarah initially adjusts better than her husband.

My wife could have her mother move in and deal with it. The last thing in the world I could do is have *my* mother move in. There's just no drama in somebody who has an easy time with it. So I'd make the financial circumstances force Molly to move in with Sarah.

If my wife and I were in a different financial situation, I wouldn't let my mother move in, even if I had to put her in a doghouse. I just wouldn't do it. Linda would want her mother to move in, and it would cause a tremendous amount of tension between us. And within that, obviously, is comedy. First, I look for the dramatic tension and find the comedy off that. If these people are struggling financially, if I'm the husband, and it's my wife moving her mother in, I'd probably give up almost anything to raise the money to get her somewhere else.

So I think there's humor within that, and if they were struggling, or upwardly mobile, I mean, what would you be willing to do to get rid of your mother-in-law, and how much would you hide it? Would you take an extra job, which would give you more income and get you out of the house? The emotion drives you to dramatic beats and comedy beats.

Maybe Molly is okay when she first comes. But again, I like surprises. You expect her to have a tough time with her mother; maybe she doesn't. It's the husband who has the tough time. That's the kind of beginning I would go to. Whether any of that is anything that's any good, who knows? I would look for opportunities and openings. What gives you possibilities? What haven't you seen? Again, how to make credible that it's been three days since he died. I like the concept of it. In reality, it's pretty unlikely, so to tackle an interesting idea, or make it credible, really pushes you as a writer. Maybe you can or maybe you can't. And you have to be open to not falling in love with that idea. If you can pull it off, it is interesting. It's an interesting dynamic between Molly and Sarah, who says, "It didn't occur to you to call me?" You can also play up Molly's self-involvement because if she immediately discovered that Sarah and her husband/boyfriend were not in great financial shape, and she's broke, she'd think, "Where does that leave me?" You could go the other way: Molly was left a lot of money by her husband but does she want to give it to Sarah?

Next, I ask questions related to Molly coming to live with her daughter and son-in-law. How big is the apartment? Is it an apartment? Is it a house? Is it a condo? Is it Sarah's? Is her husband just moving in with her? Is it his place? All those things, to me, are the choices, and the kind of stuff I didn't think of when I was doing sitcoms, thinking from all the points of view.

How uptight is the mother about moving in? If he's not a husband, but a boyfriend, does Molly know that he's living there? Is he really living there? Are they dating? Is he kind of living there? How conservative or liberal is she? Who are his parents? Is he a

Republican? Is Molly an aging hippie? Without hitting the audience over the head, what are the variations on those themes?

What I would do is this: I would just list these things. What's a plot point? Potentially, what's a character trait? What's a line you might use? And I tend to lay it out in sections and take the best guess I can, and treat it literally like a puzzle. I have a degree in math and physics and I went to graduate school in math. So I have this very unusual background of organization. People are always saying, "What a wasted background," but it's actually very helpful with plotting.

PD: So you approach writing like an engineer?

ES: I didn't know I did that, and I didn't notice anything unusual. I actually didn't know that other people didn't do it and I'm always kind of amazed by how disorganized some writers are. I actually hired one writer who I'd lay out a plot with, and she'd come back with these insane tangents. The only way I could get her to stop and think is that I brought her Brio trains. They're like little wooden train sets that the kids used to have. I got her a piece of Brio train track where it's a straight track with a little curve that goes off. I got a little stop sign, and I put it on her desk. I put the stop sign half off, half on the little curve and I said, "Every time you come up with a beat, whether we gave it to you or not, I want you to think, "Am I going this way [Elliot indicates a straight line], or am I going this way [Elliot indicates a curved line]? If you even *suspect* you're going this way [Elliot indicates a curved line again], look at that little stop sign and come into my office." And that's the kind of thing that tells you maybe you're going the wrong way. To me, the biggest part is what ultimately is your best guess about the right way to tell a good story. I kept on people about this. "It doesn't matter how good a chunk you came up with." They'd be polishing and polishing and you can't get them to bring the f--king script in. You may be polishing stuff that's in the scene that we're not going to use.

PD: You closed the circle for me when you said you had a math/science background. A lot of the writers we've spoken to say, "You've got to get conflict." You used the word *puzzle*. You look at it like a problem-solving situation for the audience.

ES: The story's everything. The beginning and end are really easy because the beginning is whatever you came up with as your premise, and the end is either a happy or a sad ending.

PD: The story's got to be logical and credible, but there has to be something in there that's puzzling.

ES: Right. Therein lies the problem, and therein lies the creativity. It's a very fine line. I think everybody has to relate to what you're saying, and yet within that you have to surprise them. I discovered that you need to have a good combination of the familiar and the surprising, and what that proportion is, who knows? But there's got to be some familiarity in a really good story.

What's so amazing about the stupidity of television is, I was known as a very good show runner who could do stories, but it became the mark against me at the networks: "Is the guy funny enough?"

I certainly can write comedy, but it wasn't my priority. Running a staff is like running a baseball team. You have to manage the whole thing. When you're also around better comedy writers, your comedy becomes better. Just like I think and hope when comedy people are around somebody like me, their story skills get better. When Marley Sims [his collaborator on *Home Improvement*, whose interview is also in this book] and I wrote together, she learned a lot from my story sense. But when it comes to dialogue, things come out of her mouth that are just unbelievable. When I'm writing with her, my dialogue becomes better.

JD: You talked about being influenced by Norman Lear. Can you give us an example?

ES: On *Home Improvement* we were the number one show and I kept trying to integrate an occasional serious episode about the family and I got Tim onboard. Marley and I wrote a script. I pitched an idea to the network. The idea was twenty-four hours in the life of a family where your kid has this serious medical testing and may have cancer, and what that twenty-four hours is like. And they just went crazy against it, even though we had the power to do it. And they said, "You can't do a cancer episode." And we said, "Well Jonathan Taylor Thomas and Tim will do it." What was tricky was the network's reluctance. They said, "Where's the humor?" I said, "I don't know yet, this is a tricky one. I understand that it's hard, but you just have to trust it. It may have to be found during the week and the original table reading may not have much of it. But that's what we want to do."

So I said to Tim, "This is one time you have to throw your weight around." He was onboard and we did it. It came in number one. It was the last time the show came in number one. And sure enough, ABC called and said, "What else do you have? What other serious things?" They were thinking of doing the *tragedy of the week*. It was unbelievable. But, even within the cancer thing, we found humor.

PD: That kind of tension relief, when you get it, is huge.

ES: Absolutely. As a matter of fact, we did a really a crazy trick. At the beginning before they go up to the doctor's appointment, there's a lemon meringue pie, and Tim's wife says to Tim, "Don't eat that no matter what, because we're taking it to my sister's." So she goes, and he looks around and he takes a spatula, and he cuts off the top, lifts it, and scoops out a whole chunk of the lemon, and then he puts the top back. And we just left it in. Then she comes back and they break this news about how their kid may have cancer and there's a really heavy scene between the two of them, and she's gone crazy, and we really distracted the audience. And at the very end, she says, "I don't know what I'm going to do with myself. I've got to have a piece of the pie." And he panics. And she digs into the pie, and there's no bottom to it. And it got this tremendous laugh.

We found this gimmick where we really weren't cheating on cancer jokes, but the audience got it, and they forgot completely about the pie; it's just sitting there. You're worried about cancer. But once she went for that fork, there was a tremendous relief, and that really took some chicanery. And that came with building these two end pieces to it. So it's all these little odds and ends and that wasn't a dishonest moment. It's tough. It doesn't always work.

JD: Were the people in your family funny?

ES: Not really. I think my humor developed as a defense mechanism. My father was a terrifying character. I locked myself in my room and watched sitcoms. I had no idea that I'd learned this. When I got on *Maude* and I was so overwhelmed, Schiller and Weiskopf used to take me out to lunch. We used to go to the Brown Derby and Farmer's Market. They would tell stories about *I Love Lucy* episodes. They had done a lot of the *Lucy* shows. And I used to say, "No, no, no, Fred Mertz was in the other room when that happened." And they kept saying, "Are you sure?" And I'd say, "I'm positive." "Yeah, I think you're right." I kept correcting them, and I realized—and they realized—that I'd learned the craft without knowing it. I'd watched so many shows that I really knew how to do this.

I got in trouble with them once because I was desperate on a *Maude* show and I stole a line from *The Honeymooners*. I gave them the script. Rod Parker was the producer and he said, "Boy, I really like what you did, especially that joke from *The Honeymooners* that I originally wrote."

PD: You had figured out the rules for comedy writing by yourself, and all of a sudden you are thrown in with these comedy giants. Did you learn much from them?

ES: Yeah, it was like going to graduate school in comedy. And at that time, there were a handful of us who were very lucky. There were basically three schools of comedy working: There were the Lear shows, the MTM shows, and the Garry Marshall shows. And they were all different kinds of levels of how you did things, but there was a lot of mentoring and these guys really took it seriously about teaching you the craft.

I was twenty-six years old when I got job writing on *Maude*. I'd only watched the show twice; there were no tape machines to be had so you couldn't get all their tapes. I read some scripts. But we were at CBS and we were across the hall from *All in the Family*. In those days, there were only four writers on a show, so you did a ton of work. But the *All in the Family* staff and the *Maude* staff were all at least fifty-two years old and I was only twenty-six. So I got this incredible thrown-in-the-water experience of how you write and what you're doing. It was sink or swim and the guys who I worked with, Bob Schiller and Bob Weiskopf, were my mentors.

Anyway, we were across the hall from *All in the Family*, and I noticed right away that we had much later nights than they did. I couldn't figure it out. I asked Schiller and Weiskopf what it was and they said it was because they have these dumb characters. Archie could do a *malaprop*, Edith could do a *dingbat* thing back to him, or they could do a *Meathead* joke, and because it was two in the morning, they could get out of there with an old, cheap joke that would work for their audience. And it's also why, on *Cheers*, they had Coach and Woody. I learned this as a trick.

I'm not saying in the middle of the night I wouldn't go to that formula, because on *Home Improvement* we certainly had the ability to do a dumb joke and when you're in trouble on a show like that, it's the handiest thing in the world, and I'll do it, but I wouldn't do it by choice. On *Maude* there were no shortcuts. The audience was always oriented toward some great *Maude* high-end, clever line, and the only shortcut was, "God will get you for that," which Bea Arthur would say. But you could only use that four times a year.

But what I also learned, which was a sitcom trap, is that everything was written for *her*. The other characters—even though talented actors played them—weren't really developed. You didn't write scenes from other characters' points of view. And that's the real sitcom trap. When we did *Home Improvement*, we always wrote for each character. What I've been learning with the playwriting and screenplays is to see scenes from everybody's point of view.

I once said to Schiller and Weiskopf, "How can I ever thank you guys for what you've taught me?" Weiskopf said, "Just pass the craft on." And that's one of the reasons I love doing theater and nurturing young writers, because it's a very terrific situation. But they taught me everything: They taught me all the crazy terminology. It was so funny at the beginning. I was sitting there totally intimidated, and I'd be laying out my story with them, and they'd say, "All right, just stick in a House Number for now." I had no idea what a House Number was. And I'd be asking everybody, I'd go across the hall, "Can you do me a favor and tell me what a House Number is?" A House Number comes from the garment center.

In the garment center, they used to say, "I've got a beautiful shoe for you, but I don't have it in stock. It's the heel of this one, the sole of this one, and it'll have this color." And that's how they put together a sample. And somehow it got into the comedy vernacular. A House Number is just the kind of joke you *would* put in, but it isn't the joke because maybe you haven't found it yet. At *Home Improvement,* I came up with the offshoot, a "House Laugh," which is something that we laugh at, but nobody else in the world is going to find funny.

PD: How do you know when you write something funny?

ES: It's in your bones. Somebody once said to me, "How come when we're working together, you go to lunch and you have some unbelievable adventure every time? I go to lunch and *have a sandwich.*" "It's just the way I see it." I learned that my descriptions were funny, and you just kind of have the confidence, and it's a crapshoot because sometimes you're right and sometimes you're wrong. You're running a show and people pitch things. It's your judgment to say, "This is funny. This isn't funny."

PD: Would an example of a joke that doesn't violate the character or the story be, "How much do you tip a guy on the way to commit suicide?"

ES: To me, that's an intelligent joke because you've set it up and you don't see it coming. I really tried over the years to learn how to do things where you don't see it coming. That's the other thing on a lot of sitcoms: You just see it coming a mile away.

Yeah, the hardest thing on a sitcom is dealing with the punch-up guys. They drive you crazy. "Oh, it's funny, it's funny, it's funny!" And you have to really be very delicate about how you reject them. There was a guy on *Maude,* let's call him Bill. Bill was a stutterer.

Bill could write brilliant jokes, but some of his were terrible jokes. Schiller said to me, "Watch this," he said. "If he says it without stuttering, it's a great line. If he stutters, even though he thinks it's a great line, it isn't a great line." There was some deep part of him that must've known. But then he'd fight for it and nobody wanted to insult him and say, "But you stuttered the line."

I learned so much from those guys. Like I said, it was graduate school, only they paid me. The other terminology I learned from the Lear school is the *turnaround joke*, which is, "There's no way he's going to show up." *Ding-dong.* So it's that kind of thing. He also called it the *ding-dong joke*. Again, very cheap laughs—you see it all the time, cutaways to that. "A hundred percent I'm not going for Chinese food." *Cut to the Chinese restaurant.* A hundred percent of the time it'll get you a laugh from the general audience. There's a million variations on the turnaround joke. You would have a hard time during my era finding a turnaround joke in *Home Improvement*, even when it was late at night, because I hate that more than anything—it's just so easy.

FROM THE WRITERS' TABLE
TO THE KITCHEN TABLE

 An Interview with Cheri and Bill Steinkellner

A partial list of Cheri and Bill Steinkellner's credits as show
runners, writers, and creators includes *Cheers*, *The Jeffersons*,
Who's the Boss?, *Teacher's Pet*, *Benson*, *Hope & Gloria*,
The Facts of Life, and *Family Ties*, and they currently write
books for stage musicals, including *Sister Act*.

Writers are usually most at ease behind a desk. The
Steinkellners are most comfortable around the antique
oval table in their spacious kitchen. The setting is
perfect, since Cheri and Bill Steinkellner are all about family.
Picture Cheri seated behind the keyboard of her Mac while Bill
paces the length of the room, offering us coffee and assorted
treats. This multiple Emmy Award—winning team, whose
marriage has been running as long as their partnership, start
developing the premise with a simple newspaper article: Go
directly to using what they know best—their family. They blend
in some wonderfully funny stories about their kids and themselves
and mix them together to create an imaginative and contemporary
story.

As they work, the maid, the gardener, and a FedEx guy come
and go. The Steinkellners never break stride. They work together

with fondness and respect, with a little teasing mixed in. As you read this interview you'll get the feeling that this is how they've always worked together. In fact, for us the magic of this particular interview is that it's impossible to tell where the partnership ends and the marriage begins, or the other way around.

⊠ ⊠ ⊠

CS (CHERI STEINKELLNER): Billy just cut out an article on helicopter moms. I'm sending it to our son to show him, "Hey, see, I'm not that bad."

BS (BILL STEINKELLNER): You're a low-flying helicopter mom.

CS: No, I'm high-flying. I'm not hovering.

"I really do think that with baby boomers, this phenomenon of watching over our children well into adulthood in a very hands-on way is pretty interesting."

BS: Oh, you're not hovering, no, no. That's an interesting idea. Let's go with that.

CS: It's a new phenomenon that hasn't yet been overexplored. I really do think that with baby boomers, this phenomenon of watching over our children well into adulthood in a very hands-on way is pretty interesting.

BS: It would be really difficult for you if your mom could just do everything. You're just starting out. Your friends adore her.

CS: It's like me!

BS: Yeah, like you. I was pitching you.

CS: I got that! I always have to stop myself because I'll just want to come in and sit and talk with my kids' friends because they're so interesting, fun, and lively. I have to remind myself to be age-appropriate and developmentally appropriate.

BS: When we took our son to college, all the parents were supposed to leave at one point, leave the kids alone, and say, "Good-bye, good-bye." So we say, "Good-bye," and then we go back just to fix a few things in the dorm room, and Cheri's lugging things in, and she's moved the bed out and is moving things out. All the other parents have already left.

CS: I'll explain that and you'll understand. Our son had a power strip with all the plugs right next to where his pillow was, and I just thought that the electromagnetic field was just not going to be healthful. I thought, "I really needed to move it a little bit away from him."

BS: If Molly did that, it would be funny. She would extend it just a little bit because some people might find it funny that he had an electromagnetic field near his head.

CS: Yeah, unless he gets brain cancer. Then who's laughing? I request that our children speak on the speakerphone instead of holding it by their ear and getting brain cancer. They have good brains and I don't want them to get cancer.

BS: Don't color me as the one who lets them have brain cancer because that would be wrong.

CS: I'm trying to think. *The Gilmore Girls* covered the whole, "We're mother and daughter, but we're really the same age and we really have the same problems. We're just like sisters, even though we're mother and daughter" thing. They did every possible permutation

of that. But I think the idea of *really* overparenting is usually
something that's relegated to a side dish. It's usually someone like
Holland Taylor (the mother on *Two and a Half Men*), over on the
side making acerbic comments, and coming in all glam.

BS: I think I'd change the daughter to a son.

CS: I think maybe I'd give Molly two kids. Or three.

"Certainly it's a fun pilot where the kids are so worried about Molly, and she's basically Auntie Mame."

BS: There's really something about this because it would take it away
from *The Gilmore Girls*. This way the kids actually have the mother
present where they have to deal with her. And maybe some kids see
her as extremely valuable. And the thing is, when we were at Stanford,
you really got the sense that these parents love their children, and
these kids love their parents. You didn't get the feeling like, "Oh,
thank God they're gone" from the kids or "I couldn't wait to get away"
from any of the parents. You know the parents work really hard. They
just didn't check in on the kid every five years and go, "How're you
doing?" And then they end up at a good university. I think there're a
lot of people probably out there who would watch this.

CS: Certainly it's a fun pilot where the kids are so worried about
Molly, and she's basically Auntie Mame. She's so irrepressible that
it's like, "Oh my God, back off, Mom." I think it's probably a good
idea to have a younger generation just because for television you
need to have young, pretty people and their funny friends.

BS: You'd have to figure out how she was able to be there.

CS: What if she's left widowed or divorced? It's probably funnier if she's divorced.

BS: Because she's available.

CS: It's probably funnier. If her husband walks out on her, you can bring him back and have lots of good stories. Okay, so let's say her husband leaves her. So Molly is starting life anew. The kids are on their own. *Mother Is a Freshman*. Have they done that since 1948?

BS: They may not have.

CS: But it's so common now. We know someone who was going to UCLA. She was going back for her MFA, but she was an acting student, so she was getting *all* the roles. She was sewing up all the age-appropriate roles. The kids were a little pissed. What if Molly's kids were already at UCLA, just because we know UCLA. She's got two or three children. It's a Bruin family, and the mom just sort of lands there, because she's grief-stricken.

BS: There's your act break. The last kid is moving out.

CS: Her son?

BS: Yeah, her son. And he sits her down for the big talk. "You have to find your own life now. I know it's going to be difficult."

CS: Oh, she's helping him move into his dorm at college?

BS: Yeah, yeah. "It's going to be difficult, but you go out there." She says, "You're right, you're right! Thank you." And then you come back from the act break and she's enrolled.

CS: She's made friends in the dorm. She's the housemother. It could work if he's the last one to leave, and Molly's just been left with an empty nest. The kids are all really worried about her. She's just had this blow from Dad dropping her for a senator at the beginning of the summer, and now they've all been hovering around her, taking care of her. Now they've got to go back to school, and Molly is helping her son move in and she says. "I'm not going back. I'm selling the house." You could definitely do it in an organic way. Although she wouldn't be able to get into school right away, she could come in as a "winter admit." There are so many ways in, if she's really lively, friendly, and funny.

BS: Like you.

CS: Does this mean I can go to Stanford with our son?

BS: You know what, it's actually possible to be permanently embarrassed. If your mother did that, you would have a flush on your face all day long.

CS: Our daughter would love it.

BS: Our son would hate it.

CS: But you could have the siblings at different levels of acceptance, embarrassment, and control. I think you'd have to have it both ways.

That would cause a lot of sibling disharmony. And there are certain things, as a parent, you really shouldn't know about your children when they go away to school. You really aren't supposed to know if somebody's staying over in their dorm, or that they went to a frat party. And you don't want to know. That's why distance is a little bit nice.

BS: Sometimes when I go to visit, it's like they're still in high school.

CS: But also she's got one kid—I think this is Sarah—who's pretty conservative, pretty by-the-book, and Molly tries to tell her, "This is your time to test the boundaries." Maybe it's something the Mom never did, either. Maybe she never tested her boundaries and went wild. Although she would have, if she's in her fifties, she would have, because she would've grown up in the sixties.

PD (PETER DESBERG): When I was at USC in the sixties, it was a very conservative school. There were girls from Orange County who had angora sweaters in their closets.

CS: So maybe that's her thing. She missed the sixties. They flew right by her. She missed disco because she was so busy playing by the rules.

BS: "What happened? I kept meaning to, but never quite got around to it."

CS: She missed Reaganomics. She missed the whole "Gordon Gecko, Money and Power" thing. Now she's getting to catch up on all these things that she missed out on. Of course, none of this works if you don't cast it perfectly.

It has to be somebody who's got elegance and charm. Christine Baransky! It has to be somebody who's so truly fun that you can see where it's not going to be a huge drag for anybody except for her children. And an overpowering personality. I'm trying to think of who else. It's just anybody who could play Auntie Mame. Theater personalities because they're comfortable being larger than life, and just a little bit more "out there." But there are other people. Kirstie Alley could do it. She would be fun; she'd be a blast. Who else is just so out there?

BS: I say go to England and you'll find somebody.

CS: Oh, yeah, just bring Emma Thompson over, and call it a day. That'd be fantastic. But you wouldn't want her to be English.

BS: Oh, she wouldn't have to be English. Gregory House isn't English. Get rid of the accent. The Brits are very good at that.

CS: It seems like then you start the show in a campus setting. Is that a good thing? Do you want it to be a public university, like a big UCLA campus setting? Or do you want it to be Ivy League, or do you want it to be small?

BS: Traditionally, America's kind of scared of campus settings.

CS: So what do you do then?

BS: Maybe make it a high-tech school, like Austin.

CS: That's good. Wherever it is, she's got to be the fish out of water. She's got to be invasive.

BS: It could be NYU.

CS: Oh, that's kind of cool.

BS: You're right in the urban area, but you're still in college.

CS: That's actually pretty neat, especially if they're from someplace like Indianapolis. If they're from someplace that's the opposite of Manhattan. I like that. All right? NYU. What else? A subset of the helicopter parent is the Black Hawk parent. With a Black Hawk parent, the children don't know what the parent is doing. They don't know that someone like Molly is going in there and advocating for them. Checking their e-mails. Checking their Facebook page. And you know what I always tell our son, "Don't put anything on Facebook you don't want us to see."

BS: During a commercial, you've got to have something to do.

CS: So now all you have to do is start hitting on a senator so I can go back to college and live it. Then we'll get the story.

BS: I'm trying to think: Are all the good-looking ones gone?

CS: He could be a governor; it doesn't have to be a senator. Although, Barbara Boxer was pretty cute on *Curb Your Enthusiasm*.

BS: She's very cute.

JD (JEFFREY DAVIS): How do you feel about that dark versus light argument we hear a lot about?

BS: I'm not very dark. We appreciate people who do it. For the most part, critics like dark, but I don't think the general audience is like that. I mean, how many things that are dark fail?

CS: Is *House* dark? Is *The Office* dark? Is *Curb Your Enthusiasm* dark?

BS: Well, we did put a gay senator in here. So, I think we've definitely started in that direction.

CS: I really love *Curb Your Enthusiasm* and *House,* where it feels natural. It doesn't feel "sitcom-y." I think it's so interesting to have sort of complex, multifaceted, surprising characters, like on *The Office*. They behave out of character, but really just like human beings where they don't always react in the same way to the same stimuli. So I think I'd be interested in that.

PD: So how might you do some of that with Molly going to college?

CS: You'd want to build the surprises into the pilot, to let people know that these people aren't reacting in the standard ways. A lot of shows have done that, like *Arrested Development*. They did that in a really good comedic way. Our best success has been just staying pretty low-concept. Low-concept, high-dialogue characters and relationships. After *Cheers*—and in all the shows that we worked on, including the animation and everything we've done—we've been swayed toward higher concept and more of a hook. I think the hook can be a real trap.

BS: By the time you get to that second or third episode, the hook doesn't mean anything anymore.

CS: So you get into the rhythm as an audience member, you expect the show to fulfill your expectations, and then when it doesn't, are you delighted or are you annoyed? I'd want to set up as few expectations as possible, so that as writers we could feel our way through it, instead of having to retell the same story every week. That's what I would want to do. What would you want to do?

BS: I would want to do what you want to do.

CS: The secret of our partnership!

BS: I think it would be interesting to do a series that was so low-tech that that would be the funny thing about it—sort of like a comedy version of *The Blair Witch Project,* only it would be a comedy. Not like every other show.

CS: But that's what *The Office* is, isn't it? Yeah, *The Office* is low-tech. I mean, look at those sets. Could they be more beige?

BS: You go back and you look at the sets for *The Honeymooners.*

CS: I would like the characters to be colorful, so the sets don't have to be. Oh my God, when you see these sitcom sets, and this wall is lavender and this wall is melon. I'd like all the color to be in the character, and for the setting and the costumes and the hair to look real. That's what I really like about *The Office.* Pam's hair does not look like she just came out of a salon. It's real hair, and I love that.

BS: Now this is sort of true of us across the board. In theater, we like . . .

CS: . . . minimal.

BS: Minimal, minimal. We like crummy little theaters. We like small theaters.

JD: How did you start working together?

BS: We were in the Groundlings.

CS: Billy was teaching improv there, and also in private classes in an underground theater (literally, under the ground) on Sunset. One day he had an idea to improvise a modern-day *Our Town*, set in Los Angeles. I thought it was a great idea, but instead of improvising it, he should write it. Did you say, "Let's write it together" or did I say, "Let's write it together"?

BS: I'm going to choose you said, "Let's write it together."

CS: We wrote it, then put it in a drawer. It was a fun exercise— nothing more. Then, many months later, we were doing an improv show at the Déjà Vu Coffee Shop on Vermont, in the worst part of Hollywood. The owner, Smitty, had just taken over a small theater next door. We asked him what show he was going to open it with. He said, "I don't know. You got anything?" And I said, "Yeah" (because we had this play in the drawer, you see). He asked, "Can you have it ready in two weeks?" I said "Sure." Because you can't pass up an opportunity like that. He had a theater—a barn—we could put on a show! So we went home, got it out of the drawer, called all our friends to be in it. Asked our next-door neighbor, Xander Berkeley, to direct it, and just put it on. It was during the LA Olympics Arts Festival—and because it celebrated LA it became sort of a go-to play. Later we moved it to a theater uptown—on Melrose.

BS: It was called *Our Place* because the big Olympic slogan was, "LA's the Place." It was really fun. Basically, it was a long exploration of why we lived in LA when all our friends were moving to New York. It was our excuse for an appreciation of Los Angeles.

JD: What's it like working with a spouse?

BS: The only time we actually had a husband-and-wife tiff was when we were on *The Jeffersons*. We got into some argument—it was my fault—and we couldn't get out of it. It kept spiraling down, and we were just like baby writers at the time. We shouldn't have even been talking, and it spiraled down and down, and we had told these guys—they were great guys, Peter Casey and David Lee—that when we had a fight at home, the animals would go under the couch. So all the guys around the table went under the chairs.

JD: Did you like the writers' room?

BS: I liked the room.

CS: He loved it. It gets in my way.

BS: She just wants to get the work done, and everybody else is willing to talk. That's what I like.

CS: I wanted to get home and be with the kids. But sidetracking is one of Billy's special talents. It's listed under "Special Skills" at the bottom of his résumé.

BS: "Able to lead conversations down avenues and in directions not conceived of."

CS: I don't know if you've noticed, but he's good at it.

BS: Everybody needs a skill.

CS: And I have learned to appreciate that skill in you.

BS: Here's my impression of Cheri: "All right, all right, we're on page so-and-so line so-and-so." It's a much more valuable talent to have.

CS: Well, if you want to go home. If you *don't* want to go home, then it's good to sidetrack. I was not well-suited to it once we had children.

BS: Once we were running shows, because of Cheri, we just got stuff done in a saner way. Our goal was to drive home with our lights off. To be home in time for dinner. Later, I worked on other shows as a consultant and I'd call Cheri and say, "They just spent two and a half hours on one joke, and it's not even a very good joke." When we ran shows, if it got too late, and the staff was punchy and no longer producing good writing, we'd pack it in. We'd say, "Go home, get some sleep, we'll write Act II in the morning." Well, the network and studio couldn't understand that. They'd see half a script the next morning and go berserk. They panicked, as if we weren't going to finish. But we came back, rested and with perspective, and got it done.

CS: We had it written before the actors even got to it. And it was better. But we were definitely breaking form. TV comedy writers aren't supposed to sleep until they write "Fade Out."

We said, "We will have it before the actors get to it."

BS: "We'll have it in the morning."

CS: "It will be in front of them before they're ready."

JD: Do you think having smaller staffs and giving out fewer assignments the way they used to has made television better?

BS: I don't know. They do all this rewriting. A lot of the rewriting seems to just go sideways, as opposed to the old days. They would just write it and that's it!

CS: And I don't understand that whole "parceling out" method. The way that works is different people are working on different parts of a script. I know they do it on a lot of shows. They do it on *Desperate Housewives*. Doing it this way, how can they know that all these different parts of a story are going to work together? How can they know it's not going to have to be cobbled together at the back end?

BS: How many things in life work when a committee is working on them? Not many.

CS: Comedy is so much clearer when there's a strong, unified voice. Like Larry David's. The stories on *Curb Your Enthusiasm* are so intricate, and you know that any little detail he lays in at the beginning is going to pay off at the end. And I don't know how you would do that when you have five rooms going.

JD: Does tabling always make a script better?

BS: Tabling can make it better, if great minds are thinking alike, and we're all on a roll, cracking each other up, and sharpening every line and story beat. But if it becomes "making an elephant by committee," and everyone argues, so the only beats and jokes that survive are the common denominators, not necessarily the boldest moves—then, no, it makes it worse.

Now as far as table readings go, sometimes that table is the best the show ever is. It's when the actors are fresh to the material and discovering it for the first time. We used to think, "Boy, if only . . ."

CS: Unless you've got trained theater actors, who are going to be able to re-create that discovery, that spontaneity that comes with saying it the first time, sometimes they get a little bored. They get a little stale. And so you've got to think of some new jokes. And they don't want to say the same thing to the audience twice because it's just not going to have the same effect the second time. So you've got to think of something new and sometimes it just doesn't come off the top of your head. We had actors on *Cheers* who could hit it precisely every time and that joke was gold from day one until shooting. But there were other actors who you just had to keep feeding them new material and then it got so you'd have to retake it and retake it and set up the shots. It's a long process.

BS: One of the issues on a long-running show is the actors get popular, and are picked off to act in movies. That means, several days a week we don't have them around to rehearse, so other people have to fill in for them. On *Cheers* one day, we watched a whole rewritten script performed by the first AD, the second AD, and the prop guy. The prop guy did a pretty good Woody.

JD: What did your teachers teach you about writing for television?

BS: Lowell Ganz, who was on *Laverne and Shirley* and *Happy Days* as a writer/producer and wrote movies like *Parenthood* and *City Slickers*, taught a class at Sherwood Oaks. He would say things like, "TV is not radio."

CS: Yeah, except then later on, we got to the Charles Brothers, who said, "*Cheers* is a radio show." Which is to say it lived in the dialogue. You could hear it without seeing it and enjoy it just as much.

BS: Actually, TV is radio. Sure, you do some physical stuff, but very often physical stuff will get lost and you always need someone to say something. Always.

THE BEST OF INTENTIONS ...
THE WORST OF OUTCOMES

☞ An Interview with Leonard Stern

A partial list of Leonard Stern's credits as a creator, show runner, and writer include *I'm Dickens, He's Fenster; He and She; The Steve Allen Show; The Good Guys; The Honeymooners; Get Smart; The Phil Silvers Show; Operation Petticoat; McMillan & Wife;* and *The Jackie Gleason Show.*

Leonard Stern was there at the birth of situation comedy on shows like *The Honeymooners* and *The Phil Silvers Show.* For nearly sixty years, he has enjoyed an unbroken string of successes in TV, film, theater, and publishing, as co-founder of Price, Stern, Sloan, the inventors of *MAD LIBS.* And yet for all his accomplishments, his humor about himself and his work is sometimes self-effacing and always witty and enthusiastic.

Leonard Stern is proud of making comedy in which conflicts arise from good intentions between people who genuinely care about one another, intentions that have unintended consequences. Of the writers we've interviewed for this book, some like to start by asking questions about structure, while others talk about characters. Leonard, a consummate professional, gets right down to work, dimensionalizing characters and developing story. It all comes from love, which makes Leonard Stern unique among comedy writers.

⊠ ⊠ ⊠

LS (LEONARD STERN): I generally find something that would amuse and interest me and have some subtext of currency. Right away as I read this, I said, "Do the parents live better than the child?" The child makes more money today than children ever made before, but the world has changed and the economics of the world are dramatically different. Baby boomers can own a house that they bought for 10 percent of what you would pay today, and they have security. The daughter, Sarah, if she were married, I have a feeling that she and her husband would both work, because it would be a requirement. And they would never catch up to the parents. They'd be dependent on the parents, in this case, Molly.

So my tendency is to have the daughter have a husband, as opposed to a single's existence. It would appeal to me because I feel television has noticeably ignored this tremendous life situation that is probably taking part in one or more family's relationships. The father and the mother and the daughter and the son, and their lifestyles are not comparable. And I would want them to mesh.

So I would see Molly becoming a business partner of the daughter, Sarah, so that it brings it to another level. She's not a meddler, she's not interfering. They're just a generation or two apart in thinking. So their concepts of music are radically different. And when I started to think like that, I said, "What kind of business would I put them in?" Something where they would be polarized in taste. And as a consequence, Sarah would be much more the businesswoman; the mother much more the social animal in the premise, and the mother contemptuous of contemporary music. "Where is the melody? Where are the rhymes?" And discouraging sales by telling people not to buy that. And so you start to have a dramatic premise. If they have to go home together, and what if, indeed, Sarah's separated from her husband and now living with her mother, how do you separate your office life from your home life? And suddenly you're not in a clichéd situation. You're off on an experiment, which is, I believe, a true reflection of what is happening today in our society, certainly in the middle class. Now if you want to ask questions, you're certainly welcome to, if you're still awake!

PD (PETER DESBERG): I love the way you set it up. What kind of business would you put them in?

> **"Affection is somewhat of an embarrassment to most comedy writers, and not to be revealed unless you break the glass."**

LS: Well, I would have them own a video/DVD and CD store on a college campus. And also they'd have a little version of Starbucks going. I would give the mother some kind of background that she had during a moment in her life where she knew celebrities. So suddenly she has an importance in a college community. And she also decides to take classes. And suddenly Sarah realizes where she got her drive from. It wasn't the father, as she suspected. It was her mother. And then Molly is trying to apply everything that's new, except taste. Her taste stays rooted in the past. And so you get a paradox, and you get a conflict. But it's a fun conflict. It isn't demeaning to either person. I think I can say with equanimity and conviction that most of the times the shows I developed were based on liking, not negativity, not putting someone down. Consequently, it's harder to write comedy of love and caring. It's—what's the word?—"spritzing" is much more acceptable, and you get more writers capable of that. Affection is somewhat of an embarrassment to most comedy writers, and not to be revealed unless you break the glass.

JD (JEFFREY DAVIS): Why do you think that is?

LS: Because comedy writers are at war with society, I think, innately. Not intentionally, but it's there. I was kind of handicapped. Most of the people I know who were successful writers had dysfunctional families. Everybody in my family liked each other. I had to forgive them—it handicapped me. Others had this marvelous head start. I think it's also social—a way of fitting in, by being the odd one out. The paradox is of minor significance.

PD: When you're writing more positive comedy, is it more difficult to find conflict?

LS: Not necessarily, because the conflict can come out of caring. *He and She* was a show I did and I think we did thirty-two episodes, and it received every nomination for a writing award in comedy from the Writers Guild, and the same from the Emmys. We had four different writers on the shows; teams competed with each other. And that was the ultimate compliment. That show was a very prideful hug of each other. There was this inordinate respect that they had for each other. They were bright and eccentric, and they made it permissible.

I think we introduced the first fop in television in a character Jack Cassidy played, who was both their best friend and their greatest irritant. I just love that show, and it's radically etched in my mind.

JD: How would you bring conflict into a happy mother/daughter relationship?

LS: It's working already because there's a difference, as I said, primarily in taste, and then there's the belief, "But how could you feel this way when you're my daughter?" And that could be a discussion; it doesn't have to be spiteful or hateful to be funny. I know if the daughter needed a dress for an occasion and it doesn't fit into the budget at the moment—say, the store had a bad month—the mother says, "Wear this." And she says, "Mom, thank you, but it's not me." And suddenly, that's enough of a reason to have a problem when she learns that her mother was offering her the dress in which she was married. Then, Molly says, "You look terrible." But the mother feels good about it. And yet you've had a problem. It's much more fun because you go on an untraveled road. It's much easier to do pejoratives and put-downs.

PD: You structured it so you have at least three generations working here because you've got the mother's generation, the daughter's, and then they're on a college campus, which is still younger.

LS: I thought, when you're marching, you find yourself occasionally out of step, and that would be part of this. And I love the fact that the mother's strong opinions affect business. Some people won't come in because she's there. "They're free to do what they want, but this is my feeling about that."

JD: Does that come from something in your life?

LS: No, probably gestation. The professor suddenly is smitten with the mother. That in itself is interesting. But he's ultraconservative. That's the one thing she can't stand about him. And yet, he's interesting. So you're dealing with a political situation, but an important one, to make the character realize that conservatives can be lovable.

"Most good comedy is character-oriented. There can be eccentricities, or exaggerations, or hyperbole."

PD: Rather than just having a conflict between two people who don't get along, you're saying they don't get along with this *part* of a person. You're looking at the traits as what causes the conflict.

LS: I'm glad you're making these distinctions. Most good comedy is character-oriented. There can be eccentricities, or exaggerations, or hyperbole. I was a great admirer of Laurel and Hardy, before it was fashionable to be, and the very first show I did on my own was *I'm Dickens, He's Fenster*, the wellspring of which was Laurel and Hardy. To my great astonishment, I received a fan letter from Stan Laurel. I didn't believe it, because everybody who worked with me on *The Steve Allen Show* knew how I loved Laurel and Hardy, so I figured it was a prank. But ultimately, Steve Allen said to me, "Have you ever heard from Stan Laurel?" So I figured now I know who wrote the letter. It turned out he was doing a book, *The Funny Men*, and he had interviewed Stan Laurel. Steve had said, "Is there any show you like very much?" And he said, "I'm enjoying one tremendously. It's called, *I'm Dickens, He's Fenster*." As Steve was about to say, "I know who wrote it; he was my head writer," Stan said, "I even wrote the creator and never heard from him." And so Steve said, "That can't be." So he told me the story that Stan had written me, and at the time I thought it was Steve who had written me. And right then and there Steve had his little book and we called Stan Laurel, and he became a critic of the show, and critiqued it every Monday. It was on Friday night. And we became friends.

He was slightly paralyzed in the face, but I almost talked him into coming to the show, and the last moment he felt uncomfortable. A remarkable human being, and this was an endorsement of what

I believed. We had great fun with paranoia. Laurel and Hardy had that—they were against each other, unless somebody interfered with the team, and then they were beautifully wedded and welded together. And this was exciting. And they had the world in microcosm, beautifully etched. I remembered Stan would do something remarkable with his fingers. [Leonard makes a gesture with his fingers.] He'd be able to do something adroit with his fingers, and Hardy would try to do it unsuccessfully through most of the film, and then he'd turn around and hit Laurel. Then you understood it. And it's marvelous. And they remained friends because Laurel understood it as well. At worst, he'd get tearful.

PD: As you were looking at Molly and Sarah, is there a particular way you go about looking at their traits?

LS: Well, there I probably borrow from life, because I was a collaborator for many years. I worked with Marty Ragaway in the beginning, then Sid Zelinka on *The Honeymooners*, and of course, your dad, Jeffrey, on *The Good Guys*. You learn how to tolerate—I'll use a euphemism—the eccentricities of your partner, and adjust to them, but they don't leave you completely unscathed. Because ultimately, you have this paranoia. You always assume the other one's plotting against you. So you always have to be on the lookout. So it's a sustained truce.

PD: So here we have a mother and daughter. Give me some ways you might flesh out the characters to bring out the conflict.

LS: Well, we have the foundation of a woman—the daughter gave up a job. I assume we're staying with the format that she was formerly working for a man, and she recognized that there was no promotion. The mother and she had to obtain a loan to get their new business off the ground. So the daughter looks like she'd be the one to be concerned about making the payments. And the mother would decide to seduce the person to whom they owed money. So this is reprehensible until you realize it's done in major corporations all the time. So you're starting to see it be dimensionalized. And suddenly the mother's wearing something low-cut, so there's an argument. "We're not doing that; we're not stooping that low," Sarah says. "I'll just bend over once," Molly says. And you can see—minute you start thinking—jokes emerge unknowingly. The foundation is right, and survival is at the bottom of this always. I don't think we ever did a *Honeymooners* show where the problem wasn't money. But I don't know if most people's problems aren't the lack of funds. And so that's always painful, and it's difficult to contemplate. And also suddenly, I see the mother preparing a list of donations she's going to make, and things she's going to give away, and they don't have any money. And I love that premise, because it doesn't mean we won't have it, and "If I should die suddenly, I want to have this distribution of wealth," and then, of course, it's imaginary wealth. If you imagine it long enough it will exist, it'll be palpable.

PD: You mentioned the nice, normal family you grew up in. Were they funny people?

LS: No, they were extraordinarily prideful. My father was an extremely gregarious man. He talked to anyone, and he had that persona that people would talk to him. But it was an embarrassment to me. He'd stop the mayor of New York. And he'd be talking to him. I'd feel embarrassed for the mayor. But here's a marvelous example of my father's personality. It took me a long time to understand it, and his ways.

We did *The Honeymooners* in a huge theater—it sat three thousand people, so it was enormous—and it was live. So it was opening night every week, and my parents came to every show, same theater. One Saturday, it was raining torrentially, and Sid Zelinka and I had to get back to the theater. We'd broken for lunch. And the front entrance was closest, so we knocked on the door, and said, "Writers," and the usher said, "Stage Entrance." We said, "It's raining out." He said, "Stage Entrance." We said, "Come on, it's pouring, you've seen us here . . ." and we're making no progress whatsoever. And suddenly the head usher came up and as he opened the door, he said, "That's okay. That's Mr. Stern's son."

PD: How did you learn to do what you do? How did you learn your craft?

LS: That was something I wanted to do. I almost had no choice. I wrote my first play, strangely enough, when I was thirteen in a French class. Mrs. Blankenstein—we always called her Frankenstein—decided to put it on. She would direct it. I loved the response it got, and it was humorous. I was very fortunate to go to a high school that had a strong drama department and did musicals twice a year—original musicals with a sixty-piece orchestra, thirty-five people in the choir. And I wrote three of those in a period of a year and a half, while I was in my last half of junior year and then the full senior year.

JD: Is there any question in your mind that a show with a daughter and mother in her fifties could find an audience?

LS: If it's good and fun, it will. But it has to be fun, and it has to not use a laugh track. It has to earn its laughter. It has to be done live. It's abysmal and subversive what's happened. My grandchildren have been victimized by the laugh track. They assume that "Hello" is funny. And if you add a curse word behind it, that's insurance. There was a marvelous sketch in a Writers Guild awards show that was brilliantly written by Carl Reiner and Mel Brooks. They did a sketch, where they were two guys who sweetened a show, did a laugh track, added it, and by error, they've gotten Lincoln's Gettysburg Address. And they start to edit, judging what "Four scores" were, and played back the laugh track. And it's the best indictment of the absurdity that has been happening now for too many years.

JD: What's going on with the *Get Smart* movie?

LS: [This interview was done a year before the movie was cast.] I'm subject to the same rumors you are. I have no idea. This is common indictment of the thinking when they do a remembered, or revered television show. They don't hire any of the original writers, even as consultants. And they change the characters, or lose the essence. If you're going to make *Get Smart*, why not do *Get Smart*? *Bilko* was a good example. The essence of Phil Silvers' character—that was the support for the whole show, the pillar that held it up—and they changed that, and it's frightening to me. We sold *Get Smart* for a movie, and we had what we thought was a marvelous premise. It was a gay, autocratic designer, who wanted to own the world so he could dress it. But the studio decided to do it in an entirely different way. And I kept saying, "Why? Why are you doing it this way?" And they said, "We don't want to do the television show." And I said, "Then why did you buy it?" And then they added a title, *The Nude Bomb*. They thought that would be a draw.

It was our premise, but it wasn't our script.

PD: Can you tell when your stuff is funny?

LS: Pretty much, because it's character-oriented. I know the character will work. I don't know if everything the character will say will work. But that led to a series of remarkable characters for the show, and led to catchphrases. I think there were probably more catchphrases on the shows I did, because they were reflective of a character. *Get Smart* had seven or eight. We probably tried forty, but it was a pretty good percentage.

JD: How did that work? Did you, Mel Brooks, and Buck Henry sit in a room together?

LS: No, no. Mel and Buck wrote the first draft of the pilot show, and ABC turned it down. And a rewrite was done, and Danny Melnick said, in selling it, "If you don't like it, you can have your money back." Within twenty-four hours, they asked for their money back. So we were stuck with the script. And miracle of miracles, it was postpilot time, but NBC had Don Adams under contract and was desperate to use him in this given year. And so, we had a meeting with them, and Grant Tinker responded favorably to the idea, and I agreed to adapt it for Don, with whom I had worked on *The Steve Allen Show*. So I did the dialogue changes to his cadence and rhythm, and I added the secret doors, and things like that, so that the final version, I guess, Mel, Buck, and I worked on. And then Mel got a movie, *The Producers*, shortly after that, and the show sold, so Buck remained as the story editor, and Mel went on to glory. And the next year Buck got *The Graduate*.

JD: Well, I love what you did with this mother/daughter premise. I think you're the only person who said you could derive conflict from love.

LS: You've met with hostile people.

ADDING OUR 15 PERCENT

Our original idea for this book title was *Make It 15 Percent Funnier*. This phrase comes from a well-known story about legendary writer Larry Gelbart, who was going over his script with a network executive. The executive began the meeting by saying, "I love the script, but can you make it 15 percent funnier?" Comedy writers often cite this incident when pointing out how crazy their business is, and how little understanding "suits" have about the comedy writing process. But this wasn't the strangest story we heard during these interviews. In this wrap-up, we want to share some of the things we learned along the way.

Spinning a Web of Comedy

We would like you to read this final chapter with three things in mind. We hope that you get some additional insights into the way these writers work. We also hope that you will come up with some insights of your own that we didn't see, and that you'll share those insights with us on our website (www.showmethefunnyonline.com). Due to space considerations, we had to omit three interviews. Since we loved them all, we randomly selected three of them. Fortunately, you can find them on our website in their entirety.

The Beginning of Our Conflicted Humility Lesson

We wanted to see if writers would start with character or story. We were surprised to discover that the answer was generally neither. They all went for *conflict*. Most of them told us that character or story structure is what they use to create conflict. And, when they didn't find conflict, they created it. Dennis Klein went even further.

When there wasn't conflict during the interview, he created it right there in the room.

The word *conflict* conjures up images of people screaming and hitting each other. Our interviews reveal that there are two types of conflict: hostile and helpful. Helpful conflict comes out of love, mixed with incompatibly good intentions. Hostile you know . . .

Some wrote from inner conflicts, others from something they knew about, and, of course, many from their own direct experiences. Many changed the situation to make it mirror what they relate to better. Elliott Schoenman, Cinco Paul and Ken Daurio, and Peter Casey quickly changed Molly and Sarah to father-and-son characters because they thought they could write it better from their own experience.

As Heide Perlman was drawing Molly's character, she related this story from her history. Her mother had a habit of saying, "Right?" after she said something. This forced people to agree with her. Her mother would say, "'Oh, you love tuna fish, right?' 'No, I don't.' 'Yeah, you love it, right?' And then even if you try to move on, if you don't say, 'Yeah,' it's like, 'Whatever,' 'Right? Right?' Like just forcing the issue, and you're thinking, 'What does it matter if I say, 'Right?' I know I don't like tuna fish, but it's just like . . . the fact of being forced into agreement is frustrating." She built that frustration-generator into Molly's character.

Sherwood Schwartz's uncle married a girl who wasn't Jewish. They thought it would devastate one of the highly observant family members, so they hid the fact from her for thirteen years. When they finally had to tell her, she just responded with, "Oh." Everybody was stunned. After Sherwood told the story, Lloyd immediately incorporated it into Sarah's life.

Seeing People in 3-D: Dimensionalizing Characters

A dimensional character can be created without knowing the conflict or story. It is more than just giving the character an interesting tick or personality trait. Many writers want to know what their character wants or needs before they can start writing. All the writers spent considerable time adding color and dimension to their characters. The way they go about it varies widely from Lew Schneider, who used a specific example of one of his neighbors, to Yvette Bowser, who has a specific questioning strategy for giving each character dimension.

If You Write It, They Will Air It: Commercial Considerations

A number of writers first considered how to make the premise commercially viable. Bob Myer began his development by casting the main characters. He discussed how different actors and genders would affect the commercial viability of the show. He was very aware of what networks were buying at the present time.

Marc Sheffler and Paul Chitlik have gotten to a point where they say if they can't get a producer or director position, they don't want to write anymore. They are tired of having their work tampered with. Charlie Peters talks about being disheartened having to pitch ideas to "embryos." In contrast, Yvette Bowser says she likes to play by the networks' rules. She sees that as a challenge. She accepts this arena and likes to compete within it.

You've Got to Be Joking

Jokes are worthless unless they fit the occasion and character exactly. A *joke-joke* is an old industry term that refers to a stand-alone joke that doesn't need a story or character reference. Historically, when producers told comedy writers that they needed three jokes per page, these jokes found their way into many TV shows and movies. Today, good writers dispose of them whenever possible.

There is an industry term called a *show schmuck*. This comedy writing term describes a character who is always available for a cheap laugh that comes from character. Coach on *Cheers*, the brother on *Raymond*, and Jack on *Will and Grace* are examples.

Elliot Schoenman said that on *Home Improvement* a lot of writers fell in love with their jokes and were willing to bend a story to keep them in. The scripts were really funny and interesting halfway through and then they took a dive in the second half. It wasn't that the jokes were better in the first half. When they rewrote the story, the whole episode became funny.

The ability to write a good joke often means the difference between getting hired or not. Heide Perlman wrote a spec script for *Cheers*. She said, "The joke that I think they really liked was the one where Diane's cat dies and Sam takes advantage of her emotional distress, to try to hook up with her. The joke I wrote in my outline, which they loved, was that Carla comes up to Diane and says, 'Oh, I'm so sorry about your cat. I've been through it all with the kids—the turtle, the fish . . .' Diane says, 'Yeah, but cats are different' And Carla says, 'Yeah, you can't flush a cat.'"

Who Showed the Funny?

Because there are so many writing programs, books, and workshops teaching comedy, we were curious about where our writers got their training. Three writers—Tracy Newman, Jonathan Stark, and Bill Steinkellner—started at the Groundlings, but they all say that their education really began when they got into the writers' room. Like Michael Elias and Marley Sims, they never took classes.

Heide Perlman talked about wanting to be a serious writer and ended up doing a spec *Cheers* script. She was given some outlines and scripts and learned structure by studying them. Michael Elias refers to himself in his early years as a "radical, renegade criminal actor." He was a member of the revolutionary group the Living Theater before doing stand-up on the *Tonight Show* with Johnny Carson.

Elliot Schoenman and Walter Bennett learned structure from watching TV sitcoms. Walter was a playwright before he wrote sitcoms and believes he learned structure from theater. When Charlie Peters was a teenager, he ghostwrote a funny advice column for teenage girls with his mother. He learned discipline by getting paid by the word in the tradition of Dickens.

Does Anyone Know What's Funny?

We asked the writers how and when they knew something was funny. Did they go to other people? Do they have a built-in device like Hemingway's "shock-proof sh-t detector"? Most of the writers believe they have a pretty good sense of what was funny. Ken Daurio said, "Having two people automatically helps that whole thing, knowing whether you're funny or not." Tracey Newman and Jonathan Stark cracked each other up during most of the interview.

Elliot Schoenman also talked about how difficult it was to deal with the punch-up guys. Every time they'd come up with a joke, they'd say, "Oh, it's funny, it's funny, it's funny!" As show runner, he had to be very delicate about how he rejected them. He told a story about a writer on *Maude* who could write brilliant jokes, but also awful ones. Bob Schiller pointed out to Elliot that the writer was a stutterer. Interestingly, when he told a joke without stuttering, it was generally a great line. But when he stuttered, even though he said it was a great line, it wasn't. It was as if there were some deep part of him that knew.

Many of the writers had stand-up experience, including Bob Myer, Lew Schneider, Marc Sheffler, and Michael Elias, to name a few. They say knowing what's funny is a survival skill. The feedback is immediate—unlike having to wait anywhere from a few minutes to a few months to find out if something will get a laugh.

Ed Decter talks about how the networks determine what's funny through testing. They play your pilot in a room full of people who have their hands on dials. The girls have dials and the guys have dials. When something's funny, they turn the dial one way and when it's not they turn it the other way. The guys' responses show up as blue lines; the girls' are pink lines. There is also an average of those lines as the show is being projected in a secret room where the writers are. Based on the results, they'll say, "Let's do a reshoot, or let's add some things to the editing to make it spike."

Making Room at the Writers' Table

The writers' room on *Frasier* was considered exceptional. Here's how Peter Casey described it. The composition of the staff was constantly changing because they were like a sports team. Some of the best players would leave because they got more lucrative offers so they had to find new writers who could fit in. New writers, when they'd begin, often talked about how intimidated they were in the room because everyone was just so good. But the staff made sure that the environment was always supportive. People never had to be afraid if their joke bombed, although he admitted that the silence could be quite brutal.

Bill Steinkellner points out that not many things in life work when a committee is creating them. Michael Elias got to the point where, on *Head of the Class*, he wouldn't enter the room—and he co-created the show. While jokes may be improved by the process,

Michael believes you need that single voice and doesn't like modern writers' rooms.

The credit for writing a joke is a serious business in the writers' room. Walter Bennett remembers being a new writer and pitching what he thought was an incredible joke. Everyone said, "Oh, no, that's not it." Later, someone else told the exact same joke and someone said, "That was brilliant." When Walter said, "I just said that," another writer said, "Oh, come on now. Let's not get that way."

Phil Rosenthal disagrees. Here is his view of the value of writers' rooms:

> You get to have these different, hopefully brilliant heads, challenging your ideas and coming up with their ideas of what's good and what's not, and then debating it, discussing it. Many people hate the writing-by-committee approach. I only loved it because if you had bright, funny people in the room, they only made you better. Yes, you should have a strong sense of what you think the show is.

The writers' room on *Everybody Loves Raymond* was legendary. Almost no one left the show during its entire tenure because they all liked it so much. Phil fondly told us about one of the pivotal roles in the room—the Room Monkey. On *Everybody Loves Raymond*, Lew Schneider played this role. Phil was quick to point out that it was the role he usually assumed on previous shows. The Room Monkey contributes pure energy, creativity, and inventiveness. He provides necessary spontaneity and enthusiasm. He's the spark plug that ignites a room full of tired writers.

Yvette Bowser tells the story of being on a show that was so difficult for her, she called her agent and said, "Get me off this plantation." She said, "They didn't know what they were doing. And they were treating me badly, (a) because I was a girl, and (b) because I was black. And I had come from a very nurturing environment, where what I had to say as a woman and, particularly as a black woman who was just out of college, was very relevant to the show that I was working on, which was *A Different World*."

Zen and the Art of Tongue Thrusting

In an old Zen parable, after just three months at the monastery, a novice approaches an elderly monk and asks him if he is truly on the one true path to enlightenment. The monk smiles patiently and replies, "Tuesday will never come if the rose doesn't grow straight." That's why we didn't interview any Zen monks.

This story also represents the way we look at any expert who tries to sell you on the one true way to write or create—especially comedy. We hope the next time you look at a comedy writing book or hear any expert preach, "*The way* to write comedy is . . ." you will involuntarily stick your tongue out in that expert's direction. If you're enrolled in a university writing class, and concerned about your grade, you can hold your overpriced textbook up to cover your face, but make sure to still stick your tongue out. The interviews in this book prove that there are as many ways to create as there are writers who do the creating. To end where we began, here's another story about Larry Gelbart. At a Q&A about *M*A*S*H*, he was asked what the rules of writing comedy were. "There are fifty-five of them," he said, "Unfortunately, nobody knows what they are."

We hope to see you on the website . . .

GLOSSARY

ARC (of the story or series) The evolution of the plot and characters of the story.

BEAT An important joke or moment in a story.

COVERAGE A summary report of the contents of a script or project with an evaluation of its viability.

FOUR-BOX MOVIES The four basic age groups that a movie or TV show appeals to.

GROUNDLINGS Los Angeles based improv group and improv/comedy school. Graduates include *SNL*'s Kristen Wiig and Phil Hartman.

HEAVY A villain.

HIGH CONCEPT A TV show or film that is largely based on a simply stated premise, rather than a more complete character development and broader story.

HOUSE NUMBER Derived from the garment industry, a substitute for a joke that specifies its characteristics; used to mark the location of a joke that will be created.

HUMANITAS AWARD An industry award for enriching human understanding dealing with important social issues.

HYBRID PILOT A pilot in which some scenes are filmed on location, and others on a soundstage.

LOCK A defined situation or relationship in the script.

MIDDLE-SLICE PILOT A pilot that combines introductory information about a series, but takes place as if the series were ongoing.

OMEGA DOG One of the lowest-status members of a writers' room.

ONE-CAMERA SHOW A TV show shot like a movie using only one camera. Not performed live with an audience.

PIPE An industry term for background information.

POSTPRODUCTION Sound and editing enhancements made to film or video after filming.

PREMISE PILOT Introduces a series, giving the necessary background and presenting the characters.

PUNCH UP Adding comedy to an already written script. Often done by specialists, although sometimes done in the writers' room.

ROOM MONKEY A member of the writers' room whose function is to provide energy, often using a broad approach to comedy.

SHOW RUNNER A writer-producer who runs the writers' room, and is involved with every aspect of the show.

SPEC SCRIPT A speculative script written with the intention of selling it or getting work as a writer.

SPRITZING A comedy term for spitballing ideas.

TABLE READING Actors sitting around a table reading a script. An initial step done to see how the script works.

TABLING is done by a group of writers in the Writers' Room to develop stories and punch up scripts.

THREE-CAMERA SHOW A TV show performed live in front of a live audience. It uses three or even four cameras to catch all the different actions in real time.

TUMMLER A social director or comedian, who stimulates audience participation.

Acknowledgments:
A Serious Thank-You
for a Book about Comedy

We would like to begin by expressing our gratitude to our editor, Laura Swerdloff. She stepped in and supported us from the start. Actually, except for being bright, dedicated, hardworking, and caring, she didn't add that much.

All books come together through the generosity of spirit of countless individuals, but a book of interviews, especially one that is by its nature a little offbeat, requires the kindness of friends, acquaintances, and sometimes even total strangers. From the inception of this project, people enthusiastically stepped up to assist us many times over, sometimes without our even having to beg. Without them, this book could never have been completed. We want to thank each of these generous friends:

Barbara Alexander, Carolyn Bauer, Larry Brezner, Neal Dodson, Jay Douglas, Julie Fleischer, Stephen Galloway, Bill Gladstone, David Goldbeck, Mark Goldberg, Gary Grossman, Jack Heller, Peter Heller, Shirl Hendryx, Monica Horan, Deborah Langford, Jackie Oleeski, Julie Sayres, Bill Tanner, Bryna Weiss, and Frank Wuliger.

We'd also like to thank the following transcribers for their dedication, perseverance and creativity: Sal Cardoni, Diana Levy, Ivana Lyon, Ori Seron, and Lauren Wilson.

. . . and of course, we'd like to thank all the writers we interviewed for giving us their time, talent, and tolerance.

Index

Author Biographies

One out of every 150 people in America bought a copy of a joke book that
Peter Desberg has written. Unfortunately, Scholastic sold the most popular
one for $1 each, so he still has to work. Counting his five joke books, he has
had twenty books published. In addition to this lucrative writing career, he is a
licensed clinical psychologist who specializes in the area of stage fright. He has
worked with many top stand-up comedians, who are regularly confronted with
massive cases of flop sweat. He also has been moonlighting as a Full Professor
at California State University–Dominguez Hills for over thirty years. He has
done extensive research on the psychology of humor and is a frequent consultant
to business presenters on how to use humor persuasively. No stranger to media,
for ten years he hosted his own cable TV show on technology. In the areas of
humor and stage fright, he has done many radio and television interviews and
is frequently quoted in national publications, including the *Wall Street Journal*,
Reader's Digest, the *Los Angeles Times*, *Psychology Today*, and *Cosmopolitan*. He has
to be a humor expert because he has a daughter who is about to turn nineteen.

Jeffrey Davis's earliest memories are of sitting around the writers' table at Nate &
Al's Delicatessen, where his father and his comedy writer cronies gathered over
corn beef and Doctor Brown's Cream Soda, told war stories, and tried to fix third
acts. He began his own career writing jokes for *Thicke of the Night*. Among his
situation comedy credits are *Love Boat*, *House Calls* with Lynn Redgrave, *Give Me
a Break*, *Diff'rent Strokes*, and *Night Court*. He has also written for such shows
as *America's Funniest People*, *America's Funniest Home Videos*, and *Small Wonder*,
and has had film projects developed by Bette Midler's All Girl Productions
and Arnold Kopelson, among others. He has written documentaries for A&E,
Discovery, and the National Geographic Channel, and written a variety of
corporate and informational videos. His plays have been produced in New York
and Los Angeles. His most recently published play is called *Speed Dating*. He is
an Associate Professor of film and TV writing at Loyola Marymount University.
His one night of stand-up at the Comedy Store convinced him that he should stay
permanently seated at his desk.